ECONOMIC LIFE

ECONOMIC LIFE

Process Interpretations
and Critical Responses

Edited by
W. Widick Schroeder and Franklin I. Gamwell

C

S

S

R

Center for the Scientific Study of Religion
Chicago Illinois

Studies in Religion and Society
Center for the Scientific Study of Religion

For a complete list of other publications in the
series, see the back of the book.

Center for the Scientific Study of Religion
5757 University Avenue
Chicago, Illinois 60637

ISBN: Cloth: 0-913348-26-0
       Paper: 0-913348-27-9

Library of Congress Catalog Card Number: 88-71051

Table of Contents

Preface

Historically, almost all human beings have spent most of their lives striving to secure the food, fiber, and shelter necessary to sustain themselves. A few sought "well-being," but most were preoccupied with "being."

Beginning in the West in the seventeenth and eighteenth centuries, and extending to parts of the rest of the planet in the nineteenth and twentieth centuries, technological innovations, increased capital investment, and economies of scale have permitted more people to attain more material goods with less expenditure of time and toil than was the case in earlier historical epochs. As a result, larger segments of the populations of many industrialized countries have been able to devote more time to activities outside the economic sphere.

To be sure, the possibility of the pursuit of well-being has not resulted in as widespread attainment of well-being as one might hope. War, the threat of war, civil unrest, poverty, economic instability, pollution, market hedonism, religious intolerance, racism, domestic violence, child abuse, sexism, or some combination of these evils continue to plague industrialized as well as transitional societies.

With the increasing economic productivity of modern societies, the character of economic institutions and their relations to other spheres of social life have increasingly become subjects of scholarly discussion and debate. Interpretations which seek to account for the economic disparities among differing nations of the world, to describe present economic conditions and predict probable developments, and to evaluate or prescribe for economic activity are invariably controversial. In spite of fundamental disagreements, however, it is widely recognized that the dynamics of market capitalism have been and continue to be central to the dramatic economic changes of modern life as a whole, so that no attempt to understand the past and/or prescribe for the future can be adequate without an interpretation of forms of economic organization.

Convinced of the importance of the subject and persuaded that the mode of thought known as process philosophy might provide resources with which to enrich the discussion, the editors invited four persons familiar with process thought to join them in reflecting upon economic life by addressing the topic, "Process Philosophy and Forms of Economic Organization."

Initiated by the seminal work of Alfred North Whitehead and Charles Hartshorne, process philosophy has attracted a substantial number of philosophers and philosophical theologians in the two generations since Whitehead formulated his ideas at Harvard in the 1920s and 1930s. In more recent decades, increasing numbers of religious social ethicists have been exploring the implications of process thought for their field.

The editors also invited six religious social ethicists to share in this project by developing critical responses to the essays. Most of these persons are not constructively informed by process thought, but they all have written on the topic of social justice and economic life. To promote reflection and dialogue, then, each of the six essays in this volume is followed by a critical response by one of these religious social ethicists.

Several seminal ideas recur in all the essays. All of them explore "oughtness" as well as "isness" or seek to prescribe for as well as to describe economic life. In process philosophy, the fully concrete things are said to be events that are constituted by a valuation of other things. As a consequence, process thinkers reject the separation of fact and value which is found in the work of social scientists who are implicitly or explicitly informed by the neo-Kantian tradition.

Again, all of the essays address the nature of human freedom and its relation to economic life. Freedom is fundamental in process philosophy, because the constitution of each concrete event is said to be *causa sui*, or self-determined. Still, these events are also constituted by their relativity to others, and all of the authors understand human life to be essentially social, that is, all affirm a reciprocal understanding of the relations between individuals and community. It follows that interpretations of economic life must include attention to equality and community as well as freedom, and this leads all of the contributors also to discuss in some manner the relation of economic activity to other spheres of social life, including especially the government.

In spite of the recurrence of these topics, the contributors differ in their appreciation of them and draw contrasting implications for economic life. This "family quarrel" is a sign of the vigor of process thought in religious social ethics. Every substantial movement of thought develops some diversity in relation to common elements.

The contributors differ in their views on the nature of and the relations between freedom, equality, and community. They also differ in their views on the priority of consumer preference in allocating economic resources, on the relative importance of considering the impact of public policy proposals on economic growth and efficiency, on the bases for inordinate human self-interest, and on the prospects for the future reduction of inordinate self-interest through personal and/or social transformation. Based partly on contrasting generic notions and partly on contrasting prudential judgments about the probable consequences of alternative public policies, the contributors offer varied proposals to promote the quest for human good.

It is our hope that these essays and the critical discussions of them will stimulate further work on economic life and its significance for the being and well-being of humankind. Even though the contributors draw from process modes of thought, the issues addressed are of interest to all who are concerned about the social ethics of political economy.

Several of the essays were discussed at sessions held during the annual meetings of the American Academy of Religion during the mid-1980s. We want to thank the participants in those sessions for their help in developing this project. We want to express our appreciation to the contributors to this volume for the thought, time, and energy they expended in the elaboration of the topic. We thank as well Brent W. Sockness for constructing the indices, and, finally, we thank Pan O'Sea Typesetters for their cooperation and usefulness.

W. Widick Schroeder   Franklin I. Gamwell

ECONOMIC LIFE

CHAPTER 1

The Philosophy of Organism as Critique of Economic Individualism

William M. Sullivan

Introduction

Alfred North Whitehead was not primarily a social thinker and he wrote ittle that could be termed political philosophy or political economy in the strict sense. Yet he developed his mature philosophy, from *Science and the Modern World* of 1925 through *Process and Reality* of 1929 and *Adventures of Ideas* of 1933 to *Modes of Thought* in 1938, with explicit reference to the intellectual, cultural and social development of modern Western civilization. Whitehead was that rare synthetic figure: a mathematician turned metaphysician whose speculation was intended as a tract for the times as much as a reaching out to the timeless. In fact, it was of the essence of his vision that reality was temporal through and through. But more particularly, Whitehead's philosophy was aimed at overcoming the imbalances in modern life which he took to be the twentieth century's only partly digested inheritance from the revolutions in thought and practice which had progressively swept through Western civilization for three hundred years. Or, put differently, one can read Whitehead's efforts at philosophical vision as an effort both to understand and to shape modernity.

Like Bergson, James and Dewey, Whitehead shared an early twentieth century turn of mind that Arthur O. Lovejoy termed the "revolt against dualism." All these "philosophers of process" strove to go beyond the cultural oppositions between science and religion, utilitarian economics and culture, materialism and idealism that had defined the nineteenth century. In his "philosophy of organism," Whitehead sought a way to reconcile within a dynamic understanding of nature and culture the cognitive power of modern science with the spiritual claims of religious faith, ethics and art. He was insistent that, without denying the determining forces at work in history, ideals and human agency played the decisive role by either succeeding or failing to integrate the potentials of an age into the harmony of "civilization." The scientific developments of evolutionary theory and twentieth century physics increased Whitehead's hopes of mediating, through a philosophy, the interdependence of individual "creativity"—a word of his coinage—and the stabilizing matrix of a shared and mutually sustained environment. This was a view of nature and culture as "progressive" yet indebted to the past, as sparked by individual achievement yet dependent upon complex interdependence for endurance.

This guiding aim at dynamic mediation led Whitehead to develop his well-known critique of the mechanistic view of nature he termed "scientific materialism." Whitehead's complaint was not that modern science has been false. Rather, its relentless concentration on one set of explanatory ideas had, with the tremendous success of scientific explanation in rendering nature pliable to human interests, crowded out the equally essential human concerns for orientation, meaning and a sense of the wholeness of things summed up in the notion of religion. That is, the analytical and instrumental thrust of modern culture gave modern civilization new powers, but could not by itself provide that connection of the whole within which those new powers could find a stable place. Whitehead's repeated historical juxtaposition of the nineteenth century culture of romanticism, with its admiration for intuition, passion, beauty, faith and tradition, to the rationalizing schemes of materialist thought was designed to pose the problem of wholeness of vision which his philosophy tried to address.

The social import of Whitehead's line of thinking is not hard to grasp in its outlines. For in the practical world, too, instrumental calculation as refined by the development of commerce and modern industry had brought great gains in productive power and social wealth. The new potentials generated by technology and the capitalist economic order were a creative advance. But in their nineteenth century forms they seemed to Whitehead dangerously one-sided, emphasizing competitive dominance by individuals, firms and nations to the exclusion of all else. Economic individualism seemed likely to impoverish the possibilities for a more inclusive and richly developed civilization in the twentieth century. Thus, economic individualism, the familiar liberal confidence in the market as a self-directing engine of progress was, for Whitehead, itself a cultural force, an ideal and an abstraction of great simplicity and power. But, by virtue of its simplicity, it was also a dangerous abstraction, one in need of the balance and softening that location in a wider harmony could give it. To provide a vision of such a mediating context was the aim of much of Whitehead's social philosophy. His effort, as we shall see, was only partly successful.

However, today, the development of a new and still poorly understood world economy once again seems to have focused attention on the struggle to compete and to survive almost to the exclusion of all other concerns. Is there something to be learned by examining more closely the attempts by Whitehead and his contemporaries to think through the issues of enterprise and competition within a concern for the wholeness and integrity of social life? What follows will try to make a case for a positive answer to this question.

I.   The Revival of the Entrepreneurial Ideal

"Success," according to a cover of *Esquire* magazine in the spring of 1985, "is the religion of the 80's." At the same time, President Reagan announced that this was "the age of the individual," the "age of the entrepreneur." There is little doubt that the past decade in America has been marked by a revival of the old ideal of the entrepreneur, now presented as a moral hero, a selfless benefactor of society at large.[1] Only, unlike the previous great wave of American enthusiasm for entrepreneurship almost exactly a century ago, the current exhortations have a less promotional and more defensive tone about them. To extoll self-reliance and commercial initiative, figures such as George Gilder spend much energy arguing against the moral evil of a large-scale, paternalistic government which saps the initiative of individuals. Yet one of the most popular books of the genre has been Lee Iacocca's *Autobiography*, a story whose context is entirely that of massive corporations and in which timely governmental aid is a necessary means to its happy ending.[2]

The appeal of tales of successful entrepreneurship is akin to the appeal of the Western and the detective story. In both, the courageous, self-reliant individual challenges overwhelming odds and, often, oppressive tyranny to vindicate the value of fair play and initiative. But the hero of the Western, like the great detective, is rarely an ordinary citizen, and typically the story ends with its hero feeling as much an outsider to his society as he was at the beginning. Settled, "civilized" life is viewed with ambivalence. It is the guarantor of safety and comfort, but at the same time the story-line tells us that the heroic traits of the founders of great enterprises, such as Henry Ford, do not survive the first generation, so that the regularizing of a great business, like the taming of the West, is really the beginning of the end of moral virtue. Its comfort tempts the individual to passivity and dependence, frequently corrupts successors of the founder. And so the stage is set for the arrival of the next hero who will reinvigorate the moral energy of the frontier, at least for a time. Given this kind of cultural backdrop, it is not surprising that the heroics of business success have until very recently been considered by most an exclusively masculine achievement.

Yet there is something about evocations of this archetypal story of entrepreneurship in the 1980s. After all, the United States is not, and has not for a long time been, a nation of self-reliant business people. Fewer than 16% of Americans are self-employed; the great bulk of our citizens are employed by big businesses, either directly or through myriads of franchise chains and affiliates.[3] Besides, none of the leading competitor nations in Europe or East Asia operate on entrepreneurial lines. The economic development of those nations has been heavily directed by central banks and governments rather than by the free-wheeling practice of business entrepreneurs.[4] Thus, in the call to renew our national faith in self-reliant economic individualism one can hear the wish to return America to an idealized vision of a past conceived as prosperous, benign and free from complex organizations, above all free of Big Government. Can one not also hear in this call a deep suspicion about the entanglements of social complexity, and so a fear of being engulfed by a world grown too dense and too near?

Trying to reinvigorate American entrepreneurship, then, is a more complex task than some of its proponents may think. It is, after all, a recurrent effort in American history, and one so recurrent across decades as to suggest that it is an articulation of a widespread sentiment. The ideal entrepreneur is both idealistic and practically shrewd, fervor-driven and ingenious. The ideal derives from the venerable Old World wish to acquire an "independency" of sufficient holdings to maintain a dignified and independent household, an ideal which the American Revolution placed at the center of general aspiration.[5] Thus, economic enterprise was invested with republican moral meaning to produce the kind of independent yet community-minded citizens Jefferson hoped for and Alexis de Tocqueville thought he encountered in the nineteenth century rural and small-town United States.

However, that earlier American pattern was changed almost beyond recognition by the stressful transformation of American life which took place in those pivotal decades on both sides of the turn of this century. During most of the nineteenth century, American economic life was small-scale, and the majority of working people—themselves largely white males—were also "businessmen," entrepreneurs in the market for themselves. But the age of the great entrepreneurs changed the nature and scale of business so much that by the century's end most working people had become employees dependent on the "labor market." To date, this change has proved irreversible.

II.   The Pragmatic Philosopher's Critique of Enterprise

One way to begin recovering the context for the current interest in entrepreneurship is to recall that public discourse in the United States has, since the agitation for independence from Britain, concerned itself with the balance between individual freedom and the general welfare. First, preaching and theology bore the central burden of this effort at public moral argument, partly transformed as well as supplemented by an increasingly secular and scientific educated opinion. Then about the beginning of the century, with the institutionalizing of the scientific ideal in new research universities, the philosophy of pragmatism entered the public forum, allied with the new social sciences.[6] A chief concern of this new philosophy was to bring together a scientific tone of mind with moral concerns about the great changes in American life then taking place. Thinkers as diverse as Josiah Royce, William James, John Dewey and the British-born Alfred North Whitehead sought to shape public understanding of practical issues by enlarging the accepted frame of reference. They sought above all to articulate ways to play off creatively the spirit of freedom and innovation against the need for interconnection, community and loyalty. Perhaps the tone and vision of that era in American philosophy was summed up by Whitehead's admonition that "The problem is not how to produce great men, but how to produce great socieities. The great society will put up the men for the occasions."[7]

In the early decades of the century, John Dewey advocated the application of scientific methods to practical social life. However, he did not speak only from within an academic specialization simply to other specialists. In an important sense, John Dewey was a public philosopher, indeed a public figure, continuing the traditional role of cultural leadership which had been the special calling of the clergy. Moreover, Dewey was of the party of reform before the First World War, and after the national mood turned to embrace the corporate, consumer capitalism which had emerged in strength by 1920, Dewey remained its outspoken critic. Dewey's dissent from the post-war settlement in America set the tone for philosophy's public role as essentially constructive criticism, persuading toward "reconstruction," a role which continued until just before World War II.

Dewey's analysis of the shortcomings of the American economic order during the 1920s and 30s sheds useful light on the current revival of the entrepreneurial spirit. Essentially, Dewey argued that the lionizing of business enterprise which ruled the culture of the 1920s was simple-minded and short-sighted. (To many contemporaries, the Depression seemed to vindicate Dewey's analysis.) In *The Public and Its Problems* of 1927, and even

more pointedly in *Individualism: Old and New* of 1929, Dewey characterized the American economy as precarious. Pervasive, disruptive
technological change guided only by the blind market force of profit maximization spread a pervasive undercurrent of insecurity. This insecurity in
turn fed both a wild appetite for consumption and an anxious drive toward
competitive self-aggrandisement. As Dewey saw it, the Roaring Twenties
was marked by worry and restlessness even for the prosperous.[8] All this
was fed by an anachronistic and destructive moral individualism which the
industrial order had liberated from its old restraints only to turn loose in a
competitive scramble which undercut the aim at "wholeness which is urged
as the essence of religion." But for Dewey, "the attempt to cultivate it
(wholeness) first in individuals and then extend it to form an organically
unified society is fantasy." The only way to bring active individual striving
together with a self-sustained social order would be "membership in a society which had attained a degree of unity."[9] Dewey sought to adapt the
methods of natural science to the purposes of a social intelligence conceived
as at once moral, aesthetic and technical. He thought Americans could
create a society in which the moral impetus of individual enterprise would
be expressed "through personal participation in the development of a shared
culture."[10]

It was during the 1920s that Dewey was joined as exponent of a public
philosophy of social and moral reconstruction by the recently transplanted
British philosopher, Alfred North Whitehead. Like Dewey, Whitehead was
a member of the generation who reached maturity before 1914. As an
Englishman, Whitehead was heir to the British tradition of reform
associated with the social liberalism of T.H. Green and L.T. Hobhouse and
the pre-war Liberal Party. While Whitehead saw himself primarily as a
speculative philosopher in the grand tradition rather than as a social advocate, his lectures and publications during the 1920s were consciously
crafted with an approving eye on Dewey. Whitehead announced his own
work as allied to Dewey's thought and described himself as trying "to rescue
(it) . . . from the charge of anti-intellectualism, which rightly or wrongly
has been associated with it."[11] Despite differences in approach, Whitehead's
writings embodied and elaborated Dewey's claim that moral theory is "all
one with moral insight, and moral insight is the recognition of the relationships at hand."[12] Whitehead and Dewey shared, to different degrees, an
Anglo-American liberal spirit of reform which associated the good of the
nation with democracy and social justice.

III.   Whitehead's Philosophy as Critical Vision

Writing in the economic boom of the 1920s, Alfred North Whitehead concluded his Lowell lectures with an essay on "Requisites for Social Progress." Revised and expanded as *Science and the Modern World* in 1925, these lectures assessed the larger cultural meaning of what Whitehead called the three-century epoch of modern science. He there put forward the claim that primacy of the notion of "matter" as occupying a uniform space had proven finally inadequate as a way of making sense of the world opened up by twentieth century scientific discovery.

Whitehead argued that as a guiding metaphor for popular understanding the scheme of "scientific materialism" also had deleterious practical effects, particularly in the realm of economic life. The seventeenth century philosophers' separation of active mind from passive matter oversimplified things dangerously. It had passed into popular understanding. There, it suggested a legitimating metaphor for purely self-centered behavior, and it focused attention exclusively on the utilitarian aspects of the natural and social environment. "The doctrine of minds as independent substances," Whitehead wrote, "leads directly not merely to private worlds of experience but also to private worlds of morals." The cruelty and social destructiveness of nineteenth century industrialization were logical effects of a moral vision in which "self-respect, and the making the most of your own opportunities" occupied the central position.[13]

Thus, the long-term consequences of early modern mechanistic science have been to increase human control over natural processes, but only at the price of ignoring "the true relation of each organism to its environment," while reinforcing "the habit of ignoring the intrinsic worth of the environment."[14] Not surprisingly, Whitehead judged modern business civilization as an instance of these same imbalances, in which the economic actor, the entrepreneur, was conceived as related to the social world only mechanistically through the workings of the market. Indeed, Whitehead saw the moral and social individualism of Adam Smith's political economy as of a piece with the atomistic mechanism of Newton's era. In opposition to that long-dominant cosmology, Whitehead put forward a new synthetic vision, centered on the ideas of organism and interconnection.

Thus Whitehead's critique of economic individualism is internally related to his overall speculative enterprise. Like Dewey's pragmatism, Whitehead's process philosophy, which he termed "the philosophy of organism," was an effort to rethink the relation of individuals to the social and cultural matrix within which they live. This was an essentially ecological conception of both the natural and the social world. It took as its starting point the historical dissociation, which began with the Enlightenment, between scientific culture and the moral, religious and aesthetic dimensions of life. Modern social and intellecutal life has long been predicated on this dissociation, and yet, Whitehead thought, twentieth century scientific and cultural experience made the reality of interconnection and interdependence undeniable. But once this situation had been understood, the chief intellectual task became reconceiving and redescribing contemporary experience and practice in ways which illuminated interdependence and focused attention on it. In brief, this was the project Whitehead identified as the task of philosophy: to give the best account possible of how things hold together, and to do it in such a way as to stir and guide action.[15]

For this reason, Whitehead's speculative philosophy took the form of a search for a new language to reunite the "two cultures" later described by C.P. Snow. This philosophy was conceived as a general description sensitive to the historical, practical and aesthetic awareness of "literary intellecutals," yet carefully defined with something of the rigor of scientific discourse. But the very conception of this project means that this kind of philosophy had to break with a key feature of the modern philosophical discourse since Descartes and Locke: the demand that philosophy serve as a cognitive foundation for other "special" scientific disciplines. Instead, Whitehead proposed his philosophy as a speculative, comprehensive hypothesis subject to further revision.[16] Part of the foundationalist enterprise was the further demand that philosophy be intelligible in a self-contained manner, as exemplified in the quest for self-evident truths. But, as Robert Neville has observed, Whitehead's kind of philosophy "cannot be intelligible in a self-contained manner because it necessarily makes external reference to the fields it envisions and unifies, being both informed by them and informing them."[17] Such a conception of philosophy both crucially depends upon a dialogue among a wider range of participants than disciplinary specialists and aims to bring such a public into being.

However, constituting, or perhaps reconstituting, this conception of a literate, actively engaged public was, by the time of Whitehead's writing, a very difficult task. Whitehead's own understanding of the technological society already in place in the United States by the 1920s saw the conditions of modern life as posing a formidable problem. The kind of philosophic vision he was developing had as its practical premise an active public life which the epochal economic and social transformation of modern capitalism had rendered highly problematical.

The crucial determining feature of modern societies, according to Whitehead, has been their capacity for ceaseless scientific and technological innovation. He traced this capacity to a new social formation, "the discovery of the method of training professionals, who specialize in particular regions of thought and thereby progressively add to the sum of knowledge within their respective limitations of subject."[18] The long-term effect of this accelerating rate of progress would be to render "the fixed person, with fixed duties, who in older societies was such a god-send, in the future a public danger."

Certainly this essentially liberal conception of progress through science, while it echoes Condorcet, was also a reading of the importance of the new professional and managerial division of labor in twentieth century industrial society. Whitehead drew attention to the costs this process was exacting from individuals and community life. After all, he noted, the key to this new technical order is thinking methodologically, a habit of mind Whitehead called thinking in a groove. "The groove prevents straying across country. . . .But there is no groove of abstractions which is adequate for the comprehension of human life." The danger is that the habits of mind developed by specialized training will overwhelm and distort awareness of the larger, one might say ecological, order of connections and balances, thereby narrowing attention and vision.

Given the cultural climate of individualism strong in a business civilization, the new social forms of technological society seemed to Whitehead to be leading to the belief that there were "not merely private worlds of experience but also private worlds of morals" so that "the moral intuitions can be held to apply only to the strictly private world of psychological experience." Thus, despite the increase of a kind of technical rationality, reason as a feature of social and political life was actually weakening.

> The leading intellects lack balance. They see this set of circumstances or that set; but not both sets together. The task of coordination is left to those who lack either the force or the character to succeed in some definite career. In short, the specialized functions of the community are performed better and more progressively, but the generalized direction lacks vision.[19]

Finally, he concluded that achieving a "directive wisdom" appropriate to modern societies would be one of the "most useful discoveries for the immediate future." But, then, what was to be done?

Addressing the Harvard Business School on its twenty-fifth anniversary in 1933, Whitehead told his audience that the Depression showed the insufficiency of the corporate capitalist organization of society. The root of the problem was its neglect of the larger concerns of human social ecology as a whole. His analysis was brief and in outline not very different from Dewey's argument a few years earlier in *Individualism: Old and New*. Whitehead was strongly critical of both the specialized organization of work and the tendency of mass production and advertising to "canalize the aesthetic enjoyments of the population," a theme reminiscent of Aldous Huxley's *Brave*

New World.[20] The Depression, said Whitehead, demanded "economic statesmanship" of a high order to surmount the current breakdown, above all to overcome unemployment. But this would require that the "great commercial corporations . . . should enlarge the scope of their activity . . . to interweave in their organizations individual craftsmanship operating upon the products of their mass production."[21] Here Whitehead's vision was once again ecological, with an invocation of John Ruskin's call to the civilizing and liberating effects of craft and artisanship. Whitehead continued to try to reintegrate and balance. He acknowledged that his proposals would "destroy much of the sweet simplicity of modern business policy which fastens its attention solely on one aspect of our complex human nature," but only to achieve a greater degree of social development by "stabilizing the popular requirements and widening the area of useful occupations."[22]

For despite his criticisms, Whitehead thought that modern society would remain a technical and specialized one. The issue was how to civilize it. His answer was largely to appeal eloquently for "statesmanship" and "education." Yet his liberal confidence that somehow good sense would prevail kept Whitehead from seriously addressing the difficult political problems raised by both his analysis and his vision.

IV. The Limits of Philosophy as Cultural Vision

The great strength of Whitehead's philosophy of organism was its critique of the assumptions of empiricist science and atomistic individualism. By arguing that these premises no longer made sense of the world of twentieth century natural science, Whitehead cleared the ground for his positive statement that both physical and human reality was better viewed in an "ecological" way. In human affairs this recovery of the notion of "internal relations" among entities meant that individuals were best understood as sharing with others in various matrices of interconnectedness. Thus each of us stands not simply over against others, as the old individualist culture would have it, but rather with others in as much as they are part of who we are by virtue of our common participation in shared concerns. Like Dewey and George Herbert Mead, Whitehead argues for the self as a social entity. The metaphor of organism and environment, like the Aristotelian logic of whole and part, enabled Whitehead to highlight the overriding dependence of all individual flourishing on the maintenance of a stable, though changing, matrix of interdependence.

Yet this ecological concern was not opposed to historical change. Like Dewey, Whitehead believed in progress and wanted to help direct and humanize the dynamism of modern societies. He hoped that democracy would serve as the great civilizing ideal in the technological age in somewhat the way Christianity had civilized the barbarians after the collapse of classical culture. Science, the market and technology were to be purified of their destructive potentials and given meaning by an organized effort to bring them into a coherent social and cultural order. Concretely, Whitehead admired Elton Mayo, of the Harvard Business School during the 1920s and 30s, for his efforts to reconstitute a moral community under industrial conditions through reorganizing factories into small production groups. This counter-Taylorist conception of industrial organization recalled for Whitehead John Ruskin and William Morris, with their hopes for reconstituting a polity of interdependent artisans.

Thus Whitehead's criticism of the "rugged individualism" of the nineteenth century entrepreneur was linked to this positive program of reuniting the scientific, moral and aesthetic dimensions of modern experience, the three separate spheres of Kantian philosophy, in a new aesthetic teleology of the whole. Whitehead looked to the aesthetic order of whole and part, as in the metaphor of organism, to reunite the scientific and "humanistic" forms of intelligence. In this he resembled contemporaries such as the young Lewis Mumford who, in 1924, wrote that ". . . our concern with physical utilities and with commercial values is something more than an abstract defect in our philosophy. On the contrary, it seems to inhere in the dominant occupations of the country, and it is less to be overcome by moralizing and exhortation than to be grown out of, by taking pains to provide for the ascendency and renewal of the more humane occupations."[23] In the end, it seems Whitehead looked to the attractive power of his synthetic vision to persuade leaders and "statesmen" in the various specialized fields of modern endeavour, such as Elton Mayo, to work toward weaving the "specialized functions of the community" into a social order of moral and aesthetic coherence.

The ecological conception of self and society certainly gave a sense of direction and comfort to those who felt the attraction of this goal, but according to Whitehead's own theory, persons only come to share understandings by becoming genuine partners in a common concern. American society could have gone in that direction only by deliberate, considered actions, which means that the cultural program could only have been actualized by effectively entering the realm of politics. But in its larger aims Whitehead's project failed. The two cultures of literary and scientific intellectuals have grown further apart in the decades since his death, just after

World War II, while both "cultures" have developed a great distance from the public at large. Perhaps most tellingly, process philosophy itself, like pragmatism, has become one more subspecialization among others within the highly professionalized field of academic philosophy. And as to its impact on public discussion about economic life, Whitehead's few essays on the subject never made much lasting impact.

American society has evolved since the 1930s in ways very different from the ways Whitehead or Dewey or Mumford had hoped it would. Whitehead's concern about the suppression of the sense of craftmanship in work was not so much resolved after the U.S. economy emerged from the Depression via World War II, as it was displaced for many by the attractions of a new suburban, consumer society. The new affluence of this society was made available by war-generated technological advances and government-financed social investments which aided a corporate-labor *detente*. As long as the nation maintained its economic and military world preeminence, steady economic growth seemed to obviate the need for more fundamental economic reorganization. Even the great waves of social unrest which broke over the "affluent society" during the 1960s concerned the inclusion of denied minorities in the general prosperity. It took the faltering of the post-War economic arrangements during the 1970s to place the basics of that post-war settlement more or less on the national agenda. Enter, at this point, the entrepreneur *redivivus*.

In this historical perspective, the upsurge of entrepreneurial faith appears as an effort at something like revitalizing business culture. The new entrepreneur, whether a Lee Iacocca (or John DeLorean) or a high-tech innovator, is above all a figure who breaks out of the hidebound, overly organized environment of American corporate life to conquer new markets and expand the frontiers of enterprise. Where conventional economic institutions have lost ground to foreign competitors or failed to respond to new challenges, the new entrepreneur proves again the capacity of Yankee ingenuity to succeed competitively. There is in this the Nietzschean tone of human will redeeming itself against dead mechanism. Thus for George Gilder, the entrepreneur is a generous, fructifying figure, providing needed goods and services for the community, but he is also a paradigm of energetic self-assertion who abashes the lazy herd—and returns women to their proper place!

The case for revived entrepreneurship is, then, couched in old American moral terms much of the time: industry versus sloth, self-reliance versus servile dependence. Yet there is another, far from comforting, side to the entrepreneurial revival, one which has affinities with the Social Darwinist view of nature as struggle for survival which helped justify the deeds of the turn-of-the-century commercial empire builders. Against the tidy, Newton-ian equilibrium assumptions of classical and neo-classical economic theory, which is tacitly assumed by much of the entrepreneurial literature, there is the conception of economic development put forward by Joseph Schumpeter and, more recently, by Mancur Olson. According to this view, the logic of market behavior drives in a Hobbesian direction as en-trepreneurs struggle to dominate and control markets, a process which ultimately results in oligopoly and rigidity. Economic advance comes in periods of creative destruction when old formations of capital are by-passed and destroyed by new technological advances. These are the moments of the entrepreneurs. But their role is temporary and self-limiting, as they pur-sue their self-interest in struggling to control, and so rigidify, the new markets. The Nietzschean resonance here is with the theme of the eternal return of the same rather than the triumph of the will.

Only the current entrepreneurial revival is not a return of the same. The structural realities of the world economic system have changed dramatically from the situation of the 1950s, let alone 1900. No national economy, not even our own, can operate independently of the larger environment, and all economies today are heavily dependent upon governmental involvement in the form of subsidy, planning or direct control. Even President Reagan's favorite success story, the entrepreneur of Silicon Valley, is the the direct result of federal development of the microchip through the space program, and of massive federal spending on scientific education and research. The moral evocation of self-reliant enterprise, by itself, can hardly be expected to resolve the problems of the American economy today. These problems are rooted in the complex reality of the modern world system of interna-tional investment and production. But it is precisely the social complexity of interdependence and large-scale institutions that American culture has had great difficulty making moral sense of beyond the evocation of the small community and the self-reliant hero of enterprise.

V.   An Opening toward a New Public Philosophy

One might venture that Whitehead was in large part correct, that the problem is at basis a lack of cultural vision, but that this vision must in turn become embodied in institutional and political life. The problem with the entrepreneurial ideal is its incompleteness. It conceives the self alone as the source of energy and misconceives the ecology of human interconnection as suffocating except when negotiated in terms of self-interest. What is missing is a coherent moral whole which could sustain and give a shared meaning to enterprise. The pathos of the valorization of the entrepreneur, to the exclusion of the larger institutional and social context, is the inability of this project to recover for modern technological life the cognitive and moral coherence necessary for active citizenship. Whitehead's social vision, like Dewey's, helps us see better what has been the cognitive price of progress, but also what needs to be recovered and reconstructed. But if Whitehead and Dewey were correct, the most urgent need is the recreation amid the economic and social conditions of our time of an active public, together with the institutions and the moral ecology which can sustain it.

To take just one example of what is an enormous task, consider the relation between citizenship and professional specialization, which Whitehead saw as the crux of the modern problem. Particularly as large areas of social life have been brought under the guidance of specialized agencies and business management itself has become increasingly professionalized, the interconnection between culture and politics has become more apparent.

Part of the story of the fading of Dewey's vision of philosophy was the increasing vogue of the notion that knowledge about social matters could be made technically precise and value-neutral on the model of the natural sciences. A version of this notion of technical rationality came after World War II to dominate virtually all the areas of professional practice. But since its era of ascendency in the 1950s and 1960s, confidence in this model of practice has entered a period of increasing crisis, as its claim to "solve" managerial and social problems in a purely technical manner has proven empty.[24] In ways that would have heartened Whitehead and Elton Mayo, the theory and teaching of management have been forced to give conscious attention to the social nexus of managerial practice, which the model of technical rationality had tried to supersede. Not surprisingly, this deflation of the claims of technical expertise has created new problems of self-definition for managers.

The technical model of professional practice defined the manager as an expert in the application of specific techniques to problems of resource and personnel allocation and production within complex organizations. The manager was thought to be a sort of social engineer, deploying value-neutral techniques to facilitate the achievement of agreed-upon ends. The manager as such stood outside the discussions of the purposes of the organization he or she served. But the collapse of confidence in the model of technical rationality has broken down the basic assumption of cognitive and moral distance between the manager and the managed, suddenly muddying the clarity of the managerial task by forcing moral terms such as trust and responsibility into discussions of managerial effectiveness. Of course, the force of the bottom line still operates, but the manager now must contend as well with forming consensus, leading a "team," and other activities traditionally more associated with politics than business. Certainly, this recent turn toward the "human," that is the moral and political, aspects of organizational life is of a piece with the switch from the economy conceived as a mechanism driven by the anti-heroic consumer to seeing it as the field in which the entrepreneur can exhibit moral courage. Fitfully, American culture seems to be rediscovering the practical basis of its institutions and its techniques, even if as yet only selectively.

In this dramatically changed context, the conception of the professional manager as the detached expert no longer rings true. The result is the blurring of boundaries between the manager's technical competence and his or her moral and political situation. Suddenly, the professional needs to consider his or her responsibility in a wider, more complex context. What is his or her responsibility to his or her organization, his or her subordinates, and what does he or she contribute to the community as a whole? These are no longer the questions of the technician. They are the animating concerns of the citizen. One consequence of this unsettling situation is the attempt to make the idealized entrepreneur the new role model for the manager. This approach has been proposed by a variety of writers in the business area.[25] The entrepreneurial model implicitly answers the questions of contribution and responsibility by urging the manager to conceive his or her situation in marketing terms. Yet here the simplistic moral vision of entrepreneurship runs up against the structural realities of modern conditions of work. These more and more demand team work and group loyalty, particularly in the innovative industries, rather than the old entrepreneurial competitiveness or the conformity of the "organization man."[26] The entrepreneurial ideal simply is not adequate, cognitively or morally, to the dimensions of the current managerial crisis. But, then, what is? Recognition of this problem has intensified the long-developing merger of the techniques of therapeutic management of the psyche with management of "things." Yet that is not the only alternative.

Perhaps this is the first moment in the past half-century when there is an opening in American culture for reconstituting a genuinely democratic public life. The very crisis of technical rationality which has called up the entrepreneurial ideal may also hold the potential for a recovery of the moral dimension of economic life. The ecological metaphor of Whitehead may be our best evocation of that sense.[27] To stay with the example of professional, managerial practice, the breakdown of the division between expertise and conduct is creating a kind of moral vacuum, and might it not be conceivable to fill this vacuum by reappropriating the ethical meaning of professional life? This would mean recovering the notion of a profession as a public trust, with responsibilities for the public welfare. And, in turn, such a reappropriation would mean reorganizing the conduct of management, so that it could play a consciously responsible public role.

To proceed in this direction requires going beyond Whitehead himself, while trying to continue the mediating intent of his thought. In his formulation of "economic statesmanship," Whitehead was perhaps too persuaded by Elton Mayo's focus on the manager as the organizer of community in the workplace. Not that this was entirely wrong, since as the development of similar managerial techniques in Europe, Japan and the United States indicates, managerial statesmanship may well be the key to increased worker productivity. But the focus on "humanizing" the workplace leaves unquestioned the radically unequal power relationships between managers and workers in large firms. More importantly, it also accepts without question the pressure of the competitive market environment, a pressure to maximize the return on capital or risk elimination in the selective struggle to survive. In this context, whatever civilizing of managerial practice economic statesmanship may effect will always be limited and controlled by market forces, not by ideals of ethical responsibility. This ethical limitation remains the central, unresolved problem for the professional manager.

Finally, then, it seems as if the modern manager cannot reach full ethical responsibility within the specialized function of business management alone. The professional's sense of moral obligation to the greater good of those he or she works with and for can only be discharged in his or her capacity as citizen. But how, in the complex modern polity, is that obligation to be identified among the manager's conflicting interests and obligations to employers, stockholders, subordinates, clients, consumers and the larger public? The very dynamism of the modern market seems to preclude the relative stability of the old ethic of "my station and its duties."

Here Dewey's theme that democracy is above all else a public dialogue about the interplay of needs, interests and the consequences of pursuing interests may help fill out what is missing in Whitehead's conception. Over and against the *laissez faire* image of public life as a market in the sense of a free-for-all of competitive interests and accommodations restrained only by neutral rules of fairness, Dewey sought, as we have seen, to construct a new image of the public. Dewey's public was not simply an interplay of interests, but a discussion about them. Or rather, it was a discussion of the consequences of the pursuit of interests within a context shaped by the aim at community, at a life together. Thus, Dewey continued the old liberal faith in the capacity of citizens to learn the skills of rational deliberation and compromise within the context of public life. Yet, this was not a simplistic representation of Jeffersonian optimism. In the complexity of the modern situation, citizens needed the counsel of experts with a sense of the larger situation, not simply the services of brokers of interests. And it was to public-spirited professionals of many kinds that Dewey looked to provide this needed catalyst for the democratic public. Dewey envisioned the professionals and the public checking and stabilizing each other.

However, at this juncture the same problem of professional responsibility arises again. What is to prevent the professional's vision, or that of anyone else in the public, from remaining fixed at the level of self-promotion and self-defense? Dewey's answer to this problem was incomplete and ultimately unsatisfactory, just as Whitehead's was, but it does point us toward a clearer conception of the fundamental issue that is posed by the project of mediating enterprise and community life. Dewey answered that politics must become as a process of moral education: an ancient theme but one hardly in favor—or perhaps even very credible—at present! Yet, Dewey rightly thought that a serious commitment to the ideal of democracy makes it impossible to avoid confronting the question of how to promote a genuinely active, educated citizenry.

VI. Conclusion: Revising the Topic

In the end, both Whitehead and Dewey were too optimistic about the possibilities which modern life offered for educating specialized workers and professionals in the sense of the common good required for active citizenship. It is not enough to call for participation if that means only the assertion of new interests unintelligibly juxtaposed against others. It is certainly not enough to trust managerial professionals to look out for the good of the whole when the social environment is structured primarily by the selective pressures of economic competition. Already in early nineteenth century America, Alexis de Toqueville had worried that "self-interest rightly understood" could work beneficently only so long as it was formed and guided by a religious morality that emphasized mutual solidarity over individual dominance. We might see Whitehead's struggle for a mediating understanding adequate to the diverse range of forces and ideals in modern society a continuation of Tocqueville's concern for a freedom complemented by connection and sharing. Certainly, this was the import of Whitehead's religious vision. Without the diffusion of the attractive and shaping power of a moral vision that exalts trust and solidarity over aggression and defensiveness, it is not likely that participation, no matter how widespread, nor mere communication, no matter how extensive, will by themselves produce a viable social life.

However, Whitehead's example also makes it clear that this mediating understanding, while it must represent a continuing intellectual quest, with the attendant risks of failure and cynicism, cannot be only cognitive. The sense of intellectual adventure and hope characteristic of the spirit of mediation requires the practical grounding of active trust and solidarity, which is to say that to make politics a moral education in citizenship, a society must possess a widely diffused public culture. Reconstructing this amid the complexity of modern society requires a mediating vision such as both Whitehead and Dewey attempted in their day. And this kind of sustaining vision is possible only when its practical conditions are understood and sustained by communities of trust and solidarity. But how can these communities avoid lapsing into defensive, intolerant closure, as has so often happened to efforts at sustaining a moral ecology? While there is no *a priori* guaranteed solution to this problem, the notion of the public as committed to openness and inclusion, an ideal which has in American history frequently asserted itself in the struggle with the press toward closure, can suggest that the ethos of democracy to which Dewey appealed may prove a vital resource again. In this perspective, the problem of reemphasizing the professions in a more public context becomes an important part within the larger project of refashioning the democratic life of the public.

However, the context for this discussion is no longer the United States alone, nor even Western civilization, for the emerging context of life in the late twentieth century is global, and a global interdependence at that. Ours is a moment in which nations and regions are entering more energetically and more desperately than at any time since World War II into a struggle for dominance in market and military competition. It cannot help but be a contest for survival as well.

In this new and threatening context, one clear imperative seems strength at any cost, for only the strong survive. Virtually everywhere, there is renewed emphasis on winning the economic contest and building military power. Thus, the American focus on entrepreneurship is a reflection of global tendencies to find strategies of more successful competition. There is no single economic and political power center, such as Britain before World War I or the U.S. after 1945. Instead, the present world is multi-centered and unstable. Thus, a vision that could make our interdependence morally meaningful and mutually constructive rather than destructive may be our only long-term alternative to violent efforts to establish order through world dominance. In the absence of a single cultural center which could supply such a moral vision, such as the Christian church of the European middle ages, we must look to the plurality of moral agencies on the world scene and seek to build a new integration through them. And here

Whitehead's pluralistic philosophy of emergent harmony seems to speak rather directly to the needs of our time. The Whiteheadian vision reminds us that we have a choice, that there is a possible, if not an inevitable, alternative to the escalating selective competition which may very likely prove fatal for the hopes of all peoples. That alternative is the vision of world civilization guided by a sense of the whole, of the ever-changing balance among interdependent parts through which each achieves its own flourishing. In the end, Whitehead gave a name to this vision, which he thought had stood at the center of all civilizations throughout the painful struggles of history. He called it peace.

Notes and References

1.   See George Gilder's *Wealth and Poverty* (New York: Basic Books, 1981). Gilder's book was a big seller in the early 1980s.

2.   See: Lee Iacocca, *Iacocca: An Autobiography* (New York: Bantam Books, 1985).

3.   See: James Oliver Robertson, *America's Business* (New York: Hill and Wang, 1985), pp. 241-5.

4.   See: Robert B. Reich, *The Next American Frontier* (New York: Times Books, 1983).

5.   Robertson, *America's Business*, pp. 46-7.

6.   See: Bruce Kuklick, *Churchmen and Philosophers: From Jonathan Edwards to John Dewey* (New Haven: Yale University Press, 1985).

7.   Alfred North Whitehead, *Science and the Modern World* (New York: Free Press, Macmillan, 1967, original 1925), p. 205. See also: John E. Smith, *The Spirit of American Philosophy* (New York: Oxford University Press, 1963).

8.   John Dewey, *Individualism: Old and New* (New York: Capricorn Books, 1962), esp. pp. 51-5.

9.   Dewey, *Ibid.*, p. 64.

10.   Dewey, *Ibid.*, p. 34.

11.   Alfred North Whitehead, *Process and Reality: An Essay in Cosmology* (New York: Macmillan, 1929), p. vii.

12.   John Dewey, "Moral Theory and Practice" in *Early Works of John Dewey* (Carbondale: Southern Illinois University Press, 1972), Vol. 3, p. 94.

13.   Alfred North Whitehead, *Science and the Modern World*, op. cit., pp. 195-6.

14.   Whitehead, *Science and the Modern World*, op. cit., p. 196.

15.   Whitehead's clearest discussions of these ideas are in the final chapter of *Science and the Modern World*, as cited; *Process and Reality*, as cited, Ch. 1; and the last chapter of *Modes of Thought* (New York: Free Press, 1968; original, Macmillian, 1938).

16.   Richard Rorty's *Philosophy and the Mirror of Nature* (Princeton: Princeton University Press, 1979) has argued that the "foundationalist enterprise of modern philosophy is over," ending "philosophy" as such. However, Rorty, while lionizing Dewey, dismisses Whitehead as a metaphysician. Also see: *Consequences of Pragmatism* (Minneapolis: University of Min-

nesota Press, 1982), Ch. 4, 5, and 12. By contrast, Franklin I. Gamwell has argued that only a development of something like Whitehead's metaphysics can save Dewey's theory of valuation from fatal inconsistency. See: *Beyond Preference: Liberal Theories of Independent Associations* (Chicago: University of Chicago Press, 1984), pp. 119ff.

17.   Robert C. Neville, "Contributions and Limitations of Process Philosophy," p. 4, Invited Paper, American Philosophical Association, Eastern Division Meeting, Dec., 1984, unpublished.

18.   Whitehead, *Science and the Modern World, op. cit.* This and following quotations are from pp. 282-3.

19.   Whitehead, *Science and the Modern World op. cit.*, pp. 282-3.

20.   Whitehead, "The Study Of The Past—Its Uses And Dangers," in *Science And Philosophy* (Patterson, NJ: Littlefield, Adams and Co., 1964), p. 168.

21.   Whitehead, *Ibid.*, pp. 169-70.

22.   Whitehead, *Ibid.*, p. 173.

23.   Lewis Mumford, *Sticks and Stones: A Study in American Architecture and Civilization* (New York: Dover Publ., 1955, original 1924), p. 109.

24.   See: Donald A. Schön, *The Reflective Practitioner: Toward an Epistemology of Practice* (New York: Basic Books, 1983).

25.   See, among others: *In Search of Excellence*, by Thomas J. Peters and Robert H. Waterman, Jr. (New York: Harper and Row, 1983).

26.   See: Michael Maccoby's social-psychological study of high-tech management in: *The Gamesman: The New Corporate Leaders* (New York: Simon and Schuster, 1976).

27.   I used the term "moral ecology" to describe the matrix of human interrelation ignored yet presupposed by individualistic and instrumental theories of action in *Reconstructing Public Philosophy* (Berkeley: University of California Press, 1982).

28.   These themes are developed in more detail in a jointly-authored work: *Habits of the Heart: Individualism and Commitment in American Life*, by Robert N. Bellah, Richard Madsen, William M. Sullivan, Ann Swidler and Steven M, Tipton (Berkeley: University of California Press, 1985).

CHAPTER 2

Economic Individualism and the Prospects for Civilizing Enterprise: A Response to William Sullivan

Daniel Rush Finn

Few phenomena in the modern world have rivaled economic individualism in the breadth and intensity of both its creative and destructive effects. It has created great wealth for even the "ordinary" people of the industrialized world and it has rent immense tapestries of human life in the process. So powerful are the effects of an economic structure based on individualism that both Schumpeter and Veblen predicted it would undermine the very moral foundations necessary for its own existence.

Thus, the task of understanding and responding to economic individualism is one of the most critical of our day. It is also arguably among the most difficult.

I. Just What is "Economic Individualism"?

One of the fundamental difficulties in discussing (and critiquing) American individualism is presented by the array of meanings and justifications for this phenomenon. There are at least five alternative visions of individualism in the United States, although there is some overlap and few people employ only one line of analysis to the exclusion of others.

The first is a conception of individualism as the immediate alternative to "big government." In this view, represented for example by Friedrich von Hayek's *The Road to Serfdom*, the dangers of totalitarianism are risked when the individual's autonomy is compromised. The evils of communism, and to some extent fascism, are so apparent that proponents of this view are willing to countenance significant shortcomings arising from individual activity rather than risk allowing an opening wedge to domineering government.

The second vision of individualism is an explicit appreciation of the strong and independent individual as most fully human. Among the most simplistic such defenses of individualism is that proposed in the novels of Ayn Rand, where the only really interesting people are those who are ruggedly individualistic. They are also simultaneously (and one is led to believe necessarily) more intelligent and even more magnanimous than the bleeding hearts, the sycophants and the bureaucrats that surround them. Somewhat more restrained is the defense of the individual offered more recently by George Gilder.

The third vision represents a defense of American individualism by denying the premise that Americans *are* all that individualistic in the first place. Michael Novak stands as an eloquent, if not always persuasive, proponent of this approach in his treatment of "the communitarian individual" in *The Spirit of Democratic Capitalism* and *Freedom with Justice*. By his description, "the ideal of the middle-class man or woman is not to be a rugged individual, isolated and alone. To be independent, yes, and also self-reliant. Yet also . . . to be open to appeals from the needy, to be informed about the world at large, and to care about its problems. The middle-class ideal is communitarian." (*Spirit*, p. 155.)

A fourth defense of American individualism comes in the form of Social Darwinism. Such a perspective finds the purging effects of competitive pressures as positive forces in ensuring that the "best" of the citizenry have the most influence on society and enjoy its greatest benefits. As Andrew Carnegie put it in 1899, ". . . while the law (of competition) may be sometimes hard for the individual, it is best for the race, because it insures the survival of the fittest in every department." (Carnegie, *North American Review*, June 1899.)

The fifth, and from my experience, the most economically influential conception of American individualism is the view that individualism is the most basic reality to which we owe the prosperity and vitality of American life. From this perspective, most of what we value as Americans—including our standard of living, our civil liberties and our sense of purpose—is attributable to the ways in which our individualism has taken us beyond the traditionalism, the mediocrity and/or the tyranny of our European countries of origin. In this view of things it is the dynamism of millions of individuals each acting in accord with their own values and views that propels both our economic prosperity and our civic vitality. I would refer to this as the consequentialist view of individualism since it points to the positive effects of individualism in the face of contrary moral arguments concerning social obligations.

The phenomenon of the "revival of the entrepreneurial ideal," which William Sullivan analyzes in his essay in this volume, receives its primary moral defense from the second and fifth of these conceptions. Sullivan himself presents a multi-faceted approach to the topic, making a brief summary of his argument appropriate.

II. The Argument

Any short summary is risky, but I shall attempt one in an effort to ensure agreement on what is being discussed. I understand Sullivan's argument to be roughly as follows:

1. We are experiencing a revival of a particular kind of economic individualism, the entrepreneurial ideal, although to a large extent this is a wistful anachronism in today's complex economy. (Section I)

2. Philosophers such as Dewey and Whitehead have critiqued the individualizing effects of technological change and the "scientific materialism" that left people in "private worlds of experience" and "private worlds of morals." (Sections II and III)

3. The solution Whitehead (and others) proposed is the re-creation of a "democratically active public." (Section III)

4. Whitehead's hope for this solution was rooted in the appeal for statesmanship and education, a hope which has proven ill-founded. (Section IV)

5. The ideal of the entrepreneur cannot provide "the cognitive and moral coherence necessary for active citizenship." (Section V)

6. Recent years have found the technical, purportedly value-neutral approach to management giving way to a more human managerial style where "the animating concerns of the citizen" (such as wider responsibility, team work and group loyalty) are playing important roles. (Section V)

7. This change is "perhaps . . . the first moment in the past half-century when there is an opening in American culture for

reconstituting a genuinely democratic public life." At the same time, however, whatever positive effects such changes may bring about, they will "always be limited and controlled by market forces, not by ideals of ethical responsibility." (Section V)

8. Due to this limitation, an adequate public life will come only through a "moral vision" emerging out of Dewey's conception of politics "as a process of moral education." (Sections V and VI)

Sullivan is clearly correct in arguing for a construal of the human person as a "social self." Just as clearly, many of the defenders of American individualism stand opposed to this understanding. The second perspective listed above is characterized most boldly by viewing the human person as the "individual self." Thus it is that, for example, libertarians are among the least grateful people in our society. They often appear oblivious to their intellectual, cultural and economic debt to others of their own generation and to those of the several hundred generations that preceded them in human history. Without a strong sense of the social self, any defense of entrepreneurship degenerates into an empirically naive and morally inadequate encomium.

The most blatant example of this naivete is perhaps Ayn Rand's character, Dagny Taggert, the railroad entrepreneur in *Atlas Shrugged*. Having preached the virtues and abilities of the self-directed individual throughout the story, Rand's central heroes find themselves in a remote, hidden valley. In the process of setting up life anew (and even better than on the outside), one individual single-handedly sets up the electrical system, another a copper mine, and Dagny's job (admittedly with some part-time help for her) is to *build a railroad down the side of a mountain!*

The rise in interest in entrepreneurship to which Sullivan points is indeed a form of American individualism, but its varieties equal those of individualism itself. It might have been helpful to identify these in more detail, since individualism has very different meanings in different contexts. To take two examples, it comes closer to the cult of the individual in much political discussion, including politically influential theorizing by George Gilder and others, and it comes closer to the consequentialist argument when religiously and ethically oriented scholars like Michael Novak engage the issue.

In addition, I am not at all sure of the status of this "revival of the entrepreneurial ideal" of which Sullivan speaks. Is it a primarily conceptual movement? Or has the U.S. economy *actually* changed and become more entrepreneurial—which presumably would mean being less encumbered in the social complexities of large corporate structures and less averse to corporate risk. Certain sectors of the economy, e.g., electronics, are currently characterized by both rapid technological change and relatively few economies of scale (i.e., fairly constant average unit cost over a large range of possible firm sizes), and as a result there is opportunity for entrepreneurial advantage. Yet the vast bulk of the economy is made up of either traditionally small business enterprises (where local entrepreneurship continues to wane in the face of regional and national chains) or very large corporate structures (which are generally considered to be the antithesis of true entrepreneurship). The question is: Just how much stock can we put in the "revival of entrepreneurship" as a real phenomenon likely to be influential and to endure in the U.S. economy?

III. Two Critical Correlations

If I have correctly understood the internal logic of Sullivan's paper, there are two separate correlations that are critical to it. The first is between, on the one hand, Whitehead's (and Dewey's) aim to reunite the "two cultures" and, on the other, the integration of technical and citizenly tasks in the new form of management. The second is between, on the one hand, this new form of management and, on the other, the revival in the ideal of entrepreneurship. As I read it, Sullivan relates entrepreneurship and Whitehead through this vision of a new manager which amounts to "a dramatically changed context."

Section V deals extensively with the role of corporate managers. Sullivan perceives that we have come to an end of "scientific management," a purportedly value-neutral, technical style of organizational control. Managers, he reports, now are concerned with "the social nexus," with "the animating concerns of the citizen," at least in part. In this regard I have two concerns which call into question the two correlations referred to above.

The first question is whether the sort of changes that are indeed going on in American management really reflect the kind of integration that Whitehead and others sought. Through most of Section V, Sullivan speaks quite hopefully of the possibilities. As the prior brief summary indicated, in describing the shift in management he states, "Perhaps this is the first moment in the past half-century when there is an opening in American culture for reconstituting a genuinely democratic public life." Yet the reader is forced to ask whether there really is a new appreciation for consensus formation, team-work and wider responsibility *for their own sake* or whether they are appreciated simply as techniques for greater productivity.

Sullivan is aware of this problem, which is why he observes that whatever positive effects such changes may bring about, they will "always be limited and controlled by market forces, not by ideals of ethical responsibility." Once this is admitted, however, it is not at all clear how such strong hope for "reconstituting a genuinely democratic public life" can be sustained. If he agrees that these "concerns of the citizen" are currently due to their productive efficacy, then we must admit that should they be found tomorrow to be unproductive, firms would drop them as readily as they picked them up.

The second question is whether the sorts of changes that are going on in American management are really related to the revival of the entrepreneurial ideal. As I read it, Sullivan merely asserts (Section V) that the changes in management are "of a piece with" the revival of the entrepreneur. While the entrepreneur may exert "moral courage" I fail to see how this is related to the movement to participatory forms of management. Sullivan may have more to say about this, but the correlation, critical as it may be to relating his treatment of entrepreneurship and Whitehead, appears strained.

IV. What are the Prospects for Change?

In the end, Sullivan places his hopes for substantial change in politics, as Dewey understood it: "as a process of moral education." That is, having a "moral vision that exalts trust and solidarity over aggression and defensiveness" is the only way that other proximate goals like participation and communication can bring about significantly improved conditions.

What, then, is the meaning of the revival of entrepreneurship or of the appearance of a more humane managerial style? Since these are phenomena outside the realm of politics and are limited by economic considerations, the answer would seem to have to be that they are ultimately of little significance. Sullivan makes a reference in Section VI to "the problem of reemphasizing the professions in a more public context," but how such a reemphasis would occur or what it might look like are left open. In his consideration of the broader world situation, he comes to a similarly general conclusion: "we must look to the plurality of moral agencies on the world scene and seek to build a new integration through them."

The problem in all of this is not that Sullivan is wrong in what he asserts. In fact, a more robust life of the polity *would* bring the promise of developing moral vision. The problem experienced by at least this reader is disappointment. Sullivan's extended consideration of the revival of entrepreneurship and the changes in management seemed to be leading toward an argument that these are literally crucial events from the point of view of the philosophy of organism which Whitehead developed. His conclusion seems clearly to be that they are not. I agree with him.

CHAPTER 3

Property: A Relational Perspective

Douglas Sturm

The great and chief end . . . of men's uniting into commonwealths, and putting themselves under government, is the preservation of their property (John Locke).[1]

The transformation of scattered private property, arising from individual labour, into capitalist private property is, naturally, a process incomparably more protracted, violent, and difficult, than the transformation of capitalist private property, already practically resting on socialized production, into socialized property. In the former case, we had the expropriation of the mass of the people by a few usurpers; in the latter, we have the expropriation of a few usurpers by the mass of people. (Karl Marx).[2]

I

1. Conditions of the common life of peoples have undergone a radical transformation from the seventeenth century to the present. The character of daily work, the form of family life, the structure of nations and empires in our times are fundamentally unlike those of three centuries ago. In the economic sector, property is among the categories of thought and practice whose features have been transfigured during the period.

In the seventeenth century, John Locke, siding with the Whigs against the Tories, cast his renowned argument supporting individualized property at the center of his concept of civil government. The chief purpose of civil government, he insisted, is the preservation of property. Locke's argument, despite its ambiguities, is still invoked, particularly in disputes over social legislation and progressive taxation.

However, in the nineteenth century, Karl Marx averred that the meaning and character of property have changed over the course of history and are in process of changing once again. Individualized private property has given way to capitalist private property, but the latter, in time, will give way to socialized property. More recently, C.B. Macpherson has voiced a similar judgment:

> The meaning of property is not constant. The actual institution, and the way people see it, and hence the meaning they give to the word, all change over time. We shall see that they are changing now. The changes are related to changes in the purposes which society or the dominant classes in society expect the institution of property to serve.[3]

The term, "property," has several specialized senses. It may designate the essential features of a thing (thus the "properties" of vertebrates or oak trees). It may refer to parcels of land or buildings (thus a superintendent manages "properties"). But in economic relations, property is the claim or title someone has to something tangible or intangible. Locke and Marx use the term in this last sense. And it is this sense with which I am concerned.

I intend to explore the meaning of property from a relational perspective, a perspective derived from the tradition of process thought. Throughout the exploration, I shall be focussing not so much on the law of property as on its fundamental meaning, although, to be sure, the law of property cannot finally be divorced from some construction about fundamental meaning. That is, legal forms of property enforced through, say, ancient Roman law, feudal law, or nineteenth century judicial decisions in America presuppose variant understandings about property in its most basic meaning. Moreover, such basic meanings assume, however dimly, some doctrine about the identity of self, nature, and society. In that sense, property is a symbol of cosmology.

The thesis I shall propose is that a relational perspective grounded in the cosmology of process thought incorporates—within its own setting—dimensions of the meaning of property present in the thought of Thomas Aquinas (the principle of common use), John Locke (the principle of labor), and R.H. Tawney (the principle of social function). A relational perspective therefore requires a radical revisioning of the liberal—more accurately, the individualistic—understanding of property.

In this first section, I shall describe broadly the current controversy over the liberal understanding of property, distinguish several aspects of the basic definition of property over which there is contention, and amplify my proposal. In subsequent sections, I shall deal, respectively, with understandings of property in Thomas, Locke, and Tawney. Finally, I shall show how central principles of these three understandings may be integrated within a relational perspective.

2. Property, in the liberal tradition, is a bulwark, protecting the individual against the arbitrary force of government. It specifies an arena in which no one may trespass without invitation or consent. As in the medieval distinction between *dominium* (ownership) and *imperium* (government), ownership constitutes a private sphere into which officials may not intrude. Together with civil liberties (speech, religious exercise, association), property is among the institutional principles promoted by liberalism to affirm the superiority of the individual over political authority. But property also isolates individuals from each other. Within its boundaries, each controls one's own destiny and pursues one's own life plans. Property is an exemplary institution of individualism.

Within this tradition, property and contract are key features of economic activity which is construed as a strictly private sphere, a business in which persons and groups interact independent of governmental authority. Governmental interference is perceived as a perversion of the proper order of institutional forms, a usurpation of the inviolable dignity of the individual. Private life (therefore economic life) is not only distinct from public life; it is superior to public life. Thereby a dominant tradition of social thought—from Aristotle to Aquinas—is turned on its head introducing an antagonistic standoff between politics (the domain of government) and economics (the domain of the individual).

John Locke is often interpreted as a seminal figure in the beginnings of modern liberalism in both its constitutional and bourgeois versions. Though this interpretation is overdrawn, Locke does affirm that protection of property is the chief end of civil authority and he allies the right to property with the life and integrity of the individual. On these points, Locke's doctrine is properly invoked throughout the subsequent tradition of liberalism.

Near the end of the eighteenth century, William Blackstone formulated a definition of property epitomizing the liberal understanding. Whether Blackstone is merely stating a popular and naive view of property or forwarding his own constructive doctrine is a matter of debate.[4] In either case, the definition was widely influential in nineteenth century American legal culture.

> There is nothing which so generally strikes the imagination and engages the affections of mankind, as the right to property; or that sole and despotic dominion which one man claims and exercises over the external things of the world, in total exclusion of the right of any other individual in the universe.[5]

Similarly, in the French Declaration of the Rights of Man and Citizen (1789), property is defined as "the right to enjoy and dispose at will of one's goods, one's income, and the fruit of one's labor and industry." Property, in brief, in this tradition, is the exclusive right of a person to possess, to use, to abuse, to dispose of a thing in any way one wishes. So conceived, property—"absolute property"—is a bundle of rights against all other persons and groups, official or private.

This doctrine was vigorously supported in influential circles in nineteenth century American jurisprudence. Hence Justice Joseph Story's dictum in the case of *Wilkinson v. Leland* (1829):

> That government can scarcely be deemed to be free where the rights of property are left solely dependent upon the will of a legislative body without any restraint. The fundamental maxims of a free government seem to require that the rights of personal liberty and private property should be held sacred. At least no court of justice in this country would be warranted in assuming that the power to violate and disregard them—a power so repugnant to the common principles of justice and civil liberty—lurked under any general grant of legislative authority, or ought to be implied from any general expression of the people. The people ought not to be presumed to part with rights so vital to their security and well-being, without very strong and direct expressions of such an intention.[6]

On grounds such as these, efforts by American legislatures, state and federal, to act "in the public interest" but against the economic claims of private parties were forcefully opposed in courts throughout the nineteenth and well into the twentieth century. Even with changes effected under the New Deal, support for the doctrine of absolute property has persisted.

In recent years, Gottfried Dietze composed an apology "in defense of property" out of the conviction that twentieth century social and political trends betoken a regressive move, contrary to the impulse of civilization. Civilization is "a state in which men are emancipated and able to enjoy freedom."[7] Freedom, as the absence of coercive restraint, is contingent on the institution of private property. Hence, in Dietze's judgment, the evolution of Western civilization reached a climax "in the latter half of the eighteenth century when the idea of the natural rights of man—including those of property—came to be universally accepted."[8]

During the nineteenth century, in Dietze's rendition, the natural rights of property were largely respected. But the twentieth century marks the "fall of property" and thereby the decay of civilization. Dietze is frightened by the implications of this move which he attributes to the emergence of egalitarian democracy. Classical democracy, governed by an elite, was respectful of the natural right to property. But egalitarian democracy acts without restraint; despite its rhetoric it is, in effect, authoritarian. In a revealing litany, Dietze illustrates his fear of the welfare state which, in its extremity, eventuates in socialism:

> This development implied the negation of the progress of civilization, a progress which had achieved its height in the nineteenth century. Private property, which has been one of the major incentives to human action throughout history, was deprived of that quality. The sick have conquered the healthy: social security, with benefits that are often out of proportion to needs, makes it less and less likely that the sick are eager to get healthy again and that they want to stay healthy for work. The lazy have conquered the diligent: unemployment compensation, having become more and more generous, makes it less and less likely that the unemployed are eager to get back to work, and that they do their best to stay in their jobs. The debtors have conquered the creditors: legislation having come to favor the debtor out of proportion to what is justifiable on humanitarian grounds, the debtor can take it easy in repaying his debt. To top it all, even work is being punished today: due to progressive taxation, the hard working individual will have a tax cut that is out of proportion to the amount he would pay if he did not work so hard. These examples are only a few demonstrations of the fall of property in the twentieth century.[9]

The liberal principle of property is thus set over against trends of the past century toward social legislation. In short, property and social justice are diametrically opposed.

Friedrich A. Hayek argues the same point in his tendentious treatise on "the mirage of social justice."[10] Since, he avers, society is nothing but an aggregation of individuals, it cannot act on its own and therefore cannot be just or unjust. In that sense, "social justice" is a mirage and concepts of distributive and economic justice are verbal nonsense. Unfortunately, however, such concepts are employed to excuse governmental interference into the lives of individuals thereby jeopardizing the central institution of free civilization, the market, which depends, in turn, on principles of property and contract.

Curiously, neither Dietze nor Hayek even mention the emergence of the modern corporation as a determinative reality in modern economic life, altering radically the meaning and forms of property.[11] If nothing else, the separation of ownership (stockholder), adminstration (manager), and production (worker) has split into many segments the bundle of rights gathered together in the single principle of absolute property. Such a development has "made it impossible to defend modern property rights in traditional Lockean terms."[12]

Undeniably, the institution of property as understood by the liberal tradition has been, at times, an important means of securing the liberties of the individual. However, as with most institutions, even those well-intentioned, it has a reverse side as well. Karl Marx and Friedrich Engels, for instance, point to the irony of a capitalist civilization which, constructed on a principle of private property is, in its actual import, destructive of that principle for the bulk of people under its sway. The presumed intent of property is the protection of the individual; its effect, under conditions of capitalism, is the subjugation of the individual:

> We Communists have been reproached with the desire of abolishing the right of personally acquiring property as the fruit of a man's own labor, which property is alleged to be the ground work of all personal freedom, activity and independence . . . But does wage-labor create any property for the laborer? Not a bit. It creates capital, i.e., that kind of property which exploits wage-labor, and which cannot increase except upon condition of getting a new supply of wage-labor for fresh exploitation. . . . You are horrified at our intending to do away with private property. But in your existing society, private property is already done away with for nine-tenths of the population. . . . Communism deprives no man of the power to appropriate the products of society: all that it does is to deprive him of the power to subjugate the labor of others by means of such appropriation.[13]

Later, in a contentious Supreme Court case, *Munn v. Illinois* (1877), Chief Justice Morrison B. Waite argued for the majority that private property is not absolute, that when private property is "affected with a public interest," the public, through its government, may properly control its use. Property, "affected with a public interest," is no longer merely private; it has a public aspect and is susceptible to principles of public life; the right to control passes into public agency:

> property does become clothed with a public interest when used in a manner to make it of public consequence, and affect the community at large. When, therefore, one devoted this property to a use in which the public has an interest, he, in effect, grants to the public an interest in that use, and must submit to be controlled by the public for the common good, to the extent of the interest he has thus created.[14]

The full burden of Waite's doctrine, which entails a radical revision of the principle of absolute property, was rejected by the mainstream of nineteenth century American jurisprudence and had minimal effect on the actual workings of the American economic system.

Following World War II, Walter Lippman, in his desperate call for a "public philosophy," launched a hard-headed critique of the principle of absolute property as it has worked out in practice in industrial society:

> Absolute private property inevitably produced intolerable evils. Absolute owners did grave damage to their neighbors and to their descendents: they ruined the fertility of the land, they exploited destructively the minerals under the surface, they burned and cut forests, they destroyed wild life, they polluted streams, they cornered supplies and formed monopolies, they held land and resources out of use, they exploited the feeble bargaining power of wage earners.[15]

In more recent years, George Cabot Lodge of Harvard Business School has announced the need for a radical ideological transformation given the impact of the "great corporations." The old ideology is individualistic; the new ideology is communitarian. In the old ideology property rights (in the Blackstonian sense) constituted an institutional means of assuring individual liberty. That made sense when centers of power were diffuse and social organization was localized. But it is no longer functional given circumstances of advanced capitalism in which the "central economic institution" is the "great corporation."[16] To support the lives of individuals in a corporative culture, Lodge proposes a principle of membership rights: "Today a new right has clearly superseded property rights in political and social importance: the right to survive, to enjoy income, health, and other rights associated with membership in the American community or in some component of that community, including a corporation."[17] Lodge proposes as well a new method to control the use of property. Under the old individualistic ideology, the market is the appropriate mechanism. Under the new communitarian ideology, a "criterion of community need" administered by the state is the more appropriate method to regulate the utilization of natural and human resources.

Thus a controversy of broad theoretical and practical significance has been joined over the status and meaning of property. On one side, absolute property is an essential principle of civilization; on the other side, absolute property is destructive and devisive, the antithesis of what is needed for a humane society. On one side, without sole and exclusive dominion over external things, freedom is a sham; on the other side, prevailing structures of ownership and use must be radically transformed and brought under some form of public control if freedom is to become a genuine possibility for all persons.

More profoundly, the controversy is over what J.H. Bogart calls "root ideas—ideas which constitute fundamental moral commitments."[18] Root ideas, I would add, constitute social ontologies, fundamental understandings about social reality. The root idea underlying the principle of absolute property is of the separateness of persons, a doctrine of external relations. The root idea underlying the alternative is of the connectedness of persons, a doctrine of internal relations. The two sides are at variance over the meaning of property and its place within the economy of human relations.[19] What I propose is that a relational perspective grounded in process thought is more akin to the latter side of the controversy, but it incorporates the deep respect for the creativity of the individual affirmed by the former side.

3. Several aspects are distinguishable in doctrines of property, over any one of which there are contentions: (1) *status* (what kind of entity is property?); (2) *subject* (who may hold property?); (3) *object* (what sorts of things

are held as property?); (4) *import and extent* (what are the limits of property?); (5) *origin* (how is property initiated?); (6) *purpose* (what is the function of property?). The first four aspects are evident in Blackstone's definition. Property is:

(1)	*status:*	"that sole and despotic dominion which
(2)	*subject:*	one man claims and exercises
(3)	*object:*	over the external things of the world,
(4)	*import:*	in total exclusion of the right of any other individual in the universe."

Blackstone's definition omits any reference to (5) *origin* and (6) *purpose*,
although those aspects may be the more critical ones when probing the fundamental meaning of property. Locke, for instance, is specifically concerned with *origin*, that is, "how men might come to have a property in
several parts of that which God gave to mankind in common, and that
without any express compact of all the commoners."[20] T.H. Green, a nineteenth century English philosopher, is primarily concerned with the question of *purpose*, the "rationale of property," namely, "that everyone should
be secured by society in the power of getting and keeping the means of
realising a will."[21]

(1) *Status: what kind of entity is property?* In popular usage, property
designates things—houses, land, slaves, or capital in a variety of forms. But
property is not the things themselves. It is some kind of claim over things.
Property is not the land. It is my claim to possess or to use or to dispose of
the land. It is a form of relationship between me and the land and, as such,
between me and other persons. If I have a claim, others should honor that
claim. Their actions should not conflict with mine.

According to C.B. Macpherson, a shift in linguistic usage from property
as a right or claim to property as a thing began in the late seventeenth century as the extent of the claim became increasingly unlimited. Where in
previous centuries a property claim was limited (several persons might hold
different claims to the same piece of land), the doctrine of absolute property
("sole and despotic dominion") tended increasingly to prevail. To say, "that
is my property" meant one claimed exclusive rights over the object and, in
effect, the object itself began to be considered the property.[22] If Macpherson
is correct, popular usage, seemingly innocuous, is in fact controversial. It
bears the marks of the liberal tradition of absolute property.

But even now not all property claims are to sole and despotic dominion. I
may invite friends to "my home," even though I hold it on a one year lease.
I claim possession to a seat in a theatre, though only for a night's performance. I may own a share of stock, but have no dominion over any of the

company's facilities.

As a claim, property is analogous to a promise. It is both an indicative (describing an institutional structure) and an imperative (incorporating a set of rights and obligations). Property indicates a form of relationship between persons and things, but, as a claim, it is a "performance utterance." If legitimate, it permits me to act in certain ways and obligates others to act or to refrain from acting in certain ways. At least in that sense, property seems to be a moral reality.

Whether it is strictly a moral reality, however, is the basis of another controversy. To Thomas Hobbes, private property is a creation of the state; property is therefore strictly a legal claim, not a moral reality. To ascertain the privileges and duties of a property claim, one must look to law, more particularly, to law as an expression of a sovereign political authority. That position is disputed by John Locke, to whom property is a *natural* right. Property is a claim predating positive law, a claim to which positive law must conform to be valid. To Hobbes, property is a legal reality; to Locke it is more basically a moral reality.

(2) *Subject: who may hold property?* In Blackstone's definition, the subject of property is "one man"; only a single person may hold full claim over a particular object. In accordance with the "root idea" of the doctrine, persons and things are taken as distinct and separable. No two persons may own the same thing: the bicycle is either mine (*meum*) or yours (*tuum*).

But legal systems over the centuries have varied on this issue. A.M. Honoré distinguishes two classes of legal system; unititular and multititular. In a unititular system, "only a single independent title is possible."[23] Others may have an interest in a thing; the owner may permit various uses by them; but the law acknowledges only a single title. This is the character of the ancient Roman law of property.

In contrast, a multititular system acknowledges the possibility of several owners of the same object. Several persons may hold legitimate claims over the same parcel of land or the same building. Property arrangements may be so complicated, no one person can be said to be the "ultimate owner." This is the character of the medieval English law of property.

A similar difference prevails between the Roman conception and that of the Germanic tribes. As Ewert Lewis demonstrates, the Roman conception

> was simple and individualistic. . . .ownership was regarded as indivisible and unique, absorbing the object owned. It was a maxim that there could not be two lords over the same object.[24]

Among Germanic tribes, on the other hand, property belonged to family and clan. Individuals had claims to use and to enjoy the fruits of property, but the basic right of disposal did not rest in the hands of the individual. Hence the concept of multiple ownership: "Ownership could not absorb the object; it was simply a right in regard to the object; and such rights might be numerous and widely distributed." European feudalism followed the Germanic principle.

More broadly, a distinction may be drawn among three types of property: common, private, and state. Private property is specified by the right of the individual to exclude all others from the use or enjoyment of the object owned. Nowadays, this is the image of property usually envisaged particularly when defenders champion the right of property or, like Gottfried Dietze, bemoan the "fall of property." However, in a significant twist in nineteenth century American jurisprudence, the idea of the individual person was extended to include corporations. In *Santa Clara County v. Southern Pacific Railroad* (1886), Justice Stephen Field argued that the Fourteenth Amendment's due process clause ("nor shall any State deprive any person of life, liberty, or property, without due process of law") was intended to include corporations as *personae fictae*. Thenceforward corporations were to enjoy all the "privileges and immunities" of individuals.[25] Thereby a constitutional amendment formulated to protect emancipated slaves became a legal defense enabling corporations to thwart efforts at public control. The principle of private property, for centuries an essential component of constitutionalism, became a central feature of corporate capitalism.

Common property, as distinguished from private property, is vested in a community and is specified by the right of all members of the community to access. Members have a right not be excluded from the use or enjoyment of the object owned. Highways and city streets, public parks and recreational facilities are cases of common property. A similar right extends to facilities and conveniences deemed open to the public, though in some sense privately owned, such as inns and railroads. State property, on the other hand, is vested in the public agency which, although created to serve the public, maintains strict control over that which is owned, permitting only limited access. Instances include military bases, state laboratories, administrative buildings.

How this tripartite distinction—private, common, state property—is construed is part of the current controversy over the fundamental meaning of property and its significance in the economic system. James Gewartney focusses primarily on the tension between private and state property, arguing that "the intellectual case for private ownership is stronger than at any time in the past," that " private ownership minimizes social conflict and provides a shield against oppressive concentration of power," and that "where private property is most widely respected . . . personal freedom is most secure."[26] Gewartney's ultimate interest is to support free market capitalism over against socialism.

On another side of the controversy, C.B. Macpherson focusses primarily on the contrast between private and common property, asserting that strong pressures are developing against the image of property as strictly private

> as a fairly direct result of the unpleasant straits to which the operation of the market has brought the most advanced societies. The more striking of these pressures comes from the growing public consciousness of the menaces of air and water pollution. Air and water, which hitherto had scarcely been regarded as property at all, are now being thought of as common property—a right to clean air and water is coming to be regarded as a property from which nobody should be excluded.[27]

Moreover, Macpherson argues that, under current economic conditions, property as the right of all members of the society "not to be excluded from the use or benefit of the achievements of the whole society" should include "an equal right of access to the accumulated means of labour" and/or "a right to an income from the whole produce of the society, an income related not to work but to what is needed for a fully human life."[28]

(3) *Object: what sorts of things are held in property?* Within a strict doctrine of absolute property, distinctions among kinds of things owned is unimportant. However, in recent times, distinctions have been drawn out of concern for fundamental social policy.

Charles Donahue, Jr., for instance, distinguishes property for production from property for consumption:

> What Karl Polanyi called "the great transformation" of the eighteenth and nineteenth centuries wrought a radical change in the object of property law. Family farms, of course, continued, reflecting the older pattern; but increasingly property for consumption and property for the family became disassociated from property for production, which fell into the hands of corporations.[29]

Kenneth R. Minogue extends the distinction, but suggests that the same object may function in more than one way, e.g., a toothbrush, an object of intimate hygiene to most persons, may be a tool of trade in a studio of commercial art.[30]

Nonetheless, from a socialist perspective, the distinction between personal and productive property is significant. As Hastings Rashdall remarks, "critics of Socialism seem to forget that Socialism does not aim at the extinction of private property but only at that of private capital."[31] Public control of productive property is an essential component of socialism, but that does not mean individuals and families will not hold property at all. The line between the personal and the productive must be settled from time to time by argument and experience. However, "We cannot justify the whole capitalistic system *en bloc* by the bare formula that property is necessary to the development of individual character. The most we can claim, as a general principle . . . , is that without some property or capacity for acquiring property there can be no individual liberty, and that without some liberty there can be no proper development of character."[32]

Earlier, John Stuart Mill insisted certain realities should be excluded from the realm of property altogether, citing particularly persons and public positions. These are

> things which are or have been subjects of property, in which no proprietary rights ought to exist at all. . . .At the head of them, is property in human beings. It is almost superfluous to observe, that this institution can have no place in any society even pretending to be founded in justice, or on fellowship between human creatures. . . .Other examples of property which ought not to have been created, are properties in public trusts; such as judicial offices. . . .a commission in the army, and. . . .right to nomination to an ecclesiastical benefice.[33]

Two decades ago, Charles A. Reich announced that a "new property" emerged in the United States subsequent to World War II, creating a complicated problem in public policy. The new property is an effect of the growth of multiple forms of government largess which, taken altogether, are "helping to create a new society."[34] Government largess includes income and benefits (e.g., social security, veterans' benefits); jobs (e.g., civil service); occupational licenses (e.g., physicians, longshoremen); franchises (e.g., television channels, park concessions); contracts (e.g., defense industries, highway construction); subsidies (e.g., shipping industry, scientific research); public resources (e.g., public lands, rivers and streams); services (e.g., technical information, postal service). Individuals and industries have become increasingly dependent on the effectiveness of their claims to governmental largess, that is, on the "new property." Therein lies the problem. As government gives, government may take away. The new property is not secure. Claims may be dismissed or nullified in the name of "public interest." In response to that problem, advocates of a free market economy propose the abolition of government largess altogether. Reich instead proposes that at least some of the new property be guaranteed as a matter of fundamental right: "Only by making such benefits into rights can the welfare state achieve its goal of providing a secure minimum basis for individual well-being and dignity in a society where each man cannot be wholly master of his own dignity."[35]

(4) *Import and extent: what are the limits of property?* Property, whatever its definition, is never merely an arrangement of persons (the subject of property) and things (the object of property). It betrays an on-

tological ground of broad social significance which ground bears on the issue of the extent and limitations of the practice of property.

In Blackstone's definition, property is the sole dominion a person exercises over external things to the total exclusion of other persons. That definition, straightforward on the surface, conceals its full import. The definition presupposes an understanding of self (as monadic), society (as aggregative), and nature (as instrumental). The principle of absolute property is a correlative of an individualistic understanding of the self, a contractualist doctrine of society, and a view of "external things" as a neutral stuff to be used and exploited at will.

Even within the liberal tradition, however, property is subject to some kind of limitation. Individualism contains its own boundary, namely, the being of the other individual, honored by the no-harm principle. In a now classic essay on "the 'liberal' concept of 'full' individual ownership," A.M. Honoré argues that property is not merely a bundle of *rights*. The "incidents of ownership" include *responsibilities* as well. An owner's rights and interests are "subject to the condition that uses harmful to other members of society are forbidden."

> I may use my car freely but not in order to run my neighbor down, or to demolish his gate, or even to go on his land if he protests; nor may I drive uninsured. I may build on my land as I choose, but not in such a way that my building collapses on my neighbor's land. I may let off fireworks on Guy Fawkes night, but not in such a way as to set fire to my neighbor's house.[36]

Within this conception, the responsibilities and limitations of property bear the marks of a fundamentally individualistic "root idea."

With a change in root idea, the meaning of property is transformed, the dynamics of property are viewed differently, and the responsibilities of property are delineated in new ways. Early this century, Bishop Charles Gore appropriated Leonard Hobhouse's distinction between "property for use" and "property for power" to indicate an alternative understanding of self as "in its fundamental being a *social* thing—a relation of one individual to another." Gore, at a time when corporate capitalism was coming into its own, "cannot get rid of the feeling that individualism in property has overdone itself; that it is working disastrous havoc."[37] Property for use is what people need for "true freedom" but that constitutes "a very limited quantity on the whole." As the accumulation of property by an individual or group expands, it becomes property for power: "it becomes at last the almost unmeasured control by the few rich, not of any amount of unconscious material, but of other men whose opportunity to live and work and eat becomes subject to their will."[38] Property, in short, is a political reality and must be assessed according to its effects on the structure and quality of the community.

Somewhat later, Morris Cohen proposed a similar understanding of the dynamics of property. The Romans, Cohen notes, distinguished *dominium* ("the rule over things by the individual") from *imperium* ("the rule over all individuals by the prince"). An analogous distinction—between private and public law—persists in modern jurisprudence. But, to Cohen, these dimensions are not so clearly distinguishable. Property confers on the owner a power over others, especially if they want or need those things over which the owner claims *dominium*: "we must not overlook the actual fact that dominion over things is also *imperium* over our fellow human beings." Property is a form of sovereignty.

> The character of property as sovereign power compelling service and obedience may be obscured for us in a commercial economy by the fiction of the so-called labour contract as a free bargain and by the frequency with which service is rendered indirectly through a money payment. But not only is there actually little freedom to bargain on the part of the steelworker or miner who needs a job, but in some cases the medieval subject had as much power to bargain when he accepted the sovereignty of his lord. Today I do not directly serve my landlord if I wish to live in the city with a roof over my head, but I must work for others to pay him rent with which he obtains the personal services of others. The money needed for purchasing things must for the vast majority be acquired by hard labour and disagreeable service to those to whom the law has accorded dominion over the things necessary for subsistence.[39]

In Cohen's judgment, since large property owners are holders of sovereign power over the lives and fortunes of fellow citizens, then the law should develop a doctrine of "their positive duties in the public interest."[40] Property is a political reality and should be subject to political control, that is, control by the community whose principal end is neither profit nor efficiency, but "how to promote a better communal life." Cohen thus berates individualists and socialists who limit their debate primarily to questions of productivity and distribution. The "more profound question" is "what goods are ultimately worth producing from the point of view of the social effects on the producers and consumers." That question "requires the guidance of collective wisdom."[41]

Aldo Leopold extends the context for assessing doctrines of property beyond the human community to include the "land," taking "land" as a symbol for the world of nature. Land is not merely an exploitable resource; it is our habitat, our place of dwelling.

> We abuse land because we regard it as a commodity belonging to us. When we see land as a community to which we belong, we may begin to use it with love and respect. . . . That land is a community is the basic concept of ecology.[42]

The community of land includes soils, waters, plants, animals. It also includes humans who should be identified not as owners and controllers of land (as intimated in Blackstone's definition), but as members and citizens of the living community of land. Land is not, in any simple sense, an "external thing." It is a commonwealth of which we are part and for which we hold responsibility. John Cobb, appropriating Leopold's image of the biotic community, insists we are participants in nature, part of a complicated process of life and death, growth and decay, sickness and healing. Participants have responsibilities; they are not masters. Yet we have acted as masters and wreaked havoc on the biotic pyramid.

> Man's interference in most places and at most times has reversed this process [of maximizing life] by impoverishing the soil and reducing the complexity of the biotic pyramid. To extend concern to all living things calls man to work with rather than against the evolutionary process. He must adapt his actions so that both the base and the complexity of the biotic pyramid may again grow, both for man's sake and for the sake of other species of which it is composed.[43]

Underlying the direction indicated by Gore, Cohen, Leopold, and Cobb is a "root idea" radically divergent from that of the doctrine of absolute property. Blackstone's definition supposed an understanding of self as monadic, society as aggregative, and nature as instrumental. The alternative doctrine assumes the self is relational, society is constitutive of the self, and nature is a community of which humans are a part and for whose life and health humans have responsibility. The ontology of the former doctrine is individualistic and anthropocentric; the ontology of the latter is relational and holistic.

(5) *Origin: how is property initiated?* The Blackstonian definition of absolute property does not address questions of origin and purpose explicitly. Yet these questions are more basic than the other four questions in ascertaining the fundamental meaning of property. Moreover, these two questions belong together.

Origin may be construed chronologically as beginning (when and how did property as the claim to some object first occur?) or foundationally as principle (what is the basic ground of the claim to a particular object or to objects in general?) These constructions are not necessarily unrelated, for an interpretation of the beginning of property may be intended to express its foundation.

As already intimated, Thomas Hobbes and John Locke are at variance on the topic of the origin of property. To Hobbes, private property is, strictly, a creation of law which is the dictate of the sovereign of the commonwealth:

annexed to the sovereignty [is] the whole power of prescribing the rules whereby every man may know what goods he may enjoy, and what actions he may do, without being molested by any of his fellow subjects: and this is it men call *propriety*. . . .this propriety, being necessary to peace, and depending on sovereign power, is the act of that power, in order to the public peace. These rules of propriety (or *meum* and *tuum*) and of good, evil, lawful, and unlawful in the actions of subjects are the civil laws.[44]

To John Locke, on the other hand, responding to Sir Robert Filmer's defense of royal sovereignty, property originates not in law but in the natural right all humans possess severally to their own person. The labor of their bodies and the work of their hands belong to them; therefore the results of their laboring are theirs as well. Property is an extension of the life activity of the individual. Civil law should protect property, but does not in itself create property.

I shall develop Locke's doctrine at greater length later. For the moment, I would note that, in Hobbes and Locke, questions of origin and purpose are intimately connected. To Hobbes, the origin of property is civil law; its purpose is social harmony. To Locke, the origin of property is labor; its purpose is the preservation of existence and creativity.

(6) *Purpose: what is the function of property?* In a recent study of doctrines of property in the West from Locke to Mill and Marx, Alan Ryan distinguishes two traditions about the purpose of property: instrumental and self-developmental.[45] The former is characteristic of Jeremy Bentham and utilitarianism. The latter is typical of Hegel and idealist philosophy. In some cases, such as John Locke, the traditions are intermixed. In the instrumentalist tradition, property is a means to some further end: prosperity, security, independence. In the self-developmental tradition, property is a direct expression of one's person—an unfolding of the progress of the self, the objectification of one's inner spirit.

Ryan suggests that legal systems vary in their approach to this question. Where, for instance, the English common law system is primarily concerned with what constitutes clear title to a possession but is unconcerned with how a possession is used, the Roman law system focussed on the query, what does it mean to be an owner of something?

More directly, the two traditions are linked with alternative views of work. From an instrumentalist perspective, work is a cost to get on with one's life. Working is "making a living." A job may be more or less pleasant, but in all cases it is a necessary burden to engage in activities more intrinsically satisfying. Productive work makes possible the joys of consumption. In the self-developmental tradition, work is one's mode of being in the world. It projects one's energies. It realizes one's inner being in concrete form. Some working conditions, however, distort the self: this is the point of Marx's thesis about work under conditions of capitalism entailing self-alienation.

Within the instrumentalist tradition, systems of property and work are justified when they contribute effectively to extrinsic purposes: economic progress, financial security, political independence, moral character. Within the self-developmental tradition, property and work are justified as expressive of the meaning of human existence. The difference is discernible in alternative arguments for economic democracy. Democracy in the workplace may be promoted as a means toward higher productivity. That's an instrumentalist argument. But it may also be supported as a way of showing due respect for the freedom of the human spirit.

Whether Ryan's classification scheme is adequate to do justice to modern theories of property, it serves to indicate that contentions over the purpose of property manifest a deeper stratum of understanding. The contrast between Bentham and Marx is not merely a difference in social policy. It is a difference in philosophical anthropology and social ontology. It is a difference that reaches into questions about the character of human life and social existence. Bentham's individualism and Marx's socialism manifest radically divergent comprehensions about our identity as human beings. At this level, theories about purpose and origin—final cause and efficient cause—of property are linked, as are debates about all other aspects of doctrines of property: status, subject, object, import. This, I suggest, is the level at which a relational perspective derived from the tradition of process thought has a contribution to make to reflection about the fundamental meaning of property.

4. The thesis I have proposed is that a relational perspective incorporates in its own setting dimensions of the meaning of property present in the thought of Thomas Aquinas, John Locke, and R.H. Tawney. The thesis is two-sided: historical and philosophical.

On the historical side, the thesis counters a suggestion made recently by Charles Donahue, Jr., linking the concept of property in the West with individualism:

> The Western legal concept of property has always been associated with various forms of individualism. . . .Individualism has always had an opposite. There is a tension between individualism and communalism, the individual and society, self-protection and self-giving. The concept of property in the West, however, has normally been associated with one side of this basic dichotomy. Both sides, of course, embody fundamental values, and the legal system must resolve the tensions between them. The issue . . . is whether it continues to be useful to have a legal concept that expresses what lies on one side of the dichotomy. For those who believe that something may be said for the Western concept of individualism, I suspect the answer is yes.[46]

SUMMARY CHART

Controversies over the Meaning of Property

1. Status: What kind of entity is property?	property as things	property as claims a. moral claims b. legal claims
2. Subject: Who may hold property?	unititular system	multititular system a. private property b. common property c. state property
3. Object: What sorts of things may be held as property?	i. property for production ii. property in persons & public offices iii. (old property)	property for consumption (property in things) "new property" (gov't largess)
4. Import & Extent: What are the limits of property?	self as monadic society as aggregative nature as instrumental	self as relational society as constitutive of self nature as community
5. Origin: How is property initiated?	creation of law	natural right: labor
6. Purpose: What is the function of property?	instrumentalist tradition	self-developmental tradition

Against Donahue, I propose there is a tradition of thought about property in the West transcending the dichotomy between individuality and sociality because of an understanding of the relational character of self. To be fair, we should note Donahue's focus on the *legal* concept of property; he is not directly concerned with debates over property on the philosophical level. However "legal," in Donahue's usage, refers to systems of *positive* law. There is a tradition in Western thought in which a doctrine of higher law or natural law is invoked as superior to positive law as such. Thomas Aquinas, John Locke, and R.H. Tawney—each from his own perspective—present a relational understanding of self and society which constitutes a grounding for a higher law concept of property.

To be sure, Thomas Aquinas (Dominican monk of the thirteenth century), John Locke (English statesman and philosopher of the seventeenth century), and R.H. Tawney (economic historian of the twentieth century) lived in and were responding to fundamentally different social and cultural contexts—medieval feudalism infused with the ideals of Christendom, the beginnings of modern bourgeois capitalism influenced by the spirit of Puritanism, and advanced bourgeois capitalism driven by the force of utilitarianism. However, although these three theorists belong to fundamentally different times and their doctrines of property are at variance with each other in various ways, each formulates a kind of communitarian understanding of social relations which, I suspect, derives from the influence of a Christian vision of ultimate reality. Each, including John Locke, casts his doctrine of property within an understanding of the connectedness of the world in which each individual is responsible for the welfare of all. To Thomas, Locke, and Tawney, property is not a principle simply of private life; wealth is not merely a matter for private enjoyment. Property is both a right and a responsibility of the individual. Property is to be held and used in trust as part of the common-wealth of all peoples and nations.

On the philosophical side, I propose that the central principles in the doctrines of property of Thomas, Locke, and Tawney may be transmuted into process thought as three dimensions of a relational doctrine of property. Central in Thomas's doctrine of property is the principle of common use; in Locke's, the principle of labor; and in Tawney's, the principle of social function. In the next three sections of the paper, I shall develop these doctrines. The correlative dimensions in process thought are principles of objectification (analogue for Thomas's principle of common use), creativity (analogue for Locke's principle of labor), and relativity (analogue for Tawney's principle of social function). In process thought, these three principles have an inclusive metaphysical bearing; however, my concern is strictly with their implications for social ontology. The three principles constitute a theory of human action. Creativity is a moment of freedom and innovation; it signifies that each action is *sui generis*, is unique, is something to be cherished for itself. Objectification is a moment of inheritance, of passing on to others; it signifies that each action is not just for itself, it is, as well, for all others, a datum for all future actions. Relativity means that each action has its own special place in the entire realm of things; it is not and cannot be all things; it has its own special contribution to make to the world. In the final section of the paper, I shall develop this correlation and shall demonstrate how a doctrine of property derived from such a relational perspective stands in opposition to the Blackstonian principle of absolute property.

II

1. Thomas Aquinas's understanding of the meaning of property has been interpreted in widely divergent ways. Some interpretations are over-simplified to the point of distortion.

Gottfried Dietze, for instance, locates Thomas in the Western tradition favoring the principle of private property: "St. Thomas proclaimed that property [i.e., private property] is natural and good."[47] There is a modicum of truth in this judgment, but Dietze uses it to support a position that is non-Thomistic if not anti-Thomistic. Dietze, in effect, transforms Thomas into a forerunner of modern bourgeois liberalism.

From a different angle, E.K. Hunt identifies Thomas with a conservative version of the "Christian corporate ethic," a version reflecting the ethos of feudalism. In Hunt's interpretation, Thomas argues

> that private property could be justified morally only because it was a necessary condition for almsgiving. The rich, he asserted, must always be "ready to distribute. . . .[and] willing to communicate." Aquinas believed . . . that "the rich man, if he does not give alms, is a thief." The rich man held wealth and power for God and for all society. . . .Aquinas' . . . profoundly conservative addition to the Christian corporate ethic was [his] insistence that the economic and social relationships of the medieval system reflected a natural and eternal ordering of these relationships. . . .[He] stressed the importance of a division of labor and effort, with different tasks assigned to the different classes, and insisted that the social and economic distinctions between the classes were necessary to accommodate this specialization.[48]

In sum, to Dietze, Thomas's doctrine of property is a precursor of modern natural rights theory, whereas to Hunt, Thomas's doctrine of property is irretrievably feudalistic. Both interpretations are misleading.

Thomas's understanding of property should be cast within the larger context of his thought. As Anthony Parel notes, "Aquinas' doctrine of property forms part of his wider teaching on the nature and destiny of man, of his humanism."[49] Thomas's doctrine of property is located in his theory of human action.

To Thomas, the primary question of property is the role external things are meant to play in the economy of human life. The primary principle is common use. The predominant problem is the temptation to transmute instrumental goods into ultimate ends.

According to Thomas, we live in a purposeful world. We are directed, throughout our lives, toward our own perfection. We are born weak and

deficient. But we are driven toward the realization of our given potentialities, ultimately toward the fulfillment of the *summum bonum*, toward
perfect happiness.

Material things, the stuff of property, are in some sense good, but they
are not the highest good. They are ephemeral and transitory. They cannot,
despite any pretense to the contrary, finally satisfy the inner yearnings of
the human spirit. The *summum bonum* cannot be found in "riches,
honours, glory, power, bodily well-being, sensory pleasures, even self-
preservation."[50] Yet external things are of instrumental value. As Thomas
writes, for that happiness "such as can be had in this life, external goods are
necessary, not as belongings to the essence of happiness, but by serving as
instruments to happiness, 'which consists in an operation of virtue'."[51]

The *locus classicus* of Thomas's doctrine of property is found in his *Summa Theologica*, II-II, Question 66, on the topic of theft and robbery, "sins
opposed to justice." In the first article, Thomas argues that people have a
natural dominion over external things, but not in an absolute or unlimited
manner. Their dominion extends to the use of things to sustain and enrich
human life. As such, external things are a *bonum utile*.

In the second article, Thomas asks whether it is legitimate for individuals
to possess things as their own. At this point, Thomas devises a critical
distinction. On the one hand, humans severally have the capability to care
for and to administer external things. Moreover, there are cogent reasons
why individuals should exercise that capability. First, responsibility: each
person takes more trouble to care for what is his or hers than what is held in
common by many. Second, efficiency: human affairs are more productive if
each person is charged with caring for particular things, whereas confusion
results when everyone is to look after everything. Third, harmony: people
live together in greater peace if everyone is satisfied with his or her own.
Thus there are compelling reasons for a system of private property.

However, on the other hand, humans have the capability to use external
things. Indeed, they need external things for sheer survival and, beyond
that, for the development of their potentialities as humans. Given that need,
Thomas propounds a principle that sets him in total opposition to the doctrine of absolute property: individuals ought to possess external things, not
as their own, but as common so that they may more readily communicate
them to those in need. Thomas's understanding of property is therefore synthetic, combining private or individual possession with common use. But
the two sides of this understanding are not equivalent. Individual possession is secondary. Common use is primary. Individual possession is not so
much a right or privilege to do with things as one wishes as it is a burden or
obligation to care for and to manage things in a responsible and orderly
way. The purpose of care is use, but use is common. This is why Anthony

Parel insists that, according to Thomas, "the ontological essence of property is common use."[52]

Furthermore, systems of private property are not, to Thomas, ordained directly by natural law. They are "devised by human reason for the benefit of human life."[53] But what is devised by human reason may be defeasible. The justification of private property depends on circumstances. In Parel's explication:

> It is to be sought . . . in historical conditions which vary from time and place and culture. Assuming that men are better motivated to care for material things if owned privately, assuming further that there will be less social conflict on the basis of private ownership, and assuming still further that each owner will be content with the satisfaction of his own legitimate need and will not invade others', private ownership may be necessary and beneficial. But this is something for the times, for the cultures and the good legislators to determine. Natural law itself is silent on how private property should be arrived at. That is left to human law. . . .Private property, in other words, is a historical institution.[54]

More vital in systems of property than ownership is use: "the benefit of human life."

The priority of common use over private possession is explicit in Thomas's discussions of economic surplus and economic necessity. In both cases, the principle of need supercedes the principle of private ownership.

> Things established by human law cannot derogate from natural right or divine right. Now, according to the natural order established by divine providence, inferior things are ordained to the purpose of succouring human needs. And therefore the division and appropriation of things, based on human law, can not overrule the principle that human needs are to be succoured by such things. Thus whatever one has in superabundance is due, by natural law, to the sustenance of the poor.[55]

Thomas even wonders if it is proper to accumulate a superabundance in the first place. Avarice includes going "too far" in getting or keeping material things: "In this way avarice is a sin directly against the neighbor, because with material possessions it is impossible for one person to enjoy extreme wealth without someone else suffering extreme want."[56] This is Thomas's indignant reaction to the judgment that "keeping what belongs to oneself is no injury to others." An editor of the Blackwell edition of the *Summa Theologica* adds the following gloss to the passage:

> Implicit here is the point . . . that avarice so taken is a sin directly against justice. One cannot but be impressed by the unqualified principle of social and economic justice, so flatly stated in the 13th century, that still remains an unfulfilled, even revolutionary ideal.[57]

Thomas's response to the question, whether it is legitimate to steal under conditions of economic necessity, is even more striking. Under ordinary circumstances, each person is entrusted with the administration of his or her property to assist the needy, although in neglecting that duty, "it is the hungry one's bread you withhold, the naked one's cloak you store away."[58] The goods belong not so much to the one who possesses and administers as to the one who needs, the hungry and the naked. Under extraordinary circumstances, that judgment may be enacted in extraordinary ways to the extremity of taking from another whatever is needed without consent.

> If the need is so manifest and so urgent that it is evident that the immediate need must be remedied by whatever means are available, as when a person is in imminent danger and no other remedy is possible, then it is lawful for one to succour one's need by means of another's property, by taking it either openly or secretly. And this is not, properly speaking, theft or robbery. . . .It is not theft, properly speaking, to take secretly and use another's property in a case of extreme need; because that which one takes for the support of one's life becomes one's own property by reason of that need.[59]

Avarice, defined by Thomas as the "immoderate desire of temporal things which serve the use of human life and which can be estimated in value by money,"[60] is the vice that contravenes the proper use of material things. On its psychological side, avarice is an undue desire for wealth or for any kind of temporal good. On its social side, avarice is unjust action, directed toward the getting and keeping of wealth. On both sides, avarice is a form of dehumanization. It is a perversion of human life.[61] Thomas is aware of the systemic effects of avarice. Its progeny—the "daughters of avarice"—include "treachery, fraud, falsehood, perjury, restlessness, violence and callousness to mercy."[62] Thomas would, most likely, appreciate Marx's charge against capitalism as given to a "fetishism of commodities."[63] Avarice is a disposition of the psyche, a flaw of character, but, as Thomas is aware, its effects extend to institutional forms and organizational designs.

Thus the remedies for avarice are two kinds: psychological and institutional. The psychological remedy is to transform the vice of avarice with moral virtues, in particular the virtues of liberality and justice.[64] Liberality as the right use of material things is both an attitude and an action. In attitude, liberality means detachment from wealth. Wealth is valued for what it is, but only for what it is, a stuff useful in a limited way to meet human need and to enhance human life. In action, liberality is manifest in a generosity of spirit in spending and in giving, again, for the enhancement of the human life of the entire community of humankind. The purpose of justice, according to Thomas, is to hold people together "in companionable living in common."[65] Justice, as the stable and continuous will to give each one's due, is manifest in forms of interaction through which the needs of all, individually and communally, are met. With respect to material things, justice is the application of the principle of need to the distribution of property.

The full impact of avarice cannot, however, be overcome by virtue alone. Thomas is, in this sense, a social realist. While voluntary action derived from a character imbued with liberality and justice is a vital dimension of social life, it must be supplemented with institutional remedies to assure justice in the distribution of property throughout the society. That is the purpose of political governance and human law. In the distribution of property, rulers, even where they may employ force, are not necessarily engaged in taking property from some to give it to another, but are instead serving the fundamental purpose of property as a system, namely, common use.[66] The foundation of a legitimate claim to material things is not possession but need; possession is more a responsibility than a right; among the obligations of government is to direct the interactions of the economy toward the realization of need and therefore to see to it that possessors of material things fulfill their responsibility.

Richard Schlatter remarks that

> The Thomist theory of property has been repeated in one form or another from the fifteenth century to the present day by the theologians of the Church. When they use it to demand that the state shall intervene to provide the necessities of life for everyone it seems to be a radical theory; when they use it to defend the rights of property against proposed reform it appears as a conservative doctrine.[67]

In either case, the inner sense of Thomas' understanding of property is that the common good must be served by material things, that ownership by the individual is never absolute, that property is subordinate to the higher purpose of enhancing human life.

Underlying Thomas's understanding of property are all the elements of his grand scholastic synthesis which, taken altogether, is a far cry from the relational perspective that I am proposing. Yet, historically, it demonstrates against Donahue that the Western concept of property, at least in its philosophical renditions, has not always been individualistic in any simple sense. And, constructively, it is suggestive of the notion that the world, under the principle of common use, is a repository of possibilities properly available for the general enrichment of life. It is not a set of things to be distributed according to the doctrine of absolute property.

2. John Locke is often interpreted as making a radical break in his psychology and in his political theory with medieval modes of thought and practice. He is presented as a herald of modern liberal individualistic sensibilities. In Henry Kariel's judgment:

> Determined to define a new regime in opposition to repressive feudal institutions, Thomas Hobbes, John Locke, Adam Smith, and James Madison were *compelled* to elucidate, and they did so unashamedly. They frankly proclaimed that a society was wanted in which everyone would be committed to the rational pursuit of self interest. They elaborately announced their faith in salvation through private endeavor.[68]

Similarly, Richard Schlatter identifies Locke as a champion of an emerging bourgeois class and its concern to establish a doctrine of absolute property:

> John Locke's theory of property became the standard bourgeois theory, the classical liberal theory. Wherever middle-class revolutionaries rebelled against feudal privilege and royal absolutism, they ascribed on their banners the slogan of 'life, liberty, and property'. . . .The theory that property was a natural right triumphed with the Glorious, the American, and the French Revolutions.[69]

Yet, as with intellectual history generally, interpretations of John Locke diverge radically. Since the early nineteenth century, they have ranged from a reading of Locke as a progenitor of modern socialism to a rendition of his work as supportive of modern libertarian philosophy.[70] Among the more influential of recent interpretations is C.B. Macpherson's through which, in John Dunn's words, Locke is characterized as writing "a moral charter for capitalism every bit as brutal as any that Marx alleged."

> Macpherson's analysis of Locke's discussion of property sees its key function as the removal of the sufficiency limitation on private accumulation and the consequent sanctioning of unlimited appropriation. At the individual level the effect of this is to make property a pure private right, excised from the context of social responsibility implied by the medieval understanding of the duty of charity.[71]

In Macpherson's own formulation, "Locke's astonishing achievement was to base the property right on natural right and natural law, and then to remove all the natural law limits from the property right."[72] Locke thus undermines the traditional view that property is a social function and ownership entails social obligations.

> He has erased the moral disability with which unlimited capitalist appropriation had hitherto been handicapped. . . .But he does even more. He also justifies, as natural, a class differential in rights and in rationality, and by doing so provides a positive moral basis for capitalist society.[73]

"Possessive individualism" is the social ontology of Locke's understanding of property.

Persuasive though it seems, Macpherson's rendition of Locke has been convincingly charged with neglecting the context of Locke's reflections. Given that context, Locke should be interpreted not as representative of modern bourgeois interests, but as formulating a political and economic doctrine out of a Calvinist theological interest.[74]

The immediate occasion for Locke's *Two Treatises of Government*—in the second of which appears his central statement on the meaning of property—seems to have been the Exclusion Crisis in England. The Tories favored the accession of James, Duke of York, to the throne following the reign of Charles II. The Whigs, fearing arbitrary government and a return to Catholicism under James, sought to exclude him from that office. Sir Robert Filmer published a series of tracts and a treatise, *Patriarcha*, arguing the Tory position on monarchy. Locke was provoked to respond, attacking Filmer's doctrine, but, more importantly, building a case for representative government and for popular resistance to arbitrary rule.

Yet Locke's argument is not a simple repetition of Whig conventions. He instead employs the language of natural law and natural rights within a specifically theological frame of reference. Locke's doctrine of property should be viewed as part of a Puritan understanding of the dynamics and purposes of human life.

The preeminent concern of Locke's theory of property is how individuals lay claim to a world that is given by the Divine Creator to humankind in common. The fundamental principle is that of labor which, in John Dunn's interpretation, is a version of the Puritan doctrine of calling. The chief function of government is to assure that the purpose and therefore the limitations of property are sustained.

The setting for Locke's theory of property is formulated early in the second treatise, in a chapter on the "state of nature." The state of nature is a condition of liberty, but not to do as one will, rather to do as one ought given the intentions of God: "For Men being all the Workmanship of one, Omnipotent, and infinitely wise Maker; All the Servants of one Sovereign Master, sent into the World by his order and about his business, they are his Property, whose Workmanship they are, made to last during his, not one anothers Pleasure."[75] Filmer and Locke agree on one premise: "The entire cosmos is the work of God."[76] But in keeping with his doctrine of absolute monarchy, Filmer construes this to mean that Adam and all subsequent authority, acting in the place of Adam, possessed full authority to distribute the things of the created world to its human denizens. Property is a privilege bestowed by the king.

Locke, on the other hand, construes the premise of God's creation to mean that every individual is assigned an assemblage of responsibilities and correlative rights. This assemblage is the Law of Nature: "The *State of Nature* has a Law of Nature to govern it, which obliges everyone."[77] Law, to Locke, is a directive force: "For *Law*, in its true Notion, is not so much the Limitation as *the direction of a free and intelligent Agent* to his proper

Interest, and prescribes no farther than is for the general Good of those under that Law."[78]

Out of his premise that the world, especially the world of humankind, is the "workmanship" of God, Locke announces that "the *fundamental Law of Nature* is *the preservation of Mankind.*"[79] Three basic rights are derived from this law.[80] First, all persons have a "right to their preservation."[81] That is, once having entered the world, they have the *right to life.* Second, all persons have a right to do what they must and should to assure the preservation of themselves and others. This is the *right to liberty*, but the right to liberty, it should be noted, is derived from an obligation: "Every one as he is *bound to preserve himself* . . . so by the like reason . . . ought he, as much as he can, *to preserve the rest of Mankind.*"[82] Third, all persons have a right to things needed for their preservation: "Men, being once born, have a right to their Preservation, and consequently to Meat and Drink, and such other things, as Nature affords for their subsistence."[83] This is the *right to possessions.*

These three rights—to life, liberty, and possessions (taken altogether, Locke calls them "by the general name, *Property*"[84])—are, it must be stressed, functions of an overriding obligation: to assure the preservation of all humankind. In this sense, Locke is not an individualist if that means, in Kariel's phrase quoted above, commitment to "the rational pursuit of self-interest."

Yet it is the individual who lives, acts, and enjoys possessions. Locke is therefore challenged to show "how Men might come to have a *property* in several parts of that which God gave to Mankind in common."[85] At base, the world is a commons; everyone has a right not to be excluded from the use of that commons; how, then, is that which is held in common to be distributed? How does each individual gain control and possession of that which is needed to fulfill the natural law?

Locke answers these questions in a single word: labor.

> Though the Earth, and all inferior Creatures be common to all Men, yet every Man has a *Property* in his own *Person.* This no Body has any Right to but himself. The *Labour* of his Body, and the *Work* of his Hands, we may say, are properly his. Whatsoever then he removes out of the State that Nature hath provided, and left it in, he hath mixed his Labour with, and joyned to it something that is his own, and thereby makes it his *Property.*[86]

Locke's labor theory of property has been appropriated by both socialists and libertarians to support their causes. Certainly the theory begs many questions.[87] But, assuming the fundamental theological context of the theory, it cannot be taken to sanction a Blackstonian version of the meaning of property. According to Alan Ryan,

> The natural thrust of Locke's initial claim is . . . towards a doctrine of stewardship, not one of absolute individual rights—men possess such rights over things as enable them to fulfill God's intention in creating those things. The ultimate source of property rights is God.[88]

Locke's labor theory of property is, however, individualistic in one sense: the individual is the locus of rights of possession which, in turn, rest upon the right of the individual to his or her own person and therefore to his or her own action. One's life, one's labor, and one's possessions belong to one's self as a unique individual. These rights are primordial. They obtain to the individual prior to the construction of any social organization or governmental form and constitute the *raison d'etre* of such institutions.

Yet these natural rights are inextricably conjoined with natural duties. As John Dunn remarks: "It is apt enough to note that Locke makes property a pure private right, but that in no way impairs the social responsibilities which emanate from it. The individualization of the right is matched symmetrically by an individualization of the duty."[89] More generally, Locke's labor theory of property must be understood within the context of the Protestant ethic of vocation. God calls each individual to a creative task, an activity of shaping and molding the world for the conduct of His business—the preservation and enhancement of human life.

Given this context, Locke's concept of labor must be defined broadly. It embraces all creative endeavors in response to and in imitation of the Divine Creator. It is definitive of the inner nature of being human. This is James Tully's interpretation of Locke's position:

> Labour . . . is a moral form of activity in two senses. Not only does it take place within a context of, and is the means of, performing moral duties, it is a moral form of activity itself. It is the form of activity characteristic of man . . . and so his duty.[90]

As natural law sanctions private property, though within the context of an ethic of divine calling, so also natural law set bounds on the accumulation and use of property. In his chapter on property in the second treatise, Locke seemingly proposes three principles of limitation, at least prior to the invention of money. First, whatever one's possessions are created by one's labor, there must be an adequate supply of materials remaining for others (the sufficiency principle): "no Man but he can have a right to what that [Labour] is joyned to, at least where there is enough and as good left in common for others."[91] Second, one must never own so much that any goes to waste (the spoilage principle): "As much as any one can make use of to any advantage of life before it spoils; so much he may by his labour fix a Property in. Whatever is beyond this, is more than his share and belongs to others."[92] Third, in the case of land, one may never own more than one can work (the labor principle): *"As much Land* as a Man Tills, Plants, Improves, Cultivates, and can use the Product of, so much is his *Property."*[93] These limitations are not artificial additions to the theory of property. They are logical extensions of the basic theological understanding of which the theory is a part.

However, the invention of money by the common consent of humankind effected a radical change in the conditions of human life. The hoarding of money does not necessarily violate the sufficiency principle. Money can accumulate without spoiling. And money makes it possible to till and cultivate much more land than otherwise. Hence money "introduced . . . larger Possessions, and a Right to them."[94] Moreover, through the invention of money, humankind in effect "agreed to disproportionate and unequal Possession of the Earth, they having . . . found out a way, how a man may fairly possess more land than he himself can use the product of, by receiving in exchange for the overplus, Gold and Silver, which may be hoarded up without injury to any one, these metals not spoileing or decaying in the hands of the possessor."[95]

At this point, interpretations of Locke's intentions diverge irreconcilably. Macpherson reads Locke as approving of this revolution, thereby creating a justification for market capitalism and the unlimited accumulation of wealth. "Locke has justified the specifically capitalist appropriation of land and money."[96] Tully, on the contrary, reads Locke as disapproving of at least the results of this revolution for it stimulated "a state of contention, covetousness and acquisitive desire."

> The acceptance of money brings with it the fall of man. Prior to its appearance men were motivated by need and convenience; now they are driven by the most corrupt of human motives: the desire for more than one needs.[97]

Given Macpherson's reading, civil government is introduced as a means of securing the unlimited accumulation of wealth; the state is an agent of capital. But given Tully's reading, civil government is required as a means of restoring and assuring the obligations and rights of natural law; the state is an agency

> obligated to distribute to each member the civil rights to life, to the liberty of preserving himself and others, and to the requisite goods or 'means of it'. This is a governmental duty from natural law and the public good, and it is now backed up with the threat of legitimate revolution if not discharged.[98]

The cogency of Tully's version of Locke is derived from his placement of Locke's theory of property within the broad theological-cultural context of his thought. Assuming Tully's position, Locke must not be seen as a champion of private property in any one-dimensional manner. Rather what Locke depicts is "a system in which private and common ownership are not mutually exclusive but mutually related: private ownership is the means of individuating the community's common property and is limited by the claim of all members. What particular legal form this might take in a given commonwealth is not a problem of theory but of prudence."[99]

Yet labor is the critical point, for without labor, human life is impossible. Labor is the creative formation and reformation of the conditions of human life, if not the substance of human life. Labor is the direct expression of one's self, the materialization of one's visions, the realization of one's being. Property within the framework of Locke's understanding should be viewed dynamically, not statically. It is not a stuff that one possesses and hoards. It is an activity necessary on the most basic level for survival, but needed on the highest level for fulfillment. Labor is the investment of one's energies in the conduct of history. In its origins, it depends on a common world, a world that is given—God's creation. In its intended consequences, it forms a heritage supportive of the life of all. But in its moment of immediacy, it is an individual's own special calling which is simultaneously an obligation and a right which subsist independent of and prior to all political forms.

3. R.H. Tawney is best known as an economic historian. But economic history to Tawney is not a specialty set apart. It is a branch of moral philosophy.[100] Its impetus derives from the interests of the present.

> History, as I understand it, is concerned with the study, not of a series of past events, but of the life of society, and with the records of the past as a means to that end . . . there is truth in the paradox that all history is the history of the present; and for this reason each generation must write its history for itself. That of its predecessors may be true, but its truth may not be relevant. Different answers are required because different questions are asked. Standing at a new point on the road, it finds that new ranges in the landscape come into view. It discovers that phenomena, which formerly appeared irrelevant, are a vital part of itself. It realizes, in short, and sometimes realises too late, that what is supposed to be the past is in reality the present.[101]

Tawney's famed works on the *Agrarian Problem in the Sixteenth Century* (1912) and *Religion and the Rise of Capitalism* (1926) are studies "of the resistance of groups and individuals to the imposition on them of capitalist modes of thought and behavior."[102] They deal respectively with two of the "main pillars of capitalism": the "doctrine of the sanctity of private property rights" and the "elaborate ethical support given to the creed of economic individualism by religious opinion."[103] They are studies of the historical origins and persistent character of modern capitalism as, in Tawney's judgment, the critical social problem of our age. Thus, in the closing passages of *Religion and the Rise of Capitalism*, he gives voice to his own commitment that "Compromise is as impossible between the Church of Christ and the idolatry of wealth, which is the practical religion of capitalist societies, as it was between the Church and the State idolatry of the Roman Empire."[104]

Tawney, during his college years, "became infected with socialist principles, principles which in Tawney's case were strongly infused with Christian ideals."[105] Within a few decades, he became, with others such as William Temple and Charles Gore, "one of the most influential spokesmen of Anglican socialism."[106] While the adequacy of his approach to socialism has been questioned,[107] the force of his arguments, historical and constructive, were directed toward the need for radical social transformation, including the transformation of the meaning of property as a central institution in economic relations.

According to Tawney, social transformation requires most basically a change in attitude.

> The attitude of governments to social questions is wrong, profoundly wrong. But it is wrong because the attitude of individuals to each other is wrong, because we in our present society are living on certain false and universal assumptions. . . .What we have got to do *first* of all is to change those assumptions or principles.[108]

Economic relationships, in Tawney's judgment, are not autonomous; they are reflective of the deep moral sensibilities of a people who, given the character of modern industrialism, must be brought to a new vision.

> Too much time is spent today upon outworks, by writers who pile up statistics and facts, but never get to the heart of the problem. That heart is not economic. It is a question of moral *relationships*. This is the citadel which must be attacked—the immoral philosophy which under lies much of modern industry.[109]

At the heart of that "immoral philosophy" is a principle of absolute property. Tawney asserts this at the beginning of his essay, "The Sickness of Acquisitive Society" (1919), which was later expanded to book length:

> The right to the free disposal of property and to the exploitation of economic opportunities is conceived by a large part of the modern world, and in particular by the most socially influential part of it, to be absolute, and this volume of interest and opinion rallies instinctively against any attempt to qualify or limit the exercise of these rights by attaching further conditions to them. . . .To-day that doctrine, if intellectually discredited, is still the practical foundation of social organization.[110]

The dominant concern of Tawney's theory of property is to construct an alternative to modern industrialism, an alternative inspired by a conception of equality. The central principle of his theory of property is social function which requires a transformation of "rights which are absolute into rights which are contingent and derivative, because it is to affirm that they are relative to functions and that they may be justly revoked when the functions are not performed."[111] The focus of Tawney's critique is on the perverse character and conditions of modern industrial capitalism.

In his critique, Tawney, seemingly using Weber's method of ideal types, contrasts two kinds of social order: acquisitive and functional. The former is the predominant character of Western societies since the eighteenth century. The latter, nowhere realized in fact, has long been a moral ideal and is, in Tawney's judgment, derived from the purpose—the *real* purpose—of economic relationships. Tawney is, at this point, a classical teleologist in moral analysis.

Modern societies typify an acquisitive society because their primary aim is to protect economic rights "while leaving economic functions, except in moments of abnormal emergency, to fulfill themselves." Their governing motivation is "to increase the opportunities open to individuals of attaining the objects which they conceive to be advantageous to themselves," and not "to secure the fulfillment of tasks imposed for the public service." Such societies are acquisitive "because their whole tendency and interest and preoccupation is to promote the acquisition of wealth." Such a conception, Tawney avers, "has laid the whole modern world under its spell."[112] In an acquisitive society, "the enjoyment of property and the direction of industry are considered . . . to require no social justification, because they are regarded as rights which stand by their own virtue, not functions to be judged by the success which they contribute to a social purpose."[113]

A functional society, on the other hand, aims "at making the acquisition of wealth contingent on the discharge of social obligations," seeks "to proportion remuneration to service," and esteems not what people possess, "but what they can make, or create, or achieve."[114] The main subject of social emphasis in such a society "would be the performance of function." In its economic dimensions, a functional society consists of four features. First, *purpose*: "the purpose of industry is obvious . . . to supply man with things which are necessary, useful or beautiful, and thus to bring life to body or spirit."[115] Second, *efficiency*: "pay for service and for service only, and when capital is hired to make sure that it is hired at the cheapest possible price." Third, *control*: "place the responsibility for organizing industry on the shoulders of those who work and use, not of those who own, because production is the business of the producer and the proper person to see that he discharges his business is the consumer for whom, and not the owner of the property, it ought to be carried on." Fourth, *accountability*: "insist that all industries shall be conducted in complete publicity as to costs and profits, because publicity ought to be the antiseptic both of economic and political abuses, and no man can have confidence in his neighbor unless both work in the light."[116]

These two kinds of social order—acquisitive and functional—are essentially incompatible. Their primary point of contention is at the level of purpose: "The essence of industrialism . . . is not any particular method of industry, but a particular estimate of the importance of industry. . . .[I]t is elevated from the subordinate place which it should occupy among human interests and activities into being the standard by which all other interests and activities are judged."[117] Industrialism confuses means with ends. It turns business into a fetish. It is a form of idolatry.

> The chief enemy of the life of the spirit, whether in art, culture, and religion, or in the simple human associations which are the common vehicle of its revelation to ordinary men, is itself a religion. It is, as every one knows, the idolatry of wealth, with its worship of pecuniary success, and its reverence for the arts . . . by which success is achieved, and its strong sense of the sanctity of possessions and weak sense of the dignity of human beings, and its consequent emphasis, not on the common interests which unite men, but on the accidents of property, and circumstance, and economic conditions, which separate and divide them.[118]

Because of its individualistic, self-centered character, an acquisitive society is intrinsically divisive. But a functional society is communal; it engages its members in mutually supportive endeavor. These two types of social order represent radically divergent understandings of the meaning of property.

While acknowledging that property is an ambiguous category, embracing a multitude of rights which "vary indefinitely in economic character, in social effect, and in moral justification,"[119] Tawney tends to distinguish two basic meanings of property: "property which is used by the owner for the conduct of his profession or the upkeep of his household, and property which yields an income irrespective of any personal service."[120] or, alternatively phrased, "property for use and property for power or exploitation."[121] The correlation between these two meanings of property and the two kinds of social order is obvious.

Since the seventeenth and eighteenth centuries in England and France, the principle of private property, initiated through revolutionary struggle to honor the idea of property for use, has been transformed, given changing historical conditions, to represent the idea of property for power. Originally the principle of the inviolability of private property seemed justified because of the social circumstances under which the principle became a fundamental social policy. First, property in land and in capital—a condition of effective work—was widely distributed. Second, major forces threatening property for use were the persistence of feudal authority and the fiscal policies of government. Third, private property was, in principle at least, a resource and citadel for the laborer; it protected "the yeoman or the master craftsman or the merchant from seeing the fruits of his toil squandered by the hangers-on at St. James or the courtly parasites of Versailles."[122] Under these conditions, private property was an aid to creative work. It promoted public purposes. It supported those who worked and their dependents. Moreover, given these cultural and political conditions, "the idea that the institution of private property involves the right of the owner to use it, or refrain from using it, in such a way as he may please, and that its principal significance is to supply him with an income, irrespective of any duties which he may discharge, would not have been understood by most public men of that age, and, if understood, would have been repudiated with indignation by the most reputable of them."[123]

Yet the principle of private property was transmuted into such an idea as the conditions of modern industrial capitalism emerged. The whole structure of the social order changed during the late nineteenth and twentieth centuries. At the present time, first, ownership of the national wealth is highly concentrated in and controlled by a small class of people. Second, what threatens the original intent of private property is the "insatiable expansion and aggregation of property itself, which menaces with absorption all property less than the greatest"—the small business, the family farmer, the country bank—and which "has turned the mass of mankind into a proletariat working under the agents and for the profit of those who own." Third, the modern property system does not protect the laborer. Instead, "ownership is not active, but passive, . . . to most of those who own property to-day it is not a means of work but an instrument for the acquisition of gain or the exercise of power and . . . there is no guarantee that gain bears any relation to service, or power to responsibility."[124] Tawney concludes that passive property distorts the meaning, the essential purpose, of the institution. Such property, he claims, is functionless.

Tawney draws a spectrum of kinds of proprietary rights protected by societies ranging from more active property (e.g. property as payments made for personal service, personal possessions needed for health and comfort, land and tools used by owners) to more passive property (e.g. property in monopoly profits, urban ground rents, royalties such as mining rights). Societies vary in the ratios of kinds of proprietary rights protected by them. In modern society the preponderance of property is passive. Given the inner meaning of property, the consequences of this shift toward passive property are morally unacceptable. The consequences are special privilege, institutionalized inequality, the erection of a whole apparatus of class associations, "which make not only the income, but the housing, education, health and manners, indeed the very physical appearance of different classes . . . almost as different from each other as though the minority were alien settlers established amid the rude civilization of a race of impoverished aborigines."[125]

As an alternative to modern industrialism, Tawney constructs the moral vision of a society based on the principle of function. Within the envisioned society, rights—including the right to property—are not absolute, but contingent.

> The individual has no absolute rights; they are relative to the function which he performs in the commuity of which he is a member, because, unless they are so limited, the consequences must be something in the nature of private war. All rights, in short, are conditional and derivative, because all power should be conditional and derivative. They are derived from the end or purpose of the society in which they exist. They are conditional on being used to contribute to the attainment of that end, not to thwart it.[126]

A central imperative of the envisioned society is equality—a "practical equality" given to the elimination of all forms of social inequality obstructive of the creative energies and works individuals have to contribute—given their differences in talents and abilities—to social well-being:

> it is the mark of a civilized society to aim at eliminating such inequalities as have their source, not in individual differences, but in its own organization, and that individual differences, which are a source of social energy, are more likely to ripen and find expression if social inequalities are, as far as practicable, diminished.[127]

So understood, practical equality is a means of moving beyond the intrinsic divisiveness of industrial capitalism toward the communal spirit of a humane society.

> If a high degree of practical equality is necessary to social well-being, because without it ability cannot find its way to its true vocation, it is necessary also for another and more fundamental reason. It is necessary because a community requires unity as well as diversity, and because, important as it is to discriminate between different powers, it is even more important to provide for common needs. . . .Social well-being does not only depend upon intelligent leadership; it also depends upon cohesion and solidarity. It implies the existence . . . of a conviction that civilization is not the business of the elite alone, but a common enterprise which is the concern of all.[128]

Thus equality of opportunity is a vital precept in a functional society. However, Tawney distinguishes two meanings of that precept. In one sense, the opportunities sought are "to rise, to get on, to exchange one position for a succession of others, to climb, in the conventional metaphor, the educational or economic ladder." This meaning of the precept is characteristic of the acquisitive society. In its second meaning, typical of a functional society, the opportunities sought are "to lead a good life in all senses of the term, whether one 'rises' or not." The aim of this kind of equality of opportunity is not individual self-advancement, but solidarity, participation in and contribution to the whole community.[129]

While Tawney insists that "the application to property and industry of the principle of function is compatible with several different types of social organization,"[130] he nonetheless urges a range of fundamental social policies whose implication is that industry—its wealth and its power—should be transmuted into a form of public or common property.

With respect to industrial wealth, Tawney promotes the progressive taxation of corporate enterprise to create a communal provision for social income. He interprets this policy as "the pooling of its [industry's] surplus resources by means of taxation, and the use of the funds thus obtained to make accessible to all, irrespective of their income, occupation, or social position, the condition of civilization which, in the absence of such measures, would be enjoyed only by the rich."[131] As social income, Tawney would include programs "to raise the general standard of health," "to equalize educational opportunites," "to provide for the contingencies of life" (sickness, old age, unemployment), to secure housing, and to protect the beauty of the environment.

In addition to the redistribution of industrial wealth, Tawney promotes a radical reconstruction of the corporate organization to mitigate the heavy concentration of economic power typical of modern industrial capitalism. He admits that, at times when liberty and equality are incompatible, liberty is to be preferred:

> The spiritual energy of human beings, in all the wealth of their infinite arrangements, is the end to which external arrangements, whether political or economic, are merely means. Hence institutions which guarantee to men the opportunity of becoming the best of which they are capable are the supreme political good, and liberty is rightly preferred to equality, when the two are in conflict.[132]

However, given the prevailing form of modern industry, the dominant threat to liberty is corporate autocracy. Under such conditions, an equalization of economic power is a requisite of economic liberty. Thus, while acknowledging the need for authority in economic organization, Tawney proposes more direct participation of the worker in the governance of industry—from the workplace to the board room—and more extensive subjection of major industries to public policy. Such moves, declares Tawney, will both have the effect of increasing the efficiency of industry[133] and, more importantly, give expression to the true meaning of industry "as a social function."

Industry, as the most prominent form of property in the modern world, should not be conceived as owned by its shareholders in the Blackstonian sense of absolute property. Rather, in Tawney's doctrine, it should be conceived as a public service, as a contribution to the enhancement of the whole community, as thus a kind of common property.

4. The works of Thomas Aquinas, John Locke, and R.H. Tawney were accomplished at different periods of social history. Thomas wrote during the maturity of the Western feudal and manorial system. Locke was responding to tensions and struggles of an emergent bourgeois capitalism. Tawney was engaged in interpreting and reacting to a time of advanced corporate industrialism. These differences of social and historical setting are reflected in their respective doctrines of property. Nonetheless, their doctrines of property display a remarkable continuity. On the negative side, none is supportive of the principle of absolute property formulated by William Blackstone. To be sure, Locke's doctrine has often been invoked as a case of "possessive individualism." But, if John Dunn and James Tully are correct, such an invocation distorts the actual character of Locke's argument. On the positive side, all three of these doctrines conjoin two dimensions in their understandings of property—communal and individual. Property as a claim on the use of resources is neither exclusively an individual right nor simply a matter for political and social determination. Charles Donahue's dichotomy between individualism and commualism is overdrawn and his identification of the concept of property with individualism is dubitable. At least in some of its philosophical forms, the concept of property manifests a more complicated, perhaps more justifiable approach to social and economic arrangements.

The historical side of this study, however, is subordinate to its philosophical concern, namely, to explore the meaning of property from a relational perspective. The thesis I have proposed is that a relational principle, grounded in a cosmology of process thought, embraces, in its own way, dimensions of the meaning of property found in the thought of Thomas (the principle of common use), Locke (the principle of labor), and Tawney (the principle of social function). In keeping with the continuity among these three otherwise disparate theorists, a relational doctrine of property requires a radical revisioning of the classical liberal or absolute principle of property with its strictly individualistic import.

The question of property is intimately related to a broad issue of political and economic philosophy—the relation between public and private. The doctrine of absolute property is correlative with an insistence on the priority of private life. Public life is of secondary, perhaps only instrumental, importance. In extreme form, such an insistence poses doubts about the possibility of any genuinely public life at all. What appears public is reducible to the private.

As Lois Livezey argues in her dissertation on Alfred North Whitehead's "conception of the public world," a privatistic understanding of action is incompatible with process thought.[134] Furthermore, a privatistic understanding of action constitutes a major problem in the modern world. Commenting on the diffusion of a Cartesian form of thought throughout modern life, Whitehead remarks:

> The doctrine of minds, as independent substances, leads directly not merely to private worlds of experience, but also to private worlds of morals. The moral intuitions can be held to apply only to the strictly private world of psychological experience. Accordingly, self-respect, and the making of the most of your own individual opportunities together constituted the efficient morality of the leaders among the industrialists of that period. The western world is now suffering from the limited moral outlook of the three previous generations.[135]

What is ignored is "the true relation of each organism to its environment."

In contrast, to Whitehead, each entity—each decision, each action—consists of two sides, public and private. In a concise statement of his doctrine of prehensions, he formulates this point explicitly:

> The theory of prehensions is founded on the doctrine that there are no concrete facts which are merely public, or merely private. The distinction between publicity and privacy is a distinction of reason, and is not a distinction between mutually exclusive concrete facts. The sole concrete facts, in terms of which actualities can be analysed, are prehensions; and every prehension has its public side and its private side. Its public side is constituted by the complex datum prehended; and its private side is constituted by the subjective form through which a private quality is imposed on the public datum.[136]

More precisely, to take account of "the creative advance of nature," one must understand actualities dynamically, as in process from public moment to private moment, then again to public moment. Thus Whitehead writes:

> An actual entity considered in reference to the publicity of things is a 'superject'; namely, it arises from the publicity which it finds, and it adds itself to the publicity which it transmits. It is a moment of passage from *decided public facts* to a *novel public fact*. Public facts are, in their nature, coordinate.
>
> An actual entity considered in reference to the privacy of things is a 'subject'; namely, it is a moment of the genesis of *self-enjoyment*. It consists of a purposed *self-creation* out of materials which are at hand in virtue of their publicity.[137]

Of these three moments, I suggest that Thomas's *principle of common use* pertains primarily to that of "decided public facts"; that Locke's *principle of labor* is focussed on the moment of self-creation and self-enjoyment; and that Tawney's *principle of social function* is predominantly a statement about the moment of "novel public fact." Thomas's primary concern is that the world be understood as a common resource belonging to the entire community. Locke's interest is with the manner and sense of individuation, with the particular rights of each person. Tawney's point is to direct self-creation toward the enhancement of the community's future. With this construction, these three principles are conjoined in a single understanding of the meaning of property which stands in stark opposition to Dietze's defense of a doctrine of private property as a central institution of human civilization.

Profound reservations about the doctrine of absolute property are evidenced in Whitehead's *historical thesis* about the genius and deficiencies of the prevailing philosophy of the past three centuries. In *Science and the Modern World*, for instance, Whitehead links scientific materialism with an individualistic social philosophy, expressing, among other things, his critique of the tradition of economic thought inaugurated by Adam Smith.

> It is very arguable that the science of political economy, as studied in its first period after the death of Adam Smith (1790), did more harm than good. It destroyed many economic fallacies, and taught how to think about the economic revolution then in progress. But it riveted on men a certain set of abstractions which were disastrous in their influence on modern mentality. It de-humanized industry.[138]

Along with its individualism, this philosophy assumed a principle of the value neutrality of matter, thereby inculcating "the habit of ignoring the intrinsic worth of the environment," including both the social and the physical environment.[139]

> Thus all thought concerned with social organization expressed itself in terms of material things and capital. Ultimate values were excluded. . . .A creed of competitive business morality was evolved, in some respects curiously high; but entirely devoid of consideration for the value of human life. The workmen were conceived as mere hands, drawn from the pool of labour. To God's question, men gave the answer of Cain—'Am I my brother's keeper?'; and they incurred Cain's guilt. This was the atmosphere in which the industrial revolution was accomplished in England, and to a large extent elsewhere.[140]

In *Adventures of Ideas*, Whitehead's historical thesis is both more complex and more explicit in its judgment about the modern doctrine of property. From ancient to modern times, a massive shift in social organization and social thought has transpired, redounding to the benefit of all humankind: "Slavery was the presupposition of political theorists then; Freedom is the presupposition of political theorists now."[141] This gradual development, halting and limited, has meant a growth in "the conception of the dignity of human nature" and therefore in "the idea of the essential rights of human beings, arising from their sheer humanity."[142] However, notions of human freedom and human rights, embodied in institutional and ideational form in the nineteenth century, took an ironic turn. The amalgamation of liberalism with industrialism produced a new kind of enslavement. "The mere doctrines of freedom, individualism, and competition had produced a resurgence of something very like industrial slavery at the base of society."[143]

As a result, in Whitehead's judgment, "economic organization constitutes the most massive problem of human relationships."[144] In particular, doctrines of contract and property have been eviscerated of their earlier significance by the emergence of the modern corporation as a presumed or fictitious person with all the essential rights and liberties that, gradually over the course of centuries, had attached to natural persons.

> The necessity for large capital, with the aid of legal ingenuity produced the commercial corporation with limited liability. . . .The introduction into the arena of this new type of 'person' has considerably modified the effective meaning of the characteristic liberal doctrine of contractual freedom. It is one thing to claim such freedom as a natural right for human persons, and quite another to claim it for corporate persons. And again the notion of private property had a simple obviousness at the foot of Mount Sinai and even in the eighteenth century. When there were primitive roads, negligible drains, private wells, no elaborate system of credit, when payment meant the direct production of gold-pieces, when each industry was reasonably self-contained—in fact when the world was not as it is now—then it was fairly obvious what was meant by private property, apart from any current legal fictions. Today private property is mainly a legal fiction.[145]

At this point, Whitehead directs his critique beyond the problem of corporate industrialism to the central idea of individualism on which the modern doctrine of liberalism is grounded. The alternative to individualism is an understanding of the intrinsic relatedness of human life and of the need for a new social arrangement in which freedom and coordination, individuality and participation are correlative.

> The whole concept of absolute individuals with absolute rights, and with a contractual power of forming fully defined external relations, has broken down. The human being is inseparable from its environment in each occasion of its existence. The environment which the occasion inherits is immanent in it, and conversely it is immanent in the environment which it helps to transmit. . . .There is no escape from customary status. . . .On the other hand, the inherited status is never a full determination. There is always the freedom for the determination of individual emphasis.[146]

As already intimated, underlying Whitehead's historical thesis about the ironic character of the modern world is his *cosmology*. Whitehead's cosmology concentrates on actual entities as "the final real things of which the world is made up."[147] An actual entity is a creative synthesis of a complex inheritance; it has, for a time, a life of its own; it then becomes part of the heritage for all future entities. That, in stark form, is the fundamental character of the world in all its many forms.

Three moments are distinguishable in that process: an inheritance from the past, the enjoyment of the present, a possibility for the future. Simplifying Whitehead's language, I suggest the terms of objectification, creativity, and relativity may be employed to designate, respectively, these three moments. *Objectification*, Whitehead writes, "refers to the particular mode in which the potentiality of one actual entity is realized in another actual entity."[148] Objectification is the moment an individual receives the common world, positively or negatively, into itself. *Creativity*, to Whitehead, is an ultimate category:

> It is that ultimate principle by which the many, which are the universe disjunctively, become the one actual occasion, which is the universe conjunctively. It lies in the nature of things that the many enter into complex unity.
>
> 'Creativity' is the principle of *novelty*. An actual occasion is a novel entity diverse from any entity in the 'many' which it unifies. Thus 'creativity' introduces novelty into the content of the many, which are the universe disjunctively. The 'creative advance' is the application of this ultimate principle of creativity to each novel situation which it originates.[149]

Finally, according to the principle of *relativity*, "it belongs to the nature of a 'being' that it is a potential for every 'becoming'."[150] Although each actual entity has its day and then, in a sense, it perishes, it still persists as a datum, whatever its character, to be reckoned with by all subsequent entities. As evident, objectification and relativity are correlative ideas which, nonetheless, I distinguish to focus attention on aspects of past and future as both public dimensions in the passage of life. Life moves from a common world to the solitariness of private experience, but then it moves again into the realm of the common. That is the ineluctable character of all reality.

Whitehead's cosmology is the framework for his philosophy of civilization which is his contribution to *social theory*. Where, on the cosmological level, life has a certain fixedness about it, in human association, determinate variation is possible. Civilization in Whitehead's thought is a normative concept. As such it functions on several levels: it is a groundwork for a doctrine of human rights; it is a version of common good; and it incorporates an understanding of human virtue.[151] According to Lois Livezey, of the related features that constitute civilization, "Adventure and peace represent Whitehead's novel contribution to . . . [its] defining character."[152]

Adventure is the feature of creativity in civilization. It is the character of experimentation and novelty. It is a function of the capacity for self-transcendence. Freedom is the requisite of adventure. Flexibility of association, provision for new opportunity, respect for difference, appreciation of robust debate, affirmation of the unusual are among expressions of the sense of adventure. Adventure is thus a ground for individual rights and rights of association. Peace, on the other hand, in its social dimension, is a feature of relativity. It elicits actions of mutual support and reciprocal enhancement. Loyalty and trust, concern and care, harmony and order are among its political aspects. Peace is thus a basis for the obligations and responsibilities of citizenship. Where adventure favors the sensibilities and actions of individuals and groups, peace affirms the solidarity of the total community. Together adventure and peace are responsive to a central problem of social life, the commingling of freedom and coordination.[153]

> One of the most general philosophic notions to be used in the analysis of civilized activities is to consider the effect on social life due to the variations of emphasis between Individual Absoluteness and Individual Relativity. Here 'absoluteness' means the notion of release from essential dependence on other members of the community in respect to modes of activity, while relativity means the converse fact of essential relatedness.[154]

Whitehead did not systematically set out the implications of his cosmology and social theory on the *question of property*. But, in connotation, it is evident he would stand in the tradition I have traced through Thomas Aquinas, John Locke, and R.H. Tawney. That is, given his concept of civilization as the norm for social arrangements, he would conjoin two dimensions in his understanding of property—communal and individual. The appropriation and manipulation of environmental resources, the possession and use of material things are two-sided. They are intended for the support and extension of the individual's life, but not exclusively so. They are meant also for enhancing the quality and character of the lives of others and for the life of the community as a totality. Property is a bundle of individual rights and social responsibilities. Respect for individual determination and public concern are linked. Precisely how they should be linked at any given time may depend on historical considerations. But under no circumstances is property exclusively an individual and absolute right. Likewise, under no circumstances is property exclusively a matter for autocratic concession and dictate. The meaning of property must be cast within the framework of the ideal of civilization.

Within that framework, a relational perspective on the several aspects of the meaning of property would take the following form. I have altered the order to begin with the paramount concerns of Whitehead's cosmology and social theory.

i. *Origin: How is property initiated?* Property originates in the dynamics of human life. Property in the sense of claims to environmental resources is a natural part of the interactive process of living. It is the appropriation of "decided public facts" for purposes of self-creation.

ii. *Purpose: What is the function of property?* The ultimate purpose of property is captured in the concept of civilization. Property is thus both a means and an expression of the creativity of the individual and the quality of a society. A relational perspective synthesizes the instrumentalist and the self-developmental traditions.

iii. *Status: What kind of entity is property?* Property is most fundamentally a moral claim to the appropriation and use of things of all kinds for the purposes stated above. The legal claim to property should provide whatever institutional support is necessary or desirable to advance the more basic moral claim.

iv. *Subject: Who may hold property?* Given the complexly interactive character of human life, property must be understood as multititular. No one possesses absolute or exclusive title over anything, even one's own life. Particularly in the instance of material things, a right not to be excluded from access to what is necessary or desirable for the conduct of one's life is as critical as, if not more critical than, the right to exclude others is conceived to be in the classical liberal tradition.

v. *Object: What sorts of things may be held as property?* In a sense, given the actual dynamics of human life, everything constitutes property to an extent. We even appropriate each other in the simple actions of our everyday existence. What is at stake is not so much what we appropriate as how we appropriate. More important than the question of what we command as resources is the issue of whether in the process of appropriation and in the forms assumed by appropriation, the lives of individuals are enhanced and the quality of social life, as well as the life of nature, is sustained or improved. This is sufficient reason to reject slavery and forced labor as inappropriate and to support a distinction in principle between property for consumption and property for production.

vi. *Import and extent: What are the limits of property?* The limits of property are dictated by its purpose. The limiting question is, what advances the cause of civilization? Given the breadth of the relational perspective, however, the cause of civilization must be understood to embrace care and concern for the entire ecosphere.

In sum, from this perspective, property should be conceived of simultaneously as (1) a public resource (principle of common use), (2) an individual province (principle of labor), and (3) a public responsibility (principle of social function). Within the spectrum of economic philosophies currently under contention, this conception is closer to the democratic socialism of an R.H. Tawney than to the libertarianism of a Friedrich Hayek. Process thought, in its approach to "the most massive problem of human relationships"[155] of the present time, points toward a communitarian form of the meaning of property.

Notes and References

1.   John Locke, *Two Treatises of Government*, edited by Peter Laslett (Cambridge: Cambridge University Press, 1966) II 124.

2.   Karl Marx, *Capital* (Chicago: Encyclopedia Brittanica, Great Books, vol. 50, 1952) I xxxii.

3.   C.B. Macpherson, "The Meaning of Property" in C.B. Macpherson, ed., *Property* (Toronto: Unversity of Toronto Press, 1978), p. 1.

4.   See Frederick G. Whelan, "Property as Artifice: Hume and Blackstone" in J. Roland Pennock and John W. Chapman, eds., *Property* (New York: New York University Press, 1980), pp. 114-125.

5.   Blackstone, Commentaries II 2, quoted in *ibid.*, p. 118.

6.   Quoted by James McClellan, *Joseph Story and the American Constitution* (Norman: University of Oklahoma Press, 1971), p. 214.

7.   Gottfried Dietze, *In Defense of Property* (Baltimore: The Johns Hopkins Press, 1971), p. 93.

8.   *Ibid.*, p. 39.

9.   *Ibid.*, pp. 126-127.

10.   Friedrich A. Hayek, *The Mirage of Social Justice* (Chicago: The University of Chicago Press, 1976).

11.   See Thomas C. Grey, "The Disintegration of Property" in Pennock and Chapman, eds., *op. cit.* at note 4, pp. 69-85.

12.   Richard Schlatter, *Private Property: The History of an Idea* (New York: Russell and Russell, 1973), p. 278.

13.   Karl Marx and Friedrich Engels, *Manifesto of the Communist Party* (Chicago: Encyclopedia Brittanica, Great Books, vol. 50, 1952), pp. 425-426.

14.   94 U.S. 113, 126.

15. Walter Lippmann, *The Public Philosophy* (New York: New American Library, 1956), p. 93.

16. George Cabot Lodge, *The New American Ideology* (New York: Alfred A. Knopf, 1976), p. 198.

17. *Ibid.*, pp. 17-18; see all of chapter 7.

18. J.H. Bogard, "Lockean Proviso and State of Nature Theories," *Ethics* 95/4 (July 1985) 832.

19. See John W. Chapman, "Justice, Freedom and Property" in Pennock and Chapman, eds. *op. cit.* at note 4, pp. 289-324, for a broader and more detailed spectrum of fundamental positions of economic justice.

20. John Locke, *op. cit.* at note 1, II 25.

21. Quoted in Macpherson, ed.,*op. cit.* at note 3, p. 110.

22. *Ibid.*, pp. 3-4, 6-9.

23. A.M. Honoré, "Ownership" in A.G. Guest, ed., *Oxford Essays in Jurisprudence* (London: Oxford University Press, 1961), p. 137.

24. Ewart Lewis, *Medieval Political Ideas*, vol. 1 (New York: Cooper Square Publishers, Inc., 1974), p. 89.

25. See William B. Scott, *In Pursuit of Happiness: American Conceptions of Property from the Seventeenth to the Twentieth Century* (Bloomington: Indiana University Press, 1977), pp. 137-147.

26. James Gwartney, "Private Property, Freedom and the West," *The Intercollegiate Review* 20/3 (Spring/Summer 1985) 48.

27. Macpherson, *op. cit.* at note 3, p. 11; see also pp. 4-6, 9-11.

28. *Ibid.*, p. 206.

29. Charles Donahue, Jr., "The Future of the Concept of Property Predicted from its Past" in Pennock and Chapman, eds., *op. cit.* at note 4, p. 56.

30. Kenneth R. Minogue, "The Concept of Property and its Contemporary Significance" in *ibid.*, pp. 14-15.

31. Hastings Rashdall, "The Philosophical Theory of Property" in Charles Gore, et al., *Property: Its Duties and Rights* (New York: The MacMillan Co., 1922), p. 66.

32. *Ibid.*, pp. 66-67.

33. Quoted in Macpherson, ed., *op. cit.* at note 3, pp. 98-99.

34. Charles A. Reich, "The New Property," *The Yale Law Journal* 73/5 (April 1964) 733.

35. *Ibid.*, p. 786.

36. *Op. cit.* at note 23, p. 123.

37. *Op. cit.* at note 31, p. xxiii.

38. *Ibid.*, p. xv.

39. Quoted in Macpherson, ed., *op. cit.* at note 3, p. 159.

40. *Ibid.*, p. 172.

41. *Ibid.*, p. 175.

42. Aldo Leopold, *A Sand County Almanac* (London: Oxford University Press, 1968), p. viii.

43. John B. Cobb, Jr., *Is It Too Late?* (Beverly Hills, CA: Bruce, 1972), p. 55.

44. Thomas Hobbes, *Leviathan*, II 18.

45. Alan Ryan, *Property and Political Theory* (Oxford: Basil Blackwell, 1984).

46. Charles Donahue, Jr., *op. cit.* at note 29, p. 58.

47. *Op. cit.* at note 7, p. 16.

48. E.K. Hunt, *Property and Prophets* (New York: Harper and Row, 1972), p. 11.

49. Anthony Parel, "Aquinas' Theory of Property" in Anthony Parel and Thomas Flanagan, eds., *Theories of Property: Aristotle to the Present* (Waterloo, Ontario: Wilfrid Laurier University Press, 1979), p. 89.

50. *Ibid.*, p. 92. See *Summa Theologica* I-II Q. 2.

51. *Summa Theologica* I-II Q. 4 Art. 7.

52. Parel, *op. cit.* at note 49, p. 89.

53. *Summa Theologica* I-II Q. 94 art. 5 ad. 3; see also II-II Q. 57 art. 3.

54. Parel, *op. cit.* at note 49, p. 97.

55. *Summa Theologica* II-II Q. 66 art. 7.

56. *Ibid.*, II-II Q. 118 art. 1 ad. 2.

57. T.C. O'Brien, ed., *St. Thomas Aquinas, Summa Theologiae*, vol. 41 *Virtues of Justice in the Human Community* II-II 101-22 (New York: Blackfriars & McGraw Hill, 1972), p. 243, footnote b.

58. *Summa Theologica* II-II Q. 66 art. 7.

59. *Ibid.*

60. *Ibid.*, I Q. 63 art. 2 ad. 2 .

61. See *ibid.*, II-II Q. 118 art. 1.

62. *Ibid.*, II-II Q. 118 art. 8.

63. See Immanuel Wallerstein, *Historical Capitalism* (London: Verso, 1983), chapter 13 "The Commodification of Everything."

64. See *Summa Theologica* II-II Q. 117 (on liberality) and Q. 58 (on justice).

65. *Ibid.*, II-II Q. 58 art. 2.

66. See *ibid.*, II-II Q. 66 art. 8.

67. Richard Schlatter, *op. cit.* at note 12, p. 55.

68. Henry S. Kariel, *Beyond Liberalism* (New York: Harper and Row, 1977), p. 5.

69. Richard Schlatter, *op. cit.* at note 12, p. 252.

70. See James Tully, "The Framework of Natural Rights in Locke's Analysis of Property: A Contextual Reconstruction" in Parel and Flanagan, eds., *op. cit.* at note 49, p. 115, and Ryan, *op. cit.* at note 45, pp. 18-24.

71. John Dunn, *The Political Thought of John Locke* (Cambridge: Cambridge University Press, 1982), p. 214; see generally, pp. 214-241.

72. C.B. Macpherson, *The Political Theory of Possessive Individualism* (London: Oxford University Press, 1972), p. 199.

73. *Ibid.*, p. 221.

74. See John Dunn, *op. cit.* at note 71; James Tully, *A Discourse on Property: John Locke and His Adversaries* (Cambridge: Cambridge University Press, 1980); Alan Ryan, *op. cit.* at note 45; and Eldon J. Eisenach, *Two Worlds of Liberalism* (Chicago: The University of Chicago Press, 1981).

75. John Locke, *op. cit.* at note 1, II 6.

76. Dunn, *op. cit.* at note 71, p. 87.

77. John Locke, *op. cit.* at note 1, II 6.

78. *Ibid.*, II 57.

79. *Ibid.*, II 135.

80. Tully in Parel and Flanagan, eds., *op. cit.* at note 49, pp. 127-129; also Tully, *op. cit.* at note 74, pp. 43-50, 62, 163.

81. John Locke, *op. cit.* at note 1, II 25.

82. *Ibid.*, II 60.

83. *Ibid.*, II 25.

84. *Ibid.*, II 123.

85. *Ibid.*, II 25.

86. *Ibid.*, II 27.

87. Rashdall, *op. cit.* at note 31, pp. 47-50; see also Robert Nozick, *Anarchy, State and Utopia* (New York: Basic Books, 1974), pp. 174-182.

88. Ryan, *op. cit.* at note 45, pp. 31-32.

89. Dunn, *op. cit.* at note 71, p. 217.

90. Tully, *op. cit.* at note 74, p. 110.

91. John Locke, *op. cit.* at note 1, II 27.

92. *Ibid.*, II 31.

93. *Ibid.*, II 32.

94. *Ibid.*, II 36.

95. *Ibid.*, II 50.

96. Macpherson, *op. cit.* at note 72, p. 208.

97. Tully, *op. cit.* at note 74, p. 150; cf. Dunn, *op. cit.* at note 71, p. 248.

98. Tully, *op. cit.* at note 74, p. 166; see Locke, *op. cit.* at note 1, II 50 & 123.

99. Tully, *op. cit.* at note 74, p. 170.

100. J.M.Winter, "Introduction: Tawney the Historian" in J.M. Winter, ed., *History and Society: Essays by R.H. Tawney* (London: Routledge and Kegan Paul, 1978), p. 8. See also J.M. Winter and D.M. Joslin, "Introduction" in Winter and Joslin, eds., *R.H. Tawney's Commonplace Book* (Cambridge: Cambridge University Press, 1972), p. xx.

101. R.H. Tawney, "The Study of Economic History (1933)" in Winter, ed., *op. cit.* at note 100, pp. 54-55. See also R.H. Tawney, *Social History and Literature* (Leicester University Press, 1958), p. 6.

102. Winter, *op. cit.* at note 100, p. 2.

103. W.H. Nelson, "R.H. Tawney" in *Some Modern Historians of Britain* (New York: The Dryden Press, 1951), p. 334.

104. R.H. Tawney, *Religion and the Rise of Capitalism* (New York: Penguin Books, 1947), p. 235.

105. Nelson, *op. cit.* at note 103, p. 326.

106. Winter, *op. cit.* at note 100, p. 15.

107. See Alasdair MacIntyre, *Against the Self-Images of the Age* (New York: Schocken, 1971), pp. 38-42.

108. Tawney, *Commonplace Books, op. cit.* at note 100, pp. 45-46.

109.   *Ibid.*, p. 56.

110.   R.H. Tawney, "The Sickness of Acquisitive Society," *The Hibbert Journal* XVII/3 (1919) 353.

111.   R.H. Tawney, *The Acquisitive Society* (New York: Harcourt, Brace & Co., 1920), p. 26.

112.   R.H. Tawney, *op. cit.* at note 110, pp. 356-357. See also Tawney, *op. cit.* at note 111, pp. 29-30.

113.   Tawney, *op. cit.* at note 111, p. 24.

114.   Tawney, *op. cit.* at note 110, p. 356; *op. cit.* at note 111, pp. 28-29.

115.   Tawney, *op. cit.* at note 111, p. 8.

116.   *Ibid.*, p. 85.

117.   *Ibid.*, p. 45.

118.   R.H. Tawney, *Equality* (New York: Harcourt, Brace & Co., 1931), p. 271.

119.   Tawney, *op. cit.* at note 111, pp. 53-54.

120.   Tawney, *op. cit.* at note 110, p. 370.

121.   R.H. Tawney, *The Attack and Other Papers* (New York: Harcourt, Brace & Co., 1953), p. 188.

122.   Tawney, *op. cit.* at note 111, p. 56.

123.   *Ibid.*, p. 59.

124.   *Ibid.*, pp. 61-62.

125.   *Ibid.*, pp. 71-72. See also *op. cit.* at note 118, chapter II, "The Religion of Inequality," pp. 12-49.

126.   Tawney, *op. cit.* at note 110, p. 368.

127.   Tawney, *op. cit.* at note 118, p. 50.

128.   *Ibid.*, pp. 130-131.

129.   Tawney, *op. cit.* at note 121, pp. 190-191 and *op. cit.* at note 118, pp. 119-136.

130.   Tawney, *op. cit.* at note 111, p. 84.

131.   Tawney, *op. cit.* at note 118, p. 153. See the whole of chapter V, "The Strategy of Equality," pp. 149-208.

132.   *Ibid.*, p. 220.

133.   *Ibid.*, pp. 246, 262. See also *op. cit.* at note 111, pp. 139-160 and *op. cit.* at note 104, p. 232. On the other hand, see Tawney's comment in his *Commonplace Book, op. cit.* at note 100, pp. 70-71: "If industry could be so organized that the mass of workers would feel convinced that the social order was just, a decrease in efficiency wld [sic] be cheap at the price."

134.   Lois Gehr Livezey, *Whitehead's Conception of the Public World*, unpublished doctoral dissertation (Chicago, 1983).

135.   Alfred North Whitehead, *Science and the Modern World* (New York: The MacMillan Co., 1939), p. 281.

136.   Alfred North Whitehead, *Process and Reality: Corrected Edition* (New York: The Free Press, 1979), p. 290.

137.   *Ibid.*, p. 289 (italics added).

138.   Whitehead, *op. cit.* at note 135, p. 288.

139.   *Ibid.*, pp. 281-282.

140. *Ibid.*, pp. 291-292.

141. Alfred North Whitehead, *Adventures of Ideas* (New York: The Free Press, 1967), p. 13.

142. *Ibid.*, pp. 15, 13.

143. *Ibid.*, p. 143.

144. *Ibid.*, p. 62.

145. *Ibid.*, pp. 62-63.

146. *Ibid.*, see also p. 67.

147. Whitehead, *op. cit.* at note 136, p. 18.

148. *Ibid.*, p. 23.

149. *Ibid.*, p. 21.

150. *Ibid.*, p. 22.

151. This is the character of Lois Livezey's argument in her disseration, *op. cit.* at note 134. See also her unpublished paper, "Rights, Goods, and Virtues: Toward An Interpretation of Justice in Process Thought," delivered at the Annual Meeting of the Society of Christian Ethics, January 1986.

152. Livezey, *op. cit.* at note 134, p. 324.

153. Whitehead, *op. cit.* at note 141, pp. 28, 56.

154. *Ibid.*, p. 43.

155. *Ibid.*, p. 62.

CHAPTER 4

Property Rights: Another Relational Perspective

George W. Pickering

Whitehead says that "economic organization constitutes the most massive problem of human relationships." Indeed it does. Providing for the material well-being of the five billion persons who currently inhabit this planet is nothing if not massive; and that is what economic organizations are for—delivering the goods so that human beings can live, live well, and live better. So stated, we see that the problem of economic organization is intimately related to what Whitehead identified as the function of reason. It is an intellectual as well as an institutional problem. It is also a moral problem insofar as it is not self-evident what content we ought to give to the notions of "well" and "better." Wars have been fought and revolutions waged over the proper meaning of those terms. One need not be an "economic determinist" in order to affirm that the issues arising from the understandings of and arrangements for material well-being are among the chief determinants of the course and meaning of history.

From time immemorial, property of some sort has been the principal means by which groups and individuals have been able to mark off and know what is "theirs," that is, what they can more or less count on for securing and advancing their material well-being. The character of this property and the rights that go with it have always been subject to political definition. I use the word "political" here in a very broad sense to indicate that communities have always been the primary agents, through whatever instruments of authority they have, in defining what may properly be held as property and what entitlements go with the ownership of it.

In liberal societies, there has been a premium on personal property, sometimes called "private." This emphasis on the personal has indeed gone hand in hand with the liberal "cosmology." Liberals of all sorts have generally shared the intuition that each and every individual has a personal destiny to live out as best that individual can and that each and every individual is entitled to possess the fruits of personal effort as an aid to the fulfillment of that personal destiny, so long as these fruits are not achieved at the cost of harm to others or in contravention of any legitimate law. We can even say that liberal societies have provided a legal framework aimed at maximizing the creation, not simply the preservation, of property; and in this effort they have been phenomenally successful.

In liberal societies this effort has been deemed so important that property is considered a "natural right" of some sort. The question has been much debated: of what sort? John Locke's claim was that persons had a natural right to life, liberty and property. That gave property a very high standing as a common good which, it appears, Locke was not quite able to maintain in the face of his own preservationist understanding of government.[1] Under Thomas Jefferson's reformulation, these became rights to life, liberty and the pursuit of happiness. It is a good question, How does property stand in relation to these rights? Is it an outcome of their exercise and, therefore, entitled to a protected status of some sort? Yes, to some extent it certainly is. Is it also a necessary condition for their free exercise? To some extent it certainly is; but this is not the relation of "property" to "rights" with which the rhetoric of property rights has mostly been concerned these past two centuries.

The cry of "property rights" has generally been invoked by those who have some in defense of their claims for freedom to do with it as they please. Call this "possessive individualism," if you like. That is a fairly adequate description of the predominant mood, especially among the anglo-saxon countries, toward property under both "merchant" and "corporate" capitalism. Under both of these economic regimes, social and political authority has generally weighed in on the side of the creation of property and the protection of proprietary claims.

There are those, and Douglas Sturm appears to place himself among them in his essay, who believe that this "possessive individualism" is not only what Western liberalism unleashed, but that it is all it was ever about. This proposition is in a class with claims that the crusades and the Inquisition were all that Christianity was ever about. In fact the analogy is strict. Just as the crusades and the Inquisition were Christian pathologies so possessive individualism is a liberal pathology. It has exerted an undeniable and undesirable force within western liberal societies and it has proven to be an undisciplined disaster as an export to third world countries. No special pleading is required, nor should any be allowed, on this account.

There is more to Western liberalism than this possessive individualism, however, and this "more" is crucial to the rational extension of democracy into economic affairs and relations in a workable way. The issue, as I take it, for Sturm and others, liberals and radicals alike, lies in the question of what standing property should have either within a liberal society or in any alternative social and political arrangement. For liberals especially, this question is driven by the problem of gigantic multi-national corporations and the possibility that they are runaway powers that have eluded or exceeded the purview of proper governance. Since they appear to be the unruly children of liberalism, the question naturally arises: do they not represent the end of its line as a politically creative force?

There is no point in trying to deny that as a matter of both history and philosophy there has been a liberal "obsession" with property or that the notion of property rights is fundamental to liberalism. And yet whatever the mistakes and miscarriages that have turned up in the history of this obsession, there is an abiding intuition here—of cosmic proportions—whose culturally creative and socially constructive potential is, I hope to show, far from played out. Guccis and Porsches are not the last stop on the drive towards either the right to property or the pursuit of happiness.

The appeal to "property rights" need not and should not be limited to the defense of privilege; it may yet provide the grounds and the means to secure and symbolize the ultimate standing of each and every individual in the midst of nature and society. Unless property is a right of some sort, then there are no moral grounds for objecting to the division of the human world into the "haves" and the "have-nots."

Human equality is at issue both in the concept of property and in the idea of rights. It is at issue in theory as well as practice; for both property and rights are terms which must be institutionalized in practice and how this is done will contribute materially to the fundamental relationships of individuals in association.

Liberalism, even in most conservative renditions, has always taken the position that material well-being is an essential component of the pursuit of happiness. The obsession with property would seem to be decisive on that score. The notion that people with property are somehow more responsible and more reliable and more available for moderate politics originally led the framers of the United States Constitution to accept property qualifications as part of their definition of citizens in the full sense. Only by degrees did the logic of liberalism get driven to the ideal of democracy; and even now there is stubborn resistance to the extension of the democratic ideal into the realm of "economic rights."

This is no time to turn back. There was and there is a profound truth in the intuition of a reciprocal relationship between property and rights—the liberal obsession. Sticking with that intuition is the cutting edge of the democratic ideal in our time.

Those who deny that liberal democracy has any room for "economic rights" and see in the economic rights movement only a Marxist attempt to subvert the very notion of rights—that is, the United States State Department among others—not only sell the history and principles of liberal democracy short[2]; for all practical and moral purposes, they announce that there is no promise for democratic social change in the world as we know it. Their proposition comes to this: those who think that the promotion and governance of social change must include redistributive policies with regard to property as well as power should either (A) stop thinking that way or (B) look elsewhere for ideals and principles. Under the form of either (A) or (B) most of the world has taken this advice; and neither they nor we are generally better off as a result.

It bothers me that Sturm has gone along with the State Department on this score by choosing (B). He turns to Aquinas for a notion of the "common good" even though the Thomistic system, including its rendering of the common good, is riddled with supremacist assumptions, assertions and principles. He draws from Locke a liberal notion of individual creativity which is allied to a conservatively preservationist theory of government. He rests his case for equality on the vaguely socialistic musings of R.H. Tawney who is hardly in the same class intellectually with Aquinas and Locke. None of these represents a theory of governing or of property or of rights that we could actually use to advance the cause of democratic social change anywhere in the world. Nor does Sturm propose that they would. All he gets out of them is a counterfoil to the absolutistic individualism which he identifies with liberalism.

Gamwell's suggestion of two liberalisms, established and reformed, could be helpful in this context.[3] Sturm appears to equate all liberalism with *established* liberalism, that is, a sort of preferential individualism in which "common goods" are mere accidental consequences of inherently diverse interests, relationships are merely instrumental to the individual's pursuit of personal preferences, and political life is subservient to the private purposes of individuals—the real goods of this life, whatever they may be, the opportunity to acquire and control property being one of the big ones. If this were the whole of liberalism, then surely we should have to look elsewhere for ideals and principles if we somehow got the idea that human equality was a substantive issue deserving public embodiments and political expression.

Reformed liberalism, on the other hand, offers another option. If established liberalism rests its case on maximizing private interests, reformed liberalism is oriented towards maximizing "the public world" wherein the public world is conceived as the most inclusive available unification of "activities in association" or "unity in diversity." This reformed liberalism does not rule out the wide pursuit of private interests; but it does insist that there are substantive standards for the interests to be included *and* for the forms of inclusion. Maximizing the public world does not, in this case, mean maximizing governmental institutions. It means maximizing human associations especially in their voluntary character. It means actualizing as much of the communication as is possible among individuals in associations. While legitimate coercion is not ruled out, its use is limited to the protection and expansion of persuasion as the effective way of deciding what to do and how to do it.

Individuals in association are thus taken to be the ultimate unit of things human and common goods are thus those goods which sustain, support and maximize activities in association. Gamwell's constructive argument for such a reformed liberalism appeals to Whitehead's metaphysics (via Hartshorne) for the ultimate grounding of its principle of comparative advantage.

According to Mortimer J. Adler, there has been a drift towards something like this reformed liberalism in America since the nineteenth century, guided by the democratic ideals announced in the Declaration of Independence, embedded in the broad purposes proposed in the United States Constitution, but not clearly enunciated in *economic* terms until Franklin Delano Roosevelt's message to Congress in 1944:

> In that speech, the President declared that "true individual freedom cannot exist without economic security and independence. . . . People who are hungry and out of a job are the stuff of which dictators are made. . . . In our day these economic truths have become accepted as self-evident. We have accepted, so to speak, a second Bill of Rights, under which a new basis of security and prosperity can be established for all."[4]

Unfortunately these economic rights have not been "self-evident" to everyone since Roosevelt. They have been rather vehemently denied by several of his successors; and even among those to whom such ideas have been persuasive, it has not been obvious how to make good on such claims. Henry Shue, for instance, has presented an argument in his *Basic Rights: Subsistence, Affluence, and U.S. Foreign Policy* which holds that if persons have any rights at all, then they have subsistence rights, that is, rights to "unpolluted air, unpolluted water, adequate food, adequate clothing, adequate shelter, and minimal public health care."[5] These are economic rights and Shue argues that they are basic rights because people need these things in order to have any other rights. These rights generate social and political duties, it is clear. Yet Shue is quick to aver that "from no theory like the present one is it possible to deduce precisely what sort of institutions are needed, and I have no reason to think that the same institutions would be most effective in all places and at all times."[6]

James Sterba reaches a similar conclusion and incurs similar problems in his study of *The Demands of Justice*. He argues against Rawls' notion that any inequalities should be arranged so that they are of maximal benefit to the least advantaged. All that is needed for justice as fairness according to Sterba is that there be a satisfactory minimum of material goods guaranteed to all. On behalf of this, he brings forth four principles of distributive justice:

> *Principle of Need*: Each person is guaranteed the primary social goods that are necessary to meet the normal costs of satisfying his basic needs in the society in which he lives. . . .
>
> *Principle of Appropriation and Exchange*: Additional primary social goods are to be distributed on the basis of private appropriation and voluntary agreement and exchange.
>
> *Principle of Minimal Contribution*: A minimal contribution to society of those who are capable of contributing, when social and economic resources are insufficient to provide the guaranteed minimum to everyone in society without requiring that contribution or when the incentive to contribute to society would otherwise be adversely affected, so that persons would not maximize their contribution to society.
>
> *Principle of Saving*: The rate of saving for each generation should represent its fair contribution towards realizing and maintaining a society in which members can fully enjoy the benefit of its just institutions.[7]

Both Shue and Sterba argue for subsistence rights as an economic minimum and for open structures of opportunity both so that individuals can make their appropriate contribution to the rest of their society and so that they can benefit from their own endeavors; but their arguments stop short of indicating how these imperatives might be institutionalized. As stated, it would seem that their claims could be fulfilled by a combination of education, health insurance, social security, environmental legislation, a thriving business sector in a growth economy, safety net welfare programs, and a continuing "underclass" of unpropertied citizens.

It is the latter problem that Mortimer Adler tackles. If it is a question of rights, then mere subsistence will not do. The issue of economic equality must be faced because rights imply an equality of some sort. The aim should be to produce a society in which there are no economic *have-nots*, not a society in which all have the same amounts of wealth. "In a society in which all are economic *haves*, some may have more and some may have less, but all have *enough* wealth to supply them with the economic goods that anyone needs to lead a decent human life. . . . the limited equality that justice requires consists in that state of affairs in which all are economic *haves* to the degree needed for the pursuit of happiness."[8]

As Adler sees the matter, it takes real property, capital, to make the pursuit of happiness, an admitted right in the American lexicon, fully effective. This means providing that none shall be without "income producing property." This is to ensure that none are excluded from either the pursuit of happiness nor from the enjoyment of the liberties and political participation to which they are entitled as citizens of a liberal democracy.

"There would appear to be two distinct ways in which this can be done," according to Adler. "They are not incompatible and therefore they can be combined to make a third way. One is by means of income-producing property; another is by the economic equivalents of property; and the third is some combination of the first two."[9]

It is Adler's contention that Thomas Jefferson understood this intimate connection between income-producing property and political participation, but that he and his generation drew the wrong conclusion from it. "Our ancestors failed to realize that those whom they felt justified in disfranchising by imposing a property qualification for suffrage were not unfit to be citizens by any natural inferiority to men of property, but rather by the economic deprivations they suffered as wage-earners, and by the way in which they were nurtured under the conditions of life that resulted from their being economic have-nots."[10]

In the meantime, we have formally extended the full rights of citizenship to all adults; but we have a ways to go in the material implementation of those formal rights. The provision of welfare and the prospect of a full-employment economy are excellent steps along the way; but they do not provide the full entitlement which the citizens of a liberal democracy need both to fulfill their rights and to assume their duties as equal individuals in association with others.

"Economic independence is the one thing the economic equivalents of income-producing property, in the form of welfare entitlements and benefits, cannot provide wage-earners. Only individuals having sufficient income-producing property are persons of independent means."[11]

Adler's is a proposal to make capitalism work for liberal democracy rather than letting liberal democracy work for the current crop of capitalists. Capitalism has proven ingenious at the task of creating property, i.e., economic growth; but in spawning large-scale corporations, it tends to centralize both wealth and power in ways that undermine the commitment to full implementation of the equal rights and, indeed, to the natural equality of human beings which is the basis of a liberal democracy.

"Accordingly," says Adler, "the best solution of the problem of how to secure the economic rights and establish the economic equality that are the indispensible underpinnings of political democracy is by some combination of the two means of doing so: by every individual or family having a dual income, partly from wages or salaries of labor, accompanied by some welfare benefits, and partly from the revenue earned by income-producing property through the ownership of equities in capital."[12]

So, here at least is a concept of property rights which is compatible with individuals in association as the ultimate human unit. It avoids the absolutistic individualism of early capitalism which turned might into right and it rejects the corrosive communalism which turns governments into bureaucratic meddlers. It recognizes the contribution which the society as a whole makes to the creation of wealth by creating shares that can be equally distributed; but it leaves intact the incentives to individual and associational effort at self-improvement. It imposes a higher duty on the body politic than to provide mere subsistence which everyone knows creates second-class citizens; but this duty takes the familiar form of income-producing property which, however it is structured, is not a second-class form of property. In short, it gives new meaning to the notion of "property rights," as something for everybody not a privilege of the few.

As things stand at the moment, of course, the technical details for such an arrangement have not been worked out; but it hardly seems beyond the imagination of the regiments of accountants available to figure out how to set up and manage a broad-guaged mutual fund to which all businesses could contribute and in which all citizens could hold shares that could never be sold or transferred except by inheritance. There is no reason that I know of why such a fund would have to be actually managed by a government bureaucracy. It might be possible to farm it out on a competitive basis to a variety of investment firms. One thing is for sure, the less isolated its destiny is from the fortunes of the general economy, the better for everyone. A separate investment sector for publicly held trusts hardly seems desirable. Something akin to the large retirement funds seems more desirable, with investment firms competing for the business, based on their performance. In any event, all this is to be worked out, basically within institutions already functioning.

There is conceptual, technical and political work to be done if we are to make real this new notion of property rights. Whether process thought will help to advance this part of the agenda for democratic social change remains to be seen. In advocating individuals in association as the basic human unit, I believe the perspective developed here might well be compatible with a Whiteheadian social theory. I am, however, uncertain of this for two reasons.

First it is not clear that we can get a notion of rights from Whitehead strong enough to carry its weight in the liberal democratic faith. Certainly his attack on "absolute individuals with absolute rights" is justified; but it is a good question, what kind of individual with what kind of rights can we get from his thought? As Lois Gehr Livezey has pointed out, "Whitehead does not settle the question of what the relative or social character of rights comes to."[13] She seems to approach the concept of rights in process thought as work that mostly remains to be done. She does suggest a line of possible development, however: ". . . it seems to me that the sociality of human nature provides the basis on which to formulate a theory of human rights related to the creation and nurture of relationships, that is, *rights of association*. In other words, a Whiteheadian doctrine of human rights should be cast in terms of claims upon the social order for the protection and promotion of human capacities essential to the initiation, preservation, and transformation of relationships."[14]

Second, until we have more clarity on the status of rights in process thought, then I, at least, cannot tell where the "communitarianism" espoused by Sturm will take us in terms of any actual institutions, especially in the forms which property should take. I should have thought that it was a given in Whitehead's thought that any polarization of the options into "individualistic" and "communitarian" would *ipso facto* be ruled out as an egregious example of the fallacy of misplaced concreteness. What is concretely real are individuals in associations, each trying to be something both for themselves and for others, that is, engaged in what Mr. Jefferson called "the pursuit of happiness."

In conclusion, I will state the doctrine of property implied in these pages by using the categories proposed by Professor Sturm:

origin	Property originates naturally from the creativity exercised by individuals in association in their productive interactions with nature and with each other.
purpose	The purpose of property is to provide the material basis for the pursuit of happiness.
object	Such property might consist of any resource legitimately useful in sustaining and advancing the lives of free and equal individuals in association.
import	The import of such property is to secure the relative independence of individuals in association from the vicissitudes of nature and the tyrannies of history.
subject and status	It may be held by any individuals in whatever combination of associations they may agree to; and some property should, as a matter of right, be held by each individual as a means to secure the individual's place in the life of the broader community.

The major problem with property in liberal societies has been, ironically, its isolation both intellectually and institutionally from any effective doctrine of equal rights and its consequent drift into the category of mere privilege and preference.

Notes and References

1.   Ian Shapiro, *The Evolution of Rights in Liberal Theory* (Cambridge: Cambridge University Press, 1986), especially pp. 143-44.

2.   See Henry Shue, *Basic Rights: Subsistence, Affluence, and U.S. Foreign Policy* (Princeton: Princeton University Press, 1980), pp. 6-9.

3.   Franklin I. Gamwell, *Beyond Preference: Liberal Theories of Independent Associations* (Chicago: University of Chicago Press, 1984).

4.   Mortimer Adler, *We Hold These Truths: Understanding the Ideas and Ideals of the Constitution* (New York: Collier Books, 1987), p. 147.

5.   Shue, p. 23.

6.   Shue, p. 17.

7.   James Sterba, *The Demands of Justice* (Notre Dame, Indiana: University of Notre Dame Press, 1980), p. 61.

8.   Adler, pp. 150-51.

9.   Adler, pp. 151-52.

10.   Adler, p. 153.

11.   Adler, p. 154.

12.   Adler, p. 155.

13.   Lois Gehr Livezey, "Goods, Rights, and Virtues: Toward An Interpretation of Justice in Process Thought." *The Annual of the Society of Christian Ethics, 1986*, Alan B. Anderson et. al., ed., pp. 49-50.

14.   Livezey, p. 50.

CHAPTER 5

Process Philosophy and the Social Order: A Freedom-Equality Model

Kenneth Cauthen

Abstract: A process model will view society neither as an aggregate of autonomous individuals nor as a unitary organism, but as a complex arrangement having, to some extent, both of these features. The whole truth about individuals in communities is multileveled and has many facets, requiring a complicated, sophisticated analysis which allows for many dimensions to emerge under different circumstances. This thesis will be elaborated by creating three ideal conceptions of the social order: an individual-freedom model, a communal-equality model, and an individual-freedom/communal-equality model. The third will be defended, not only as illustrative of a process view of reality, but also as potentially the most productive of economic justice.

PART I

Process philosophers are persuaded that the metaphysical system they espouse will yield insights fruitful for understanding many, if not all, particular topics.[1] "Applicability," according to Alfred North Whitehead, is a test of the validity of a metaphysical scheme. If what one says about what is ultimately real is true, it follows that this grasp of reality at the fundamental level can be used to illuminate specific and/or limited spheres of the experienceable world. This could be, in part, a circular process, since, for Whitehead anyway, the metaphysical quest begins with some immediate experience and then seeks for some generality that is explanatory of the data.[2] Any hypotheses thus derived are tested and continually revised by reference to other bodies of experience until an ensemble of general principles is arrived at possessing the virtue of maximal applicability.[3] If this procedure has been successful, then no patterns or processes should be operative in any sphere which have not been anticipated, else the metaphysical task is not yet done (and never is).[4]

A test case is provided by the social order. Are the principles of process metaphysics useful in interpreting human society? Can the reality of selves in community acting and interacting in the political, cultural, and economic spheres be illuminated by its generalities? If the claims of process philosophy are taken as a guide, what interpretive clues may be derived from its basic insights that one would expect to find exemplified in the social order? What principles of justice and of the good society are implicit in, or at least compatible with, this outlook? Without trying to be exhaustive, a number of suggestions will be made. The following interpretations assume a knowledge of the fundamentals of process philosophy as found in the thought of Alfred North Whitehead, Charles Hartshorne, and others. Stated here are plausible implications for social philosophy of this way of viewing things. Within limits, alternative social philosophies and ethical principles could doubtless be constructed with equal or better grounding in process metaphysics. The only assertion made is that the interpretations offered do not violate those principles, even if they are not necessarily entailed by them.

1. Persons are neither completely independent, autonomous individuals nor merely parts of a unitary organism. Reality contains real individuals, but never as separate, discontinuous entities but always in mutually determining relations to other persons surrounding them.[5] Individuals are both free agents acting on their own and interdependent members of communities whose actions are constrained by other agents and by the whole society acting as one (through enforced laws, for example). Human societies, then, have organic features while being composed of identifiable individuals who have their own distinctive reality and character.[6]

2. A fundamental characteristic of both individuals and of human societies is that they are constituted by an aim at the good. Whitehead maintained that all life is driven by a three-fold urge: "to live, . . . to live well, . . . and to live better."[7] Hence, the function of reason is to guide

this urge toward its fulfillment. If individuals are real and if society has an organic unity and character of its own as something more than the sum of its members, then attention must be given both to the good of each person as a free agent and to the common good that embraces all in their togetherness. Individuals have a good of their own, and they have a shared good with others. Both dimensions are essential and must be taken into account.

3. Three elements enter into theories of the ideal (just and good) society:

(a) the point just elaborated, namely, *the aim at maximizing the good of individuals and of communities.*

(b) *Freedom.* If individuals are real and have a good of their own, they must have sufficient freedom from social restraint to realize their just aims. Moreover, freedom is required in order for each person to maximize the contribution he or she can make to the creation of a communal good to be enjoyed by all. Freedom, then, is not only a right of individuals; it is also a necessity for society as a means to achieve and increase the common good. Individuals are (in part) self-determining agents who seek self-realization. Hence, the rules of society should grant self-determination as extensive as is consistent with a like freedom for other individuals and with the requirements of the common good. Society must be organized to prohibit the exercise of individual freedom in ways that are harmful to other individuals or that damage the common good. But it must also be ordered so as to maximize the potential of each person to contribute creatively to the good of the whole community. The ideal is that each should realize her or his own good in a harmony with others in a cooperative effort to maximize the welfare of all in relationships involving mutuality and reciprocity.

(c) *Equality.* All experiencing subjects have intrinsic value commensurate with their capacity for depth (complexity, intensity, and richness) and breadth (range of inclusiveness) of experiencing. Thus, mosquitos have intrinsic value less than human beings but equal to that of other mosquitos. It follows that all persons as persons have intrinsic value equal to that of any other person. As social beings, individuals should have both equal liberty with others to pursue and enjoy their own self-chosen and merited good within the bounds of justice and also an equal claim with others to share in the common good. Equality is in a special sense a communal norm that arises only in settings in which individuals are bound together by common purposes and share a common destiny in the context of mutually dependent relationships.[8]

The principle of a just and good society, then, can be stated as follows: maximize individual and communal good, maximize individual freedom, and maximize the common equality of all within the constraints each aim places on the others.[9]

PART II

MODELS OF IDEAL SOCIETIES

Three models of an ideal society will be elaborated in this section. The first will be organized around the primary value of individual freedom and the quest for a private good—the Individualist-freedom Model. The second will be organized around the primary value of equality and the quest for a common good to be shared equally—the Communal-equality Model. The third will be framed as a synthesis of the first two in which freedom and equality are balanced and in which attention is given to both individual and communal good—the Individualist-freedom/Communal-equality Model.

The models will be created in two stages. The first stage will state the fundamental underlying principles in their more or less absolute, unqualified form. A refinement of the principles will follow, with the addition of other compatible ideas that do not necessarily inhere in the primordial motifs themselves.

The two models are created initially by combining four different principles[10], which can be outlined as follows:

Type 1	Type 2
The Freedom Model	*The Equality Model*
(1) FREEDOM PRINCIPLE	(1) EQUALITY PRINCIPLE
Maximum liberty for all.	Maximum equality for all.
(libertarianism)	(egalitarianism)
(2) SOCIOLOGICAL PRINCIPLE:	(2) SOCIOLOGICAL PRINCIPLE:
Individuals are the unit.[11]	The group is the unit.
The group is the sum total of	Individuals are organic parts of the
individuals. (social nominalism)[12]	whole. (social realism)
(3) VALUE PRINCIPLE:	(3) VALUE PRINCIPLE:
The good life is the pursuit and	The good life is the creation and
enjoyment of individual good.	sharing of a common good.
(individualism)	(communalism)
(4) POLITY PRINCIPLE:	(4) POLITY PRINCIPLE:
Democratic rule.	Democratic rule.
(*Equal* liberty)	(Equal *liberty*)

The sociological and value principles are independent of the freedom and equality principles.[13] In the modern world, however, both freedom and equality are prominent, and it is the peculiar combination of the first three principles in each case that produces the ideals to be elaborated. Freedom has a natural affinity with social nominalism and individualism. Equality, likewise, fits well with social realism and communalism, although the connection is not a logically necessary or exclusive one. The models developed here will use the other principle in each case as a subordinate ideal. To elaborate, the Freedom Model will use equality as a secondary principle, while the Equality Model will employ freedom in the same fashion. So doing puts each model in a better light than would otherwise be the case.

A cluster of ideas, then, forms the heart of each model. The fundamental motif of Type 1 is freedom. Stated in its unqualified form, the fundamental ideal is: unlimited freedom for all. Freedom refers to the range of unrestricted activity available to a person, the arena in which no coercion or other external restraint exists. But a kind of internal pragmatic logic leads to a modification of this original premise. The uncoordinated quest of all for a self-chosen good would lead at best to a nest of inconveniences or at worst to a "war of all with all" (Hobbes). What one conceives of as happening depends in part on how selfish or egocentric and/or aggressive and violent one believes human beings to be in their natural state. In any case, the pursuit of self-interest (meaning here what the self is interested in) can be carried on best within a framework that allows equal freedom to all and, hence, to the channeling of individual actions within boundaries that do not intrude upon the others' rights to the same pursuits. Mutual respect for and the equal protection of equal rights are to everybody's advantage.

Type 2 in its unqualified form is: complete equality for all. Equality refers to what is or counts the same in one person as in another, whether this pertains to the existence or allocation of status, power, authority, rights, privileges, and opportunities, etc., or to the distribution of income, goods, services, and other socially provided benefits. But in the principle and fact of equality, too, an internal pragmatic logic is at work. While everyone may be equal as persons or regarded as so in some respects, in many, or all, other respects, people are unequal. Some can do things others cannot or do some things better than others. People differ in merit and have different needs. Thus, in organized human societies as well as in, to use the traditional phrase, "the state of nature," all sorts of inequalities arise among persons who in some respects may be actually equal or who, according "to the law of nature" should be so regarded. Hence, the pure Equality Model requires a modified ideal in which certain types of equalities are regarded as legitimate and protected, while, in other respects, inequalities are permitted.[14] The affirmation of equal freedom as citizens and equal opportunity to succeed in all phases of society are common to the liberal, democratic philosophies of recent centuries (prominent in Type 1). The most idealistic form (emerging only in Type 2) prescribes that persons should contribute according to their abilities and receive according to their needs. This functional recognition of inequality is necessary to maximize common good and to allow equal consideration to all persons as producers and consumers of the common good.[15]

When the polity principle is added, the result—combining pragmatic and idealistic considerations—qualifies the primordial impulse of each type by taking into account the primary value of the other type. In Type 1, equality is added to freedom to produce the ideal of equal freedom for all to seek a private good.[16] The fundamental idea of Type 2 is equality, which when combined with freedom, yields the idea of equality of liberty. This is a consequence both of following out the logic of "equality in all respects for all" and of taking individual freedom into account as an independent and worthy value. Hence, Type 1 assumes that each free person has equal freedom with other persons to seek a private good. Type 2 assumes that equal persons have equal freedom, not to seek a private good but to contribute to and receive from the community as an equal. In other words, both assume that all persons are, in the meanings assigned by each, equally free.[17]

All this leads to the ideal of democracy or rule of the people. In principle this means that all may participate equally by choosing the rules by which they will be governed, or at least in selecting the people who will govern them. In the state and in many other organizations, this means majority or representative rule. In Type 1, this guards against the rule of the strong, as would likely occur if freedom were not restricted constitutionally by distributing power equally (in principle) among all citizens. Moreover, constitutional guarantees of certain rights are necessary to guard against the tyranny of a democratic majority. In Type 2 the ideal of equal freedom guards as well against the rule of the (alleged) "best" or some elite that by virtue of tradition, theory, or simply by taking power presumes to define the common good and to decide how it is to be produced and distributed.[18] Despite these modifications, the threat of the tyranny of the strong is still the corrosive factor in the Freedom Model. Likewise, the threat of the tyranny of "the best" or the elite is the bane of the equality model.[19] Without these qualifications of freedom with equality and of equality with freedom, both types would be intolerable.

Underlying the ideal of equal freedom in both types as defined here is a notion of rights which attach to individuals. Each person is a moral personality with an inalienable status and worth (whether inherent or conferred by some transcendent power, e.g., God).[20] Every individual counts and counts equally in the ideal form of both types, since each has rights that must not be violated. Obviously, the Freedom Model tends toward excesses of individualism in which some (who are more gifted, ruthless, or ambitious, or who work harder or whatever) acquire power over others so that equal freedom is threatened. In the Equality Model, individual rights may be smothered for the sake of making all equal or in quest of maximizing the common good. In the latter case the result may be that the freedom of some or of all is threatened by the ruling elite, or even by democratic processes, thus restricting liberty for the sake of the good of the whole.[21] The ideas of individual worth and of equal freedom guard against these excesses and distinguish modern democratic versions of Types 1 and 2 from their counterparts in former times.[22]

The Freedom Model leads to a concept of equal opportunity, while the Equality Model produces the notion of equality of outcomes, as well as of opportunities. At least this is the case initially and in principle. But in the end, neither goal is possible or desirable, the former being more impossible and the latter being more undesirable. Hence, in practice one has to settle for something less than what was originally posited. The question of appropriate definition becomes crucial.

Type 1 is more committed to freedom of opportunity than to equality of opportunity. As a consequence, it is reluctant to go beyond the notion that careers should be open to talent. No irrelevant criteria should be used to keep the most qualified persons from actualizing legal and moral opportunities to secure jobs, income, power, status, authority, respect, and other desirable goods and positions. Meritocracy is the norm. However, some are better endowed genetically with gifts and talents, and some have the benefit of a head start because of family or class background. Correcting differences in biological endowment is impossible for the current generation. Overcoming the social handicaps that give some unequal advantages requires interference with individual freedom, which violates the norms of the Freedom Model.

Type 2, with its priority of commitment to equality, is more devoted to both equality of opportunity and of result than is Type 1. In fact, in its boldest or purest forms, it is willing to restrict individual freedom for the sake of equality for all in both respects. But absolute equality of opportunity would require both the homogenizing of genetic inheritance (the biological component) and the destruction of the family (a major part of the social component). The first is not now possible and would not be desirable were it possible. The second is possible (if everyone agreed) but is not desirable. The norm of equality of result (the same rewards and provisions for all) not only prevents distribution of benefits according to merit, but also prevents distribution according to need.

Moreover, for functional reasons equalizing opportunities and outcomes might mean that everybody had less of everything (material goods, good music, scientific knowledge and technological advance—everything producible by the best human effort and talent). Unless the brightest and best are set free to maximize their talents in the quest of excellence, that is, given unequal opportunity, less total good will be available to share, whether defined quantitatively or qualitatively or shared equally or unequally. Biological and social inequalities, then, may in practice benefit everybody, despite the attraction of the ideal of equality in all respects. Compromise for the sake of the greater good for all seems inevitable.

The commitment to *equal* freedom creates an internal tension within Type 1. It can be argued on liberal grounds that equal opportunity must be real and effective, not just formal, if it is to be of value. Hence, efforts to equalize the opportunities of the socially disadvantaged can be defended within this framework. Likewise, the commitment to equal *freedom* in Type 2 leads to a different kind of internal stress. The emphasis on equality of outcome as well as efforts to make opportunities effectively equal for all may well come into conflict with individual freedom and merit. Each type has to struggle to resolve the tensions that result from its peculiar way of combining freedom and equality, while giving priority in each case to one or the other.

As already indicated, the principles that make up each model are relatively autonomous, though each has a natural consanguinity with the others. Nonetheless, it is possible to combine each with various versions of the other two principles to form visions of ideal societies different from the one formulated here. The models presented are those most relevant to contemporary discussions. A brief discussion of each will give further definition and contrast.

Type 1: The Freedom Model

One assumption underlying any theory of society has to do with the relationship between individuals and the groups to which they belong. The Freedom Model presupposes a view which can be called social nominalism. In this way of thinking individuals are regarded as independent and autonomous, the units of which society is composed. Organized societies arise by voluntary agreement or covenant, forming a group for the purposes of achieving ends that are mutually desirable but which cannot be had without cooperative efforts. A state may be formed on this basis. So may any number of other smaller organizations that individuals may create to further their mutual aims. Societies, then, are collections of individuals created for mutual benefit by voluntary covenant.

Individuals have rights that others may not morally violate. Central among these rights is freedom to pursue ends chosen by each individual, without interference from others and without limitation except as their exercise may interfere with the rights and liberty of others. A government may be formed to secure these rights and to protect the free exercise of liberty by each member of the contracting state. The state has the exclusive authority to use coercion to enforce its will. Its role is to prevent individuals from using coercion on each other or to defraud others of the rights assigned them by the contract which created the state initially. The state's role is limited mainly to protecting the society from outside enemies and to policing the internal activities of the society to maximize the exercise of individual freedom. The central authority may also build roads, print money, finance public education, and do other things that individuals cannot do for themselves or through voluntary organizations, or at least not as well. The private ownership of property and a capitalistic form of economic organization fit well with this model.

Type 2: The Equality Model

Type 2 presupposes a theory of social realism in which the group is regarded as the unit, while individuals are organically related to each other and to the whole. In the strongest and purest form, this internal connectedness is regarded as a natural fact—the way things are. In a modified and weaker form, the unity in community is not natural and organic but a voluntary, contractual reality. People may decide to regard the whole as the primary reality and value center and to act as if they were one—all for one and one for all.[23] The individual is subordinated to the whole, and individual good is subordinated to the common good. But when combined with the additional notions of individual worth and equal freedom for all, each person has a claim on the whole equal to the others. This sets up limits within which the individual can be sacrificed or ignored for the sake of the common good. A democratic polity is assumed in which the inevitable tensions between individual rights and communal good are resolved (or compromises worked out) in the public arena with the full participation of all.[24]

The state may be regarded as a natural or given entity into which people are born (as into a family)[25] or as a human creation designed to promote the common good and to protect the equal rights of all.[26] The state's role in Type 2 will be more extensive than in Type 1. It will not only protect the whole from outside threats and guard individual rights, but will also promote by collective means the good of the whole. It may own the basic means of production. Likewise, it will provide standards and mechanisms for the distribution of goods and services, according to norms decided upon—equally, or according to need, or some other formula aimed at an equitable sharing of the common good.[27] If the state does not own the means of production outright, it will control and direct the economic processes in accordance with public aims. The central authority may also organize, control, or coordinate cultural and social (educational, etc.) activities as well. Church and state would be separate in a democratic pluralistic society, although established religion would not be incompatible with the logic of more extreme versions of the model[29].

The two models may now be summarized and developed further. The following are logical or ideal types based on certain assumptions, although different versions are possible and more-or-less equally compatible with the underlying presuppositions.

Type 1: The Freedom Model	*Type 2: The Equality Model*
Individual freedom as extensive as is compatible with equal rights and a like freedom for others.	Maximal equality compatible with the functional requirements of maximizing the common good or meeting need.
Individual merit is a primary principle of reward.	Individual merit is a subordinate principle of reward.
Presupposes model of autonomous individuals contracting with each other, engaging in voluntary exchanges and cooperative ventures for whole in which each shares.	Presupposes model of organic (or contractual) community of interdependent individuals cooperating with each other for the good of the mutual advantage.
Democratic rule: all participate in the governing of state and society.	Democratic rule: all participate in the governing of state and society.
Honors equality of opportunity (no formal barriers to careers open to talent).	Honors equality of opportunity in effective fact and equality of result as a persistent tendency.
Meaning and reward come from individual achievement based on merit.	Meaning and reward come from participating in community, contributing to it and receiving from it.
Freedom is shaped by aim at individual good and constrained by the equal rights and freedom of others.	Freedom of the individual is shaped and constrained by good of the whole and equal claims of all.
Freedom is liberty to pursue individual good in ways non-harmful to others.	Freedom is liberty to pursue common good cooperatively with others.

Minimal state facilitates individual pursuit of private good.	Extensive state facilitates production and distribution of common good.
Emphasizes differences among people.	Emphasizes similarites among people.
Success or failure depends primarily on factors internal to individuals.	Success or failure depends primarily on factors external to individuals.
IDEAL SOCIETY IS THE SUM TOTAL OF AUTONOMOUS INDIVIDUALS WITH EQUAL LIBERTY PURSUING SELF—INTEREST THROUGH VOLUNTARY INTERACTION.	IDEAL SOCIETY IS AN ORGANIC COMMUNITY MADE UP OF MEMBERS WHO, IN A COOPERATIVE EFFORT, PRODUCE A COMMON GOOD TO BE SHARED EQUITABLY.

A third ideal type can now be outlined that combines principles from Types 1 and 2 into a synthesis which differs from either but is closer to both than they are to each other.[29]

Type 3: The Freedom-Equality Model

A preliminary word is necessary before constructing the final model to clarify the difference in logical status between freedom and equality. Freedom relates to individuals and comes into play if at least one person exists.[30] Equality relates to what is common to individuals and has no relevance until at least two persons are on the scene. A solitary female shipwrecked on an island would have freedom to do as she pleased,[31] for no one else is around (no other human being) to be equal or unequal with. (Of course, if animals were present, she would be under obligation to be kind and to do no unnecessary harm to them.) But if two persons (male and female) were cast up together, the question of equality or inequality arises. In what respects do they share something in common that justifies equality? Freedom is, of course, also a social concept referring to the range of action open to individuals unconstrained by the coercive power of society as a whole.

To put it differently in terms of the value principle, we may distinguish between the creation and enjoyment of individual good and the creation and enjoyment of a common good. Equality is a regulative concept which applies to both. If individuals are to seek and enjoy a private good, then all should be equally free to do so. If a common good is to be created and enjoyed, individuals should participate in the enterprise equally. Or one could say that two value principles pertain: maximizing individual freedom and maximizing total welfare. Again, equality is a regulative principle. Individuals should be equally free, that is, have a range of freedom or set of liberties that is equally extensive with that of others. In the other case, individuals should contribute and share equally in the creation and enjoyment of the total (and common) social well-being.[32] Hence, while freedom and equality are not logically identical in status, they may for all practical purposes be considered simply as two different value principles. In Type 3 they are to be regarded equally.

Type 3:
The Freedom-Equality Model

(1) FREEDOM-EQUALITY
PRINCIPLE:
Maximum freedom and equality
for all in all respects within the
constraints each, along with the
quest to maximize the good, puts
on the other.

(2) SOCIOLOGICAL PRINCIPLE:
Individuals are relatively autonomous in some respects and in some
settings but organically connected
to social units in other respects and
in other settings.

(3) VALUE PRINCIPLE:
The good life includes both the
enjoyment of individual good and
of common good.

(4) POLITY PRINCIPLE:
Democratic rule. (Equal liberty)

Unrestricted freedom and complete equality for all in all respects are, of course, not possible or desirable. The freedom of one person limits the freedom of another. Freedom for each is in tension with equality for all. Hence, an optimal arrangement must be sought. Freedom and equality are to be maximized within the constraints each puts on the other. Moreover, the quest to increase the happiness (the good) of all may constrain and be constrained by individual freedom and social equality.

The relationship between individuals and societies is complex.[33] Many theories fail because they oversimplify by leaving out important dimensions required by a wholly adequate view. Seen in one way, a person is both an individual and a social being. Suppose Mary says, "I am an American." Mary is thoroughly and wholly an "I"—a discrete individual not confused with any other person. At the same time, she is thoroughly and wholly "an American"—a participant in that community. Within this framework, Mary is not an individual in some respects and an interdependent member of society in other respects. She is in all respects a particular individual and in all respects a participant in that society indicated by the term "American." Individuality is real, but exists always in community.

Seen another way, individuals are neither discrete, independent units who create societies by contract or association, nor mere parts of a social organism who cannot function independently at all. Rather they are relatively autonomous, relatively interdependent selves. Hence, neither social nominalism nor social realism is solely applicable. Society, then, is neither a mere collection of individuals united only by voluntary contract nor an organism whose members are wholly dependent on the whole in which they exist and function. Individuals are fulfilled and whole only when they function harmoniously in a particular role as a member of a society in which they both contribute to and receive from the total community. A person taken out of his or her society and cast suddenly in the midst of a civilization that is totally alien in language, religion, culture, values, economic and technological organization, and so on would still be a human being, but one whose potential for achievement and satisfaction would be considerably diminished. Such a person would be unable to participate effectively in that foreign setting as a part of the larger whole.[34]

Yet the whole truth is even more complex than this. In some cases, social nominalism is more descriptive of the facts than social realism. Sometimes we do act as independent units, as when we decide which candy bar to buy. Even here, however, no candy bars would be available for purchase apart from the economic processes of production and distribution that take place in the society in which the buyer participates. Perhaps suffering is the point at which the solitariness of individual existence is most real. Moreover, we do our own dying; no one else can do that for us. We live, work, suffer, and die in a social context, as a member of various communities. But there is a particularity and discreteness about individual suffering and dying that raises our individuality, even our solitariness, to an acute point. But, even here most persons interpret pain and death with socially generated convictions. Communal tradition also creates the religious framework within which most individuals believe or disbelieve in God, although it may be true, as Whitehead says, that religion "is what the individual does with his own solitariness."[35] Individuals do have powers of self-transcendence that enable them to evaluate received traditions and to modify or reject them, or even to create novel interpretations of life, death, and destiny.

Sometimes we do contract with each other to form groups for specific purposes, as when we form a volunteer fire department. It is for the common good, as well as for our own, that we do so, but we function as individuals who enter voluntarily into a compact to achieve certain ends which cannot be attained without cooperative effort.

Sometimes we are members of groups which are prior (logically and chronologically) to us and to which we are organically related in both biological and social senses, as when we are born into a family. We do not choose to be born; nor are we offered any alternatives with respect to which set of parents will conceive us. Certainly we are not allowed to express in advance a preference with regard to their social and economic status, race, nationality, religion, and so on. Our "destiny" in this sense is a given. The family name is assigned to us at birth, and the values of our parents begin to shape us at once. While we may choose later whether to make these values our own, patterns of behavior are already being woven onto the genetic constitution we inherited before we are old enough to think for ourselves. Recent studies have shown that genetic endowment plays a considerable role in determining certain basic personality traits, even including whether we are likely to be conformist or rebellious. In these ways, we are indeed, as St. Paul says, "members one of another." Various denominations and theologians debate whether becoming a church member is more like being born into a family (the organic, communal model) or getting married (the individualistic, contractual model).[36]

What is the state like? As citizens we are both relatively autonomous and highly interdependent. As producers and consumers of goods and services in the economic order, the same duality holds. The social contract theory with its hypothetical notion of a state of nature inhabited by a collection of discrete individuals who then create the state by an agreement may be useful for some analytical purpose. But it distorts historical fact and present reality if taken as a paradigm of the whole truth. We are born into a given state that has a polity, a history, and a set of values specific to itself. Before we are able to think for ourselves we are immersed in its ethos and are absorbed into its very life in organic ways. Yet we are discrete individuals who can, in some measure, choose whether to accept and perpetuate or to rebel against its traditions and values.

Hence, freedom and equality must be viewed in three contexts: (a) the realm of existence, experience, and choice as discrete individuals, (b) our participation in organizations created by voluntary contract, and (c) the dimensions of life in which we are organically related to communal units that are logically and historically prior to us.[37]

The good life is neither exclusively the pursuit of individual good nor solely the creation and sharing of a common good. Rather it is both in a complex, multidimensional combination of private and communal enterprises.[38] We need community and the joy of cooperative effort. But we also need room for pursuing individual projects of our own choice—to do and to take pleasure in what we want for ourselves. We are neither isolated selves nor cells of the social organism, but both relatively independent and relatively interdependent. The fullest, richest life actualizes all the dimensions of selfhood. Yet the private and the communal are not themselves separate. It is for the common good that individuals realize their own private good. Part of individual good is participating in the common good, in contributing to the well-being of others and in receiving assistance from our neighbors and associates. The highest and absolute good occurs when each person considers the good of others equal to her or his own good. This is the meaning of Jesus's injunction that we should love our neighbors as we love ourselves, not as a discipline of self-sacrifice, but as a means toward achieving self-realization in community with others. It is also true, however, that sometimes the attainment of the common good does require a sacrifice of individual self-realization, as when a soldier dies in battle in a just war to protect the survival and well being of his/her country. No perfect coincidence exists between self-realization and the good of the whole, not in this imperfect world of ours. It is extremely difficult to include in just the right way all facets of these complex interrelationships.

The family provides (potentially) the best example of giving according to ability and receiving according to need. But cooperative enterprises at work and at play as well as in the fulfillment of national purpose offer other possibilities. Unfortunately, the joy of working for a common good is often most deeply felt only in wartime or in some other emergency situation. Overcoming poverty, racism, sexism, disease, and other evils do not frequently enough unite us in common purpose. It is to our individual and collective detriment that such goals do not.[39]

Equality of opportunity and equality of result each have a legitimate place in the ideal society. The ideal is that every individual with similar gifts who makes the same effort should have equivalent life chances for success. Hence, efforts must be made to overcome the hindrances of family and social background that inevitably cripple some in comparison with others.[40] Yet superior gifts with which people are born, while not deserved, do belong to them, and it is right for them to benefit from their use. A case, full of difficulties and ambiguities, can be made for selected forms of reverse discrimination to favor groups that have been the victims of past injustices. The interdependence of citizens in a highly organized economy provides a basis for social policies that tend toward equality of outcome as far as wealth and income are concerned. But allowance must also be made for reward according to merit and contribution to the sum total of goods and services. Inequalities that benefit all are also justifiable, or at least permissible.

Working out a way to move toward equality in the sharing of goods produced by joint effort while preserving inequalities of reward based on individual merit is difficult indeed. Nevertheless, there is a compelling rationale in fact and ideals for both. One way to achieve both goals would be a socially guaranteed floor on income paid for by progressive taxation high enough to provide a decent living for those who qualify and low enough not to decrease incentive. But this solution is not perfect and involves many difficulties. Inheritance taxes could also help to re-equalize the books over generations.[41] Beyond this, the market might be permitted to allocate wealth and income.[42] Functional inequalities of wealth and income necessary for the benefit of all would also be justifiable. "From each according to ability *and* as one chooses" and "to each according to need *and* merit" indicate appropriate elements that in various combinations, in different settings, would have to be implemented with as much wisdom as possible. A more-than-minimal democratic state is necessary and justifiable to carry out these policies. The extensive state itself introduces its own problems—a large and probably inefficient bureaucracy, potential infringements on some individual liberties beyond what justice requires, the near impossibility of justly adjudicating competing claims of individuals and groups, the social conflict introduced by politicizing issues involving civil rights and redistributive efforts, and so on. Yet the minimal state so dear to conservatives is potentially and in fact an even greater threat to justice.

Priority problems of special difficulty arise when there is a family of first principles. In Type 3, three such principles have been stated: maximizing the good, maximizing individual freedom, and maximizing social equality within the constraints each places on the others. Different orderings of priorities may arise depending on the social circumstances that prevail at a given time and on the preferences of the citizens. In times of great emergency (such as an external threat) or conditions of severe poverty for all, some individual liberties and equal rights may legitimately be temporarily restricted for the sake of survival. Certain fundamental individual rights and liberties are so basic that they should be suspended only under extreme circumstances, if at all. Difficult issues arise in this connection requiring extensive treatment beyond the scope of this essay. As peace and normalcy return, the equal meeting of the basic needs of all takes priority, although in tension with individual freedom to excel. As prosperity increases, individual liberties and equal rights to share in the common good must be balanced. At higher levels of general well being within a system in which all are highly esteemed and basic needs are met, equality of results becomes progressively less essential than maintaining the most extensive range of liberties congruent with equal liberties for others. (This assumes, of course, that opportunities for all are as nearly equal as possible and desirable.) Under these circumstances the ideal will be for individuals to pursue their own ends as long as they violate no principles of justice. At every stage the basic principles of the ideal society take precedence over efficiency.[43] Efficiency must always operate within the boundary conditions prescribed by the norms of justice and the goals of a good society. Within this general framework many issues will of necessity be legitimately settled by debate and negotiation through democratic processes.

The model may now be summarized and sketched as follows:

The Freedom-Equality Model

Allows freedom as extensive and equality as complete as the constraints of each on the other permit within the framework of justice and the quest of maximum happiness for all.[44]

Presupposes model of individuals who are both autonomous and organically interdependent in various respects.

Is exemplified by democratic rule based on equal liberty for all.

Honors effective equality of opportunity and a tendency toward equality of result when each is properly understood and qualified.

Provides for meaning and rewards both from individual achievement based on merit and from participating in community, contributing to and receiving from it.

Conceives freedom as shaped by aim at individual good, constrained by equal freedom of others and

by the good of all and the equal
claims of each on what is produced
jointly and held in common.

Allows the liberty to pursue individual good in some respects and
the common good in other
respects.

Establishes a state no more extensive than necessary to facilitate
both the individual pursuit of self-
chosen interests and the collective
pursuit of the common good.

Recognizes both differences and
similarities in people.

Acknowledges that success or
failure depends on factors both internal and external to individuals.

THE IDEAL SOCIETY IS A COM-
MONWEALTH MADE UP BOTH
OF INDIVIDUALS ENGAGED IN
PURSUING PRIVATELY DEFINED
GOOD THROUGH VOLUNTARY
INTERACTIONS AND OF COM-
MUNITIES (INCLUDING THE IN-
CLUSIVE STATE) THAT PRODUCE
AND SHARE A COMMON GOOD
TO BE SHARED EQUITABLY.

CONTEMPORARY MODELS

The models described have been created by combining four underlying
principles into logical types. The effort has been to keep them pure, that is,
introduce only features that the principles logically imply, although this has
not been carried through thoroughly. Corollary principles have been introduced, although they have been incorporated in terms that do not compromise or violate the character of the resulting model.[45]

Illustrations of these models can be found in contemporary social
philosophy. Robert Nozick[46] and John Rawls [47] have recently provided

descriptions of ideal societies (ideal at least in terms of their basic framework and procedures) that reflect the principles of Types 1 and 2 respectively.

Nozick begins with autonomous individuals with inherent rights who engage in voluntary interactions and exchanges in order to maximize private interests. Holdings (income, property, wealth, goods of any kind) are acquired originally by mixing one's labor with the earth to produce goods and property. Such activities are limited only by the constraint that one leaves "enough and as good" (Locke) or provides latecomers with some appropriate minimum and does not otherwise violate the rights of the neighbor. Once justly acquired, all holdings may be used or transferred voluntarily any way the holder chooses. Any violations of just (voluntary) interactions require rectification. Hence, three principles arise: just acquisition, just transfer, and rectification of unjust acquisition and transfer. A minimal state comes into being to police and guarantee voluntary exchange and to protect from outside enemies. The state may not engage in redistributive efforts that alter the outcome of contracts and interactions freely undertaken by individuals for mutual advantage. Justice is determined solely by procedure: just acquisition and just exchange. Individuals may do what they will with their holdings, including giving it all to the poor. But justice does not require charity on the part of individuals and expressly forbids the state from taking from those who have and redistributing it to those who do not. This is a "historical entitlement" view which is opposed to all "end state" views which distribute according to some pattern to achieve certain outcomes.[48] The employment of "end state" principles prevents "capitalist acts between consenting adults" from producing their own natural outcome.[49] Making results conform to a pattern requires constant interference with the liberty of people to control and dispose of the holdings to which they are justly entitled in any way *they* choose.

John Rawls envisions a group of representative persons gathered behind a "veil of ignorance" in an "original position" (OP) to create the principles of a just society. Since the contractors in the OP are interested in their own welfare but do not know what their position will be in the ensuing society, they have to devise rules that they (and hence everybody) would be willing to live under and regard as just. Since the conditions under which the norms are devised are fair, he calls his view "justice as fairness."

Two principles result from the deliberations in the OP:

a. Each person is to have liberties as extensive as is compatible with a similar range of freedoms for others.

b. All social benefits are to be open to fair acquisition by all alike, and are to be shared equally except as an unequal distribution is to the advantage of all, especially the least well off.[50]

Principle (a) has priority over (b) in that liberty is to be restricted only for the sake of liberty and not for a mere increase in material goods or other social benefits. Moreover, the principles of justice take precedence over efficiency and maximizing total welfare. Justice also requires that any permissible inequalities that result must arise under conditions of fair opportunity for all. The state has the responsibility for arranging things so that these principles are implemented, for example, protecting individual rights, seeking to provide opportunities that are equal for all despite given biological and social handicaps, and permitting only those inequalities which benefit everyone, especially the poorest.

In terms of the models previously described, Nozick is a rather pure example of Type 1. Rawls offers a complex position which is best seen as a combination of Types 1 and 2. It would be fair to say either that he represents an example of Type 3 or that he moves back and forth between Types 1 and 2. If they were positioned on a continuum, the result would be something like this:

```
TYPE 1----------------------------------0----------------------------------Type 2
        X              Y                              Y
     NOZICK          RAWLS                          RAWLS
                 (First Principle)              (Second Principle)
```

Nozick is a social nominalist. Society is a contracted reality created by the voluntary acts of individuals. His only concession to the principle of equality is that he regards individuals as having equal rights to something roughly akin to "life, liberty, and the pursuit of happiness."

Rawls also begins with free and equal representative persons who are concerned to further their own interests and disinterested in the welfare of others.[51] However, in the OP these contracting parties agree that the talents of all should be regarded as possessed in common and that whatever is produced is to be shared (in principle) equally.[52] Hence, by agreement the community, in this respect, is to be considered the unit. His original premise, then, would appear to be equality for all in all respects or at least in terms of what he calls "social primary values, such as liberty, income, wealth, and self-respect."[53] His first principle is simply an application of the general principle of equality to the issue of liberty. However, since the first principle has lexical priority over the second, liberty takes on the status of a separate principle in addition to equality. Nevertheless, his contractual social realism and his communalism are seen in the fact that people agree to share one another's fate. Moreover, the ideal of fraternity, most closely exemplified in the family, is the affirmed value. No one will want a private or selfish advantage but will seek only those gains which benefit those who are less well off. Again, society is seen as a cooperative venture for mutual advantage.[54]

Already, it is obvious that, in comparison to Nozick's outlook, Rawls' position is complex. He moves back and forth between his libertarian principle and his egalitarian principle. For example, once a social minimum has been provided for everyone with special allowances for illness and other peculiar needs, individuals are free within a market system to seek their own interests. Individuals are also free in general to pursue a rational plan of life in quest of ends defined by themselves, though constrained by justice.[55] Hence, justice has a wide range of procedural rather than substantive meaning. On the other hand, individual merit is not to be rewarded as such, and the quest of individual excellence and private gain is not to be permitted in ways that generate inequalities except as such inequalities benefit everyone.[56] Moreover, these inequalities are not allowed unless all had fair opportunity to begin with. The qualities that enable some to outdo others are the result of inherited genetic superiority plus good family background and social circumstances which engender motivation and hard work. Individuals do not deserve these qualities nor the benefits that flow from them. They are social assets to be used for everyone's advantage. Thus are individualistic (Type 1) and communalistic (Type 2) motifs intermingled and held in a complex dialectic.

Likewise, on many other issues Nozick's position is simple, while that of Rawls is more complicated. Take equal opportunity, for example. Nozick's view is that as long as individuals have come by their assets by natural endowment and by historically just procedures of acquisition and transfer, they are entitled to the benefits that flow from their employment, even if this gives them unequal chances for success as compared to some others.

Rawls goes much further. Nozick's views represent what Rawls calls the "system of natural liberty." It simply means that there are no legal or other formal barriers to careers open to talent. But this principle simply allows the strong and the advantaged to leave their less fortunate neighbors behind. Rawls urges that efforts be made to equalize opportunity by giving special help to those who are biologically and socially handicapped. This would amount to "fair equality of opportunity." But since genetic endowment cannot be changed and since families legitimately want to pass their advantages on to their children, some will still have unequal opportunities for advancement. So he proposes "democratic equality," which means that the genetically and socially advantaged may use their unequal chances to the fullest, subject to the proviso that any resulting inequalities are permitted only insofar as everyone, especially the worst off, benefit. Once all have equality of respect and are provided a social minimum, the family need not be abolished in the interest of overcoming the unequal opportunities wealthy and healthy families provide for their children.[57]

Rawls, then, would allow at least the following interferences with market processes and the outcomes of individual actions and interactions: (a) use of social assets to equalize opportunities for all, (b) provision of social minimum (income floor and special allowances based on need), and (c) limitation of inequalities of wealth, income, etc. to those which benefit all, especially the worst off.

This comparison with Rawls is based on Nozick's first two principles: just acquisition and just transfer. If we turn to the third principle, which calls for rectification of any violations of the first two, the situation changes—how drastically is hard to tell. Critics generally agree that the combination of principles one and three provide the most unclarified and problematic aspects of Nozick's theory of justice. Should a large proportion of the continental United States be given back to the Indians, or at least compensation be made to the descendants of those unjustly deprived of their lands? Nozick admits that such issues are very complex and extremely difficult to resolve. He makes a concession with possible consequences that might make him a more radical interventionist than Rawls.[58] Nozick proposes that a possible pragmatic rule of thumb might be that society organize itself to maximize the position of whatever group ends up worst off. The assumption is that the groups on the bottom probably (though not certainly) have been the victims of past injustice. To carry out this program of rectification, a more extensive state may be necessary, though socialism as a punishment for historical sins is going too far![59]

Rawls actually allows a wide range of inequalities. It is not clear just how great inequalities of what kind for whom are permissible in order to enlarge the pie so that everyone is better off than without them. He does suggest that once a social minimum is provided and the basic needs of all are met, an efficient, competitive price system may be allowed to work, producing indeterminate inequalities of income.[60] Inequalities of inheritance are permissible as long as they conform to the difference principle and do not interfere with fair equality of opportunity or equal liberty.

To summarize, Robert Nozick is a consistent example of Type 1. He is clearly a libertarian, though some think he is not a thoroughgoing one.[61] Rawls is best seen as offering a combination of Types 1 and 2. He is, then, a libertarian egalitarian or an egalitarian libertarian. Hence, he could with some justification be called a synthesist. But his outlook is better categorized as a combination, since he moves from one type to the other rather than integrating them into an inclusive synthesis.

CRITICISM AND EVALUATION

If Type 3 is taken as the preferred model, the omissions of Nozick become obvious. The exclusive priority he gives to the motif of freedom, his social nominalism, and his conception of the good as created and experienced by independent individuals neglect the corresponding truths of Type 2. He does provide that by voluntary contract individuals can enter into cooperative enterprises. Certainly people may take pleasure in joint accomplishments. Nevertheless, his position is faulty since he does not give credence to the notion of organic connectedness, the sense of being really in union with others in a deep factual sense, rather than simply making external contracts with them.

Let us grant as well that an ethic of love is quite possible on the basis of Nozick's presuppositions. One can reach out in compassion to one's neighbors to whatever extent one chooses, even to the point of sacrificing one's own interest in their behalf. It would be unfair to accuse Nozick of espousing an ethical view that is inherently selfish, even though it is individualistic. But the basis for an adequate social ethic is lacking. He misses a dimension of social reality arising out of the internal relations that constitute selfhood in a unity in community. Moreover, he has no place for the claims of equality as a part of justice that is rooted in the interdependence and organic unity with others that is factually the case. The Pauline claim that we are "individually members one of another" (Roms. 12:5 RSV) provides an element that is lacking. His extreme libertarianism, nominalism, and individualism need to be incorporated into a synthesis with Type 2 in which egalitarianism, realism, and communalism are given their proper due. It would be superfluous to engage in a criticism of his particular social policy positions, since they are rooted in his underlying presuppositions and consistent with them. His fundamental error lies with his initial assumptions.

Rawls is much more complex.[62] Since he combines the principles from Types 1 and 2, his views are more adequate.[63] But his particular way of uniting them leaves gaps on both sides. These can be put in the following propositions:

1. *Neglect of Social Realism.* Like Nozick, in his initial set of assumptions, he is a social nominalist. The subjects of his ideal society (insofar as the basic framework of justice is concerned) are free and equal rational subjects whose interest is in themselves and their private ends. But this is only half the truth. While they agree to regard their talents as common assets, presumably, this is because it is to their advantage as individuals to do so.

2. *Neglect of Merit.* Yet despite his social nominalism, he does not allow inequalities on the basis of merit and excellence based on individual achievement. This is in keeping with the fact that he thinks that people who

do well owe most of their success to good breeding and good rearing (i.e., to factors external to the individual, a Type 2 theme).[64] At any rate, not to allow inequalities based on merit is an infringement on the principle of individual freedom. Whether one ends up at the top or the bottom of the social pyramid, surely a part of justice is that people ought to get what they deserve. Unless one's own choices and efforts are totally insignificant as a causal factor, then the principle of merit or desert has to be taken into account.[65]

3. *Neglect of Structural Interdependence as a Basis for Equality.* Rawls does create a communal society committed to equality for all with respect to social primary goods, except as inequalities benefit all. But this is a social realism based on agreement, i.e., a social contract. It does not recognize the actual interdependencies, organic connectedness, and the structural unity that belongs to social systems, which amount to something more than is created by the sum total of individual choices and acts. These structural features are intrinsic to social systems, and they are something common to all. This fact about social systems itself creates a basis for a tendency toward equality.[66] It indicates that what is actually going on is the creation and enjoyment of a common good. This principle creates an egalitarianism based on social facts. Rawls' system is built on the princple of generalized selfishness. Rules are made that guarantee that everyone gets the best of any worst possible situation.

4. *Neglect of the Enjoyment of the Non-Poor as a Possible Basis for Inequality.* Rawls produces a system geared to the advantage of the poor, the weak, the less gifted, the disadvantaged.[67] They can count on outcomes that in principle benefit them, regardless of their contribution. And even when inequalities are allowed for functional reasons, they end up better off than they would have been had the inequalities not been permitted.[68] This is a high-minded ethic geared to meeting the needs and serving the welfare of the worst off in society, an outlook with a strong basis in Judeo-Christian tradition. Despite the fact that it is produced by a kind of defensive and generalized selfishness rather than out of a concern for the other person, this is one of the most commendable features of his theory of justice.

However, if this be taken as the whole truth, a countervailing value is left out. Every potential for enjoyment in every person has some claim on resources to bring about its actualization. Still a hierarchy of needs exists so that some claims take priority over others. For example, we must eat before we can enjoy the study of philosophy. Likewise, in a family a reasonable moral rule would be: bread for all before piano lessons for anyone. Some individuals may be willing to endure severe poverty and self-neglect for the sake of living out their commitments. Some families may alter their food budget so that some gifted member may study music. The point is that the hierarchy of needs and desires may be variously arranged and priorities negotiated within broad limits, even though survival requirements are insistent and at some eventual level a necessity rather than a choice.

Nevertheless, the higher enjoyments or needs or wants do have *some* weight. They do constitute countervailing value claims once the basic necessities for survival and minimal fulfillment have been provided for all. At the social level this means that some claims on resources are produced by the needs and desires of the non-poor which must be honored whether the worst off benefit or not. While the general rule of bread for all before piano lessons for any holds for society at large as well as for families, this is not an absolute rule. Must all have indoor plumbing before any tennis courts are built? Does more lighting for a crime-ridden ghetto take absolute precedence over a symphony orchestra? If a small minority possesses unusual literary or musical talent whose exercise would benefit an elite group of the sophisticated affluent and not produce novels or music generally enjoyed by the poor, must these talents go undeveloped unless, somehow, the least advantaged are better off? It is a difficult question, but the point is that there may be grounds for inequalities that benefit some but not everyone— based purely and simply on the needs, wants, and potentials for enjoyment of those who possess them.[69] Granted that the poor take priority, but do they take absolute priority always, so that no one can ever rise the slightest bit until all rise equally and together? Must *all* inequalities benefit the disadvantaged?

The effect, then, of moving back and forth between libertarian and egalitarian principles (rather than integrating them into a unified view) is that Rawls leaves gaps that do not adequately honor either. Nevertheless, the fact that he takes into account valid elements from Types 1 and 2 means that his outlook on the whole is far superior to that of Nozick. The latter's views are fundamentally flawed from the beginning and from the ground up by his centering on one set of principles but neglecting (nearly) altogether the balancing counterparts.

PART III

PROCESS PHILOSOPHY AND SOCIAL THOUGHT

The final task is to connect the implications of process philosophy for the understanding of justice and society with the presentation of ideal types. Obviously Type 3 is the one that accords with the principles of process philosophy enunciated earlier. It is presented as a superior ideal because it incorporates valid insights from both Types 1 and 2 which each neglects in the other. This illustrates the Whiteheadian notion that when an apparent conflict is encountered, an effort should be made to transform the opposites into contrasts and to incorporate them into some larger and more harmonious frame of reference. Type 1 and Type 2 are set up as more or less polar opposites that contradict each other. Each embodies valid insights but not the whole truth. The most comprehensive and accurate rendering of the social facts requires a larger framework in which each type is both modified by the other and transformed by being set within a more adequate set of assumptions about individuals in relation to the societies to which they belong. In some settings Type 1 has the greater validity, while in others Type 2 is more relevant. Neither encompasses all that is real or just all the time. Type 3 aims at a multidimensional complexity and flexibility that makes some element of it applicable to every situation, although that is a goal too exalted for any to achieve fully. At any rate, the more inclusive vision embodied in Type 3 is closer to adequacy and applicability than its rivals.

Moreover, the synthesis more fully accounts for all our moral intuitions, although in a complex way that is full of tensions. Granted, many people would find their intuitions more in harmony with either Type 1 or 2 than with 3. Yet if there were greater agreement on the facts and on the interpretation of social reality as Type 3 presents them, there would also be more agreement that the ideals of Type 3 are required. Most people believe that what is produced by an individual alone (if that were possible or to the extent that it is the case) belongs to that individual. Most people also believe that what is produced in common should be shared in common, equally if produced that way or more ideally produced in accordance with ability and distributed according to need.[70] At least in families where love is present as the dominant motive, that form of community life is recognized. Most people also have experienced both the joy of joint effort and of individual achievement. No ideal set forth in Type 3 is foreign to experience or to moral intuitions widely shared.

The point on which people disagree most has to do with whether the nominalist, individualist, and freedom ideal or the realist, communalist, and equality ideal applies. Type 3 maintains that each set applies in various ways and in some respects. Which claim is correct? Here Whiteheadian methodology is useful. Theory tries to account for what is immediately experienced. Error may enter in a number of ways. The range of experience may be too narrow and thus lead to generalizations that are not applicable when tested by data arising in other spheres. Partial truths are made into the whole truth. Whitehead wisely warned aphoristically that "All truths are half truths." Dogmas inherited from the past may distort perception of current facts. All sorts of acquired filters may keep us from seeing things as they are. Self-interest may lead to a willing ignorance that produces theories congenial to what we desire but contrary to truth and disinterested moral intuition.

A Whiteheadian orientation would bid us to engage in continuous, critical, rigorous testing of theory by experience in the quest for interpretations most applicable to the widest range of relevant data. Rational adequacy (systematic consistency) and practical applicability (empirical relevance) are hard to come by. Error is extremely difficult to overcome, so tempted are we to enlarge a partial insight into a universal truth. Absolute claims are made for relative interpretations. Careful analysis of experienced data and constant revision of theory are needed to determine which renderings of the facts and which value judgments are most relevant in each instance and to what extent they apply in given cases.

One hunch entertained here is that many Americans have inherited a predisposition toward social nominalism, which blinds them to the systematic interdependence of individuals in today's economy. These individualistic, libertarian notions are encouraged by the rich and powerful who stand to gain by their continuing dominance. Moreover, average citizens frequently entertain hopes of becoming wealthy and so defend conservative ideologies from which they might benefit in the future. Critics of capitalism, on the other hand, all too often neglect the truths and values it embodies and too thoroughly embrace contrary ideas which may be just as limited in validity as those rejected. A case has been made here for a more complex, multidimensional view which seems to put two sets of partial truths into a synthesis which makes enough but not too much of each claim. What goes on in one setting may tend to validate Type 1, while what happens in another may corroborate Type 2. Sophisticated theories are required so that the applicable insight in particular cases may be recognized without losing sight that other truths may be more relevant in a different context. Doubtless the effort made here is not fully successful. However, any failure to grasp the fullness of truth is not the fault of Whiteheadian methodology, which urges us to a never ceasing struggle to find a more adequate theory with wider applicability in accord with the whole range of experience.

Equally rational persons with clear perceptions of the facts may differ in their moral theories. Value systems have a certain autonomy grounded in the creative imagination of selves with powers to transcend self-interest and the boundaries of their present conceptions. Hence, even if more agreement on facts and their interpretation did not produce more agreement on values, Type 3 is still set forth as an option along with other ideals in the hope that where agreement is not present, persuasion might produce more than now exists. If even this faith is naive, Type 3 is a preference in whose behalf supporting reasons can be given in harmony with the moral intuitions of some good and wise people.

Finally, the thesis of the entire paper is that this model is expressive of the metaphysical vision of process philosophy. While not everyone would spell out the implications of this outlook for understanding the social order in this way, the claim is that the approach taken here is defensible. This in no way rules out the likelihood that other theories of society and justice might be developed which are equally or more compatible with the thoughts of Alfred North Whitehead and other exponents of this point of view.[72]

Notes and References

1. "Speculative Philosophy is the endeavor to frame a coherent, logical, necessary system of general ideas in terms of which every element in our experience can be interpreted." Alfred North Whitehead, *Process and Reality* (New York: The Macmillian Co., 1929; New York: Harper Torchbook, 1960), p. 4.

2. *Ibid.*, p. 6.

3. Whitehead describes the search for first principles in terms of an airplane flight. "It starts from the ground of particular observation; it makes a flight in the air of imaginative generalization; and it again lands for renewed observation rendered acute by rational interpretation." *Ibid.*, p. 7.

4. Whitehead repeatedly stresses how tentative, partial, and relative are all attempts to get at the final truth. *Ibid.*, pp. x, 12, 14.

5. The focus of this essay is on human individuals who, along with other human individuals, exist in human communities. The metaphysical question of the relationship between "individuals" and "societies" in Whitehead's thought is subtle and complex. This is not the place to go into its intricacies. Briefly, according to Whitehead, a human being is a complex "society of societies" with a "dominant occasion" (a "soul"), defined as "an enduring object" with special characteristics of life and continuity through time that is designated a "living person." For my purposes, I am assuming that a person is an individual center of consciousness and action and, at the same time, a member of various human societies, such as the family, the church, and the state. In my view, the "mind" or "soul" exists in intimate and organic connection with a "body," and together they form a unified individual. A person both is and has a body. A distinction or duality between mind and body is essential to a proper analysis, but not a dualism. No human mind is present without a living body, and no living body functions without mental dimensions—although not necessarily consciousness. The "body" may be a complex "society of societies," existing in unity with the "soul," which—in Whiteheadian terms—is itself a special kind of "society." My intuition is that a person in totality is an individual with a continuing self-identity that guarantees responsibility for past acts as a moral agent and that is the basis for decision-making with respect to the future. Perhaps Charles Hartshorne's idea of a person as a "compound individual" constituted by a complex order of subsystems that are also "compound individuals" that, in turn, are themselves finally made up of indivisible or simple individuals (actual occasions) might serve my purposes in this connection. See Hartshorne, "The Compound Individual," *Whitehead's Philosophy: Selected Essays, 1935-1970* (Lincoln: University of Nebraska Press, 1972), pp. 41-61. For a helpful discussion of the way Whitehead thought of a person as a "society of societies," in the technical sense that he

assigned to "individual" and "society," see John B. Cobb, Jr., *A Christian Natural Theology* (Philadephia: Westminster Press, 1965), pp. 47-91. For Cobb's own views on the relationship of individuals to society, see *Process Theology as Political Theology* (Philadelphia: Westminster Press, 1982), pp. 92-108.

6.   For discussions of this aspect of Whiteheadian thought, see John B. Cobb, Jr. and W. Widick Schroeder, eds., *Process Philosophy and Social Thought* (Chicago: Center for the Scientific Study of Religion, 1981). See in particular the following chapters: Cobb, "Explanation and Causation in History and the Social Sciences," pp. 3-10; Cobb, "The Political Implications of Whitehead's Philosophy," pp. 11-28; Franklin I. Gamwell, "A Discussion of John B. Cobb, Jr., 'The Political Implications of Whitehead's Philosophy,'" pp. 29-37; Gamwell, "Happiness and the Public World: Beyond Political Liberalism," pp. 38-54; Schroeder, "Structure and Context in Process Political Theory: A Constructive Formulation," pp. 63-80; and Douglas Sturm, "Process Thought and Political Theory: Implications of a Principle of Internal Relations," pp. 81-102. See especially pp. 18-19, 35-36, 64-66, 90-91, 95-99.

7.   Alfred North Whitehead, *The Function of Reason* (Princeton: Princeton University Press, 1929; Boston: Beacon Press, 1958), p. 8.

8.   For brief discussions of freedom and equality in process philosophy, see Cobb, "The Political Implications of Whitehead's Philosophy," pp. 26-28; and Schroeder, "Structure and Context in Process Political Theory: A Constructive Formulation" *op. cit.;* pp. 66-67.

9.   This thesis is spelled out in detail in Kenneth Cauthen, *Process Ethics: A Constructive System* (New York: Edwin Mellen Press, 1984), pp. 195-310. See also the essay by Franklin I. Gamwell, "Happiness and the Public World."

10.   These models are by no means original. Similar contrasts have often been made. See, for example, George Cabot Lodge, *The New American Ideology* (New York: Knopf, 1975), who distinguishes between an "old American ideology" and a "new American ideology"; and William Ryan, *Equality* (New York: Pantheon Books, 1981), who distinguishes between "fair play" and "fair shares."

11.   The distinction between the individual and the group as the basic unit involves enormous ontological and epistemological problems. It raises many of the questions in dispute in the social sciences between the "methodological individualists" and the "methodological holists." Certainly the individual and the group have different statuses, both in being and in knowledge. The group is not an experiencing subject in the same way an individual is. Terms like "organism" and "organic" are used metaphorically, but the metaphor refers to something in reality that is not reducible to individual agents and their thoughts, attitudes, acts, etc. The common good is not experienced by some superself but by the individuals who make up the group. Yet the good experienced is created and enjoyed by them in their togetherness in a system of interdependent relationships exhibiting structural patterns and dynamic interactions that belong to the group and not to individuals alone. It is not possible or necessary for present purposes to resolve all the problems raised by the distinction between social nominalism and social realism. For the issues in debate in the social sciences between individualism and holism, see *The Encyclopedia of Philosophy* (New York: The Macmillan Co., 1967), vol. 4, pp. 53-58.

12.   Obviously, I am eliminating extreme versions of each of these sociological principles. Social nominalism taken all the way leads to extreme libertarianism and anarchism (though there may be forms of anarchism that assume a collective self-governing whole). Social realism at the other far end could mean a kind of state totalitarianism in which the good of the whole was everything and particular individuals were nothing.

13.   This becomes clear by noting social ideals from the past in which (modern secular ideas of) freedom and equality are not explicit or dominant. The ideal society in Plato's *The Republic*

is an organism in which justice refers to the proper functioning of all in their proper places, but the places are not necessarily equal, and individual freedom is limited. In the New Testament the Pauline notion of life in the Body of Christ is based on an organic conception of community in which believers are "individually members one of another" (Roms. 12:5 RSV). Notions of freedom (Gal. 5) and equality (Gal. 3:28) are present, but so is subordination (I Cor. 11:34) and slavery (Philemon). Moreover, it is not evident the extent to which freedom and equality are meant to apply to the secular order or mainly to the spiritual status of believers before God in faith. In any case, locating the good in the whole to be shared by members can be associated with organic and hierarchical conceptions as well as democratic and egalitarian ones, as Paul's analogy of the body would suggest (I Cor. 12). Historic "catholic" views of the church have certainly been organic and hierarchical, within which neither individual freedom nor equality of status, function, and authority has a prominent place.

14.   The determination of the ways in which people are or ought to be equal and are either unavoidably or normatively or permissibly unequal constitutes a large part of social philosophy. Hobbes, Locke, Rousseau, and Kant provide much of the framework for the traditional discussion, while John Rawls is the center of much of the current philosophical debate.

15.   The logic of equality is subtle. It requires that equals be treated equally and unequals unequally. To require the same contribution from unequally gifted persons is to treat them equally in one sense (by the same rule: the same contribution from each). To require contribution according to ability would be treating them equally in another sense (by the same rule: according to ability). The same logic applies to consumers. Treating persons equally (by the rule of need) means giving them different things if needs require that. By this principle giving them all the same things (an equal number of units of the same good) would be treating them unequally. Treating people equally only means treating them by the same rule, but the rule may be, in this case, giving according to need or giving the same units of the same good. Which rule is employed depends on whether "equals" refers to all human beings who each count as one or whether "equals" are regarded as those who have the same needs and "unequals" as those who have different needs.

16.   In the founding documents of the USA, the Declaration of Independence, e.g., much is said about equality. However, what was primarily meant was equal freedom, i.e., the right to elect one's rulers (political equality) and to have equal opportunity to further one's own individual goals. Certainly, they in no way intended to suggest equality for all in all respects. See Richard W. Crosby, "Equality in America: The Declaration, Tocqueville, and Today," *The New Egalitarianism* (Port Washington, N.Y.: Kennkat Press, 1979), ed. David Lewis Schaeffer, pp. 53-65. Or consider John Locke who, in urging that one could acquire private property by mixing one's labor with it, also insisted that in so doing one must leave "as much and as good" for others—an idea of equal freedom and equal opportunity.

17.   These are not necessary assumptions, since Type 1 might suppose that while all are free, some legitimately have a wider range of liberties than others (for whatever reason—noble birth, superior racial background, etc.). Likewise, Type 2 might suppose that while all are equal in many or all other respects, some should have a wider range of liberties than others (for whatever reasons—a natural hierarchy of ability which equips some to rule over others without their consent, but for their own good and the common good which all share equally, etc.).

18.   One thinks immediately of "the dictatorship of the proletarian" in Marxism and of the role of the hierarchical priesthood in Roman Catholicism. Also, within this framework one can easily understand the protest of democratic socialists against the tyrannical versions found in Soviet and other forms of Marxism.

19. One might argue that the sociological and value principles are the root sources of this model. However, the combination of these two apart from the freedom and equality principles might well, as they have in the past, produce organic hierarchical models in which power and authority are concentrated in some elite that rules by divine hereditary right, divine appointment, some natural aristocracy, etc. When biological metaphors are employed, so that society is an organism, it is easy to think of a "head" that rules over the lesser parts of the body. This is obviously not a democratic outlook.

20. This is the tradition of Locke, Kant, and the deontological school of thought. Or people may be regarded as equal in passion and desire for pleasure and happiness. This is the tradition of Hobbes, Bentham, Mill, and the teleological or utilitarian tradition. In this way of thinking, too, each person counts for one and must be taken into account. This tradition is open to the criticism that it ultimately prefers the maximizing of total good or happiness to the mode of its distribution, so that it may end up being willing to sacrifice the equal claims of all for this end. In any case, the rights tradition is being preferred here. See Amy Gutmann, *Liberal Equality* (New York: Cambridge University Press, 1980).

21. Actually, both models may make an appeal to eschatology in justifying present poverty or any kind of inequality for the sake of enlarging the total good. Type 1 never promises equality of outcome, only equality of opportunity, but it may argue that inequalities now and forevermore are necessary for economic growth and promise that the future will yield a larger piece of pie to everybody, though never equal pieces. Type 2 does promise equal outcomes (in some form that may be highly qualified in the end) but may postpone equal sharing until the new age has finally arrived, the present inequalities of opportunity and present restrictions on individual freedom being necessary either to the preservation or enlargement of the common good. See Peter Berger, *Pyramids of Sacrifice* (New York: Basic Books, 1974). It is only in the last stage of the promised Marxist utopia that the rule will be "from each according to ability and to each according to need." Hence, Type 1 promises equal opportunity but its ideals may actually result in unequal opportunities, while Type 2 promises equal outcomes but may find it necessary to postpone the realization of the dream until the new age arrives at some indefinite and constantly receding future (like the Second Coming of Christ).

22. A diagram of possibilities:

Totalitarianism	Democratic	Democratic	Totalitarianism
of the right	Capitalism	Socialism	of the Left

23. In other words, the status of the community as real may be regarded as ontological or as created contractually. I will also use the term "organic" to indicate what is here called ontological social realism. Organic suggests a biological model of a unitary organism with parts that are in fact interdependent and mutually sustaining. Social nominalism seems to be the original assumption of modern thought. Persons may agree to create a social unit for mutual benefit, but the primordial fact is real individuals who by contract create the unity. Rousseau speaks of the creation of "a single personality" by the surrender of individual rights to the social unit. John Rawls speaks of a contractual act by which free and equal individuals agree that the talents of all are to be regarded as a common asset to be exercised for the benefit of all. The contractual social realism of the modern world contrasts neatly with the medieval picture of society and of the church as an organic hierarchy in which equal worth and status and equal freedom for all (except in some ultimate theological sense of primordial status before God) were foreign notions. This is ontological social realism. The status of universals was, of course, one of the great points of debate during that period. There were nominalists and realists, and the former which developed later, after the reigning Platonism of earlier centuries, was a forerunner, philosophically speaking, of the modern world in which social nominalism has prevailed.

24. An internal tension or ambiguity is created in this formulation of the model between an equal right to participate in communal decision-making and to share equally (or proportionately) in the production and distribution of the common good, on the one hand, and freedom to seek an individual good independent of the common good, on the other hand. The former is assumed to be proper for Type 2, while the latter is reserved for Type 3.

25. The givenness of the state into which one is born might also include the hereditary divine right of kings (thought to be the case in former centuries). In any case, if the analogy of the family is taken as paradigmatic, the consequence is that the state may have its own structures and predetermined roles, which may deny equality of rule.

26. The constitution of societies modeled after Type 1 might use this same language, but common good would be defined differently, i.e., as the sum total of individual good, or as needs common to all individuals that require a unified network of activities, such as money or transportation or schooling. But the gravitational pull would be in the direction of doing as little of this as possible, while Type 2 could easily be led into an expansion of activities on behalf of all—considered as a unified whole and not simply as a collection of individuals. Some proponents of Type 1, e.g., advocate a system of vouchers provided by the state to individual families to be used to purchase education for their children provided by private schools.

27. It is difficult to know what economic and political arrangements are made necessary by the logic of the basic model and which are just compatible with it. Options equally congruent with the operational ideals might be preferred to others on grounds of efficiency or other criteria. A market system could be utilized that was controlled and directed for common rather than private ends. Or a decentralized system of relatively autonomous local activities might be created to be coordinated rather than controlled by the central authority, etc. Obviously, some common networks of transportation, communication, etc. are required, plus some way to maintain security against external threats.

Anarchistic forms of egalitarianism may regard the state as an enemy of the equality of individuals and as inherently tyrannical. Only models that allow a positive role for the state in directing the creation and distribution of the common good are developed here, though this obviously means the elimination of other ideal types that may be worthy of consideration and even, from some points of view, superior. The models that assume a positive role for the state seem most compatible with the principle of social realism, while radical forms of libertarian or anarchistic egalitarianism seem to rest on the principle of social nominalism in combination with the principle of equality.

28. Organic hierarchical versions, unmodified by democratic themes of equal liberty, might easily assume that the "head" of the "body" should be of one mind in religion and in many other areas. In this framework, freedom of thought and a plurality of life-styles are foreign and threatening ideas.

Analysis of several of the issues above suggest that a moderate or extreme version of Type 2 emerges, depending on how much it is modified by the principles of Type 1. In particular, the idea of a contractual social realism, rather than an ontological social realism, and democratic rule, rather than rule by some given hierarchy or some other elite, are characteristic of the moderate versions. The extreme versions are less characteristic of the modern world because of the importance of individualism, nominalism, and freedom. By making equal liberty and a democratic polity an integral part of Type 2 as here presented, the extreme versions have in effect been eliminated.

In particular, Type 2 is already qualified initially by making equal liberty a fundamental premise. This takes both individualism and freedom more seriously than some egalitarian models would. Without them perhaps a purer version of Type 2 would result. Yet this approach has not been followed, since Type 2 would be intolerable and (from my point of view) not very ideal to start with. What this means is that I am as much a libertarian as I am an egalitarian, so that a model which does not make equal liberty a fundamental principle is ruled out of consideration from the start. To be more precise, Type 1 without the premise of *equal* liberty and Type 2 without the premise of equal *liberty* would both be abhorrent.

29.   I have constructed a model much like this in content but quite different in form in *Process Ethics*.

30.   The contrary argument that freedom is a sociological and political concept has been maintained by numerous thinkers, including, F.A. Hayek, T.H. Green, Ludwig von Mises, and F.H. Knight. For libertarians, "freedom" refers to the sphere of individual choice and action unimpeded by the coercion of the state. In this sense, it is for them a social concept. See F.A. Hayek, *The Constitution of Liberty* (Chicago: The University of Chicago Press, 1960), pp. 12-13, 422, ns. 6 and 7.

31.   Would she be free (morally) to do physical harm to her own person or to commit suicide? My inclination is to say that she is morally obligated to honor the intrinsic worth of her own person, but that this obligation is weakened to the point of possible elimination by extraordinary conditions of extreme, pointless, and irremediable suffering. But would not suicide be an offense against God who created her and loves her? My inclination is to say yes, that is the case, but that God would be pained by her taking of her life but would not count it a sin, as it would be if one person murdered another. So high do I honor the principle of individual freedom. Granted suicide would, in one sense, be an act of ingratitude toward God; but since one did not ask for the gift, one is free to reject it as a matter of justice if its reception or perpetuation entailed unavoidable and intolerable suffering, though it might pain the giver whose loving intentions were to give a good gift.

32.   Again, to be treated equally does not necessarily mean to be treated identically. Hence, many egalitarian models end up with the notion of "from each according to ability and to each according to need." Unless factual or functional inequalities are taken into account, to treat people identically (without taking into account relevant individual differences) would be to treat them unequally in one sense.

33.   I speak now not of the Whiteheadian meaning of these terms, but of the senses in which they pertain to human beings living in communities.

34.   I am grateful to Randall Morris for directing me to T.H. Green and L.T. Hobhouse, who elaborated a social ideal that has great affinity with my point of view. Their notion was that rights and duties were to be assigned, not to individuals as such, but to persons as members of communities. Their ideal was framed in terms of a harmony of interests in which the self-realization of each person was coordinated with that of other individuals in the creation of a common good that all shared. The well-being of others is a part of the good which one ought to seek for oneself. While Hobhouse had a sense of the conflict between the good of the individual and the common good, which might necessitate self-sacrifice for the society at large, my impression is that I have a greater sense of the conflicts, ambiguities, complexities, trade-offs, compromises, and tragedies that attend the quest for justice than either he or Green. Their sense of an ideal harmony (in potential and goal, if not in fact) between individual good and the common good comes from an age and an outlook that could harbor an optimism hardly possible for the contemporary age. Nonetheless, their convictions that individuals are to be seen as members of communities, that the highest ideal is a common good that all create and enjoy, that the individual finds his or her own good in the common good, that both a one-sided individualism and a one-sided collectivism are to be avoided, and so on are in accord with my vision of the self-realization of individuals in community. See T.H. Green, *Prolegomena to Ethics* (Oxford: The Clarendon Press, 1883), pp. 160-263; *Works of Thomas Hill Green*, ed. R.L. Nettleship (London: Longmans, Green, 1886), Vol. II, pp. 335-465; L.T. Hobhouse,

Liberalism (New York: Henry Holt, 1911), pp. 116-37; *The Rational Good* (New York: Henry Holt, 1921), pp. 166-234; and *The Elements of Social Justice* (New York: Henry Holt, 1922), pp. 3-138.

35.   Alfred North Whitehead, *Religion in the Making* (New York: The Macmillan Co., 1926; Cleveland: The World Publishing Co., 1960), p. 167.

36. Believer's baptism is required by the contractual or covenantal model, while infant baptism more correctly is associated with the organic, communal model.

37.   Nozick operates within the framework of 1 and 2, while Rawls begins with 1 and sees society as created by contract, as in 2, but concludes that individuals decide to share one another's fate and to regard all biological and social assets as a common resource for the good of all to be shared equally unless an unequal arrangement helps everyone. At this point Rawls misses the truth of organic social realism by his exclusive preoccupation with the social contract model.

38.   Marc Plattner distinguishes between a traditional view in which income belongs to the earner and a new view which assumes that income belongs to the state and can thus be distributed in accordance with political and moral norms. The latter view he associates with a new egalitarianism that goes beyond the welfare state toward a redistributive state. The two views may well be associated with Types 1 and 2, respectively. Type 3 sees truth in both views. Income is a joint product of individual effort and a common network of structures that makes all workers interdependent. Moreover, the notion that the market distributes income according to some kind of merit (marginal productivity) that has moral validity will not, for many reasons, serve to justify absolute ownership of income. Hence, a redistributionist ethic need not depend on the view that all income belongs to the state, but only that some of it is produced by means common to all. The production of income is both an individual and a social process. That which is the joint product of all or many in a social process may justly be redistributed in accordance with nonmarket norms. See Marc Plattner, "The Welfare State Versus the Redistributive State," *Public Interest* (Spring, 1979), pp. 28-48.

39.   Two astute observers of the American soul have pointed to the evils of individualism without commitment to common good purposes. See Robert Bellah, et al, *Habits of the Heart: Individualism and Commitment in American Life* (Berkeley: University of California Press, 1985); and Daniel Bell, *The Cultural Contradictions of Capitalism* (New York: Basic Books, 1976).

40.   The extent of the difference made by families is debatable. Christopher Jencks and his associates concluded that only 15 % of variations in income depends on family background. Frequently enormous differences of income are to be found among brothers in the same family. See Christopher Jencks, et al, *Inequality: A Reassessment of the Effect of Family and Schooling in America* (New York: Basic Books, 1972).

41.   Questions of efficiency and of savings, as well as many other problems, arise which cannot be argued here. But see Arthur Okun, *Equality and Efficiency* (Washington: The Brookings Institution, 1975); and Robert Kuttner, *The Economic Illusion: False Choices between Prosperity and Social Justice* (New York: Houghton Mifflin Co., 1984).

42.   Questions of political feasibility are ignored in favor of stating an ideal that would be nice if people would buy into it.

43.   Efficiency means only that we seek to get the most of what we want for the least cost. But the norm of efficiency cannot come into play until the boundary conditions have been prescribed, i.e., the goals desired and the means permitted. See my *The Ethics of Enjoyment* (Atlanta: John Knox Press, 1975), pp. 64-79.

44.   Actually, a third factor enters into the notion of justice and the good society—the ideal of increasing social good. Hence, there are occasions when freedom and equality may be limited for the sake of enlarging the good to be pursued individually or shared communally as well as by each other. This has already become evident in Rawls' and my admitting that inequalities may be permitted if necessary to increase benefits to all. Freedom might similarly be limited under other circumstances. See my *Process Ethics*, pp. 195-310, for an elaboration, illustration, and defense of this view.

45.   I have in mind particularly the notions of individual worth and human rights that are not necessarily entailed by the ideas of individual freedom and social equality, though they are compatible and companion concepts. It might be the case, however, that notions of equal freedom and social equality are, in some sense, entailed by the assumption of individual worth and dignity.

46.   Robert Nozick, *Anarchy, State and Utopia* (New York: Basic Books, 1974).

47.   John Rawls, *A Theory of Justice* (Cambridge: Harvard University Press, 1971).

48.   Nozick, *Anarchy, State and Utopia*, pp. 149-82.

49.   *Ibid.*, pp. 153-64.

50.   The final and complete statement in Rawls' own words can be found in *A Theory of Justice*, pp. 302-03.

51.   I and others have wondered if this does not produce a fatal flaw in the deliberations. The rules that are produced may be prudent in that they are designed to protect one's own interest no matter where one ends up in some actual society. But are they just? Granted that the rules must apply to everyone, so that no legislator in the OP can design rules that will benefit him/her in particular. Nevertheless, the rules are designed to serve a kind of general selfishness so that one ends up with the best deal possible in any bad situation, no matter whether the bad place one lands in is one's own fault. Rawls seems to think that basically we are shaped by heredity and environment so that individual choice plays little role. The result is that he eliminates merit or desert as a rule of justice in and of itself. If his method produces a just set of rules, it is by the coincidence that a kind of generalized selfishness has that consequence. In his defense one could argue that he is providing a way to legislate the "golden rule" of Jesus or his injunction that one should love one's neighbor equally with oneself into the social order. Assuming that one might end up on the bottom, one would want the best outcome in that situation, but willing that for oneself is willing it also for the neighbor who might be in the bad spot instead of you. However, this is not done for the sake of the neighbor as such, but only because one might himself/herself be in that bad spot. Assured that one would be on top and not on the bottom, presumably one would not worry where the neighbor ended up. It is a subtle point.

52.   Rawls, *A Theory of Justice*, p. 101.

53.   *Ibid.*, pp. 62, 303. These primary values are defined as things that every rational person would want, whatever else they might want as particular individuals.

54.   *Ibid.*, pp. 84, 103. Adherents of Type 1 could also view society in this way, but when combined with the preceding points, this statement takes on more egalitarian coloring.

55.   *Ibid.*, pp. 90-95.

56.   Plattner wonders how far Rawls would go with this. Suppose that originally all have incomes of $5,000, but that if some are permitted to earn $25,000, the poorest would be raised to $6,000. Suppose further that by allowing some to earn $1,000,000 the poorest will be raised to only $6,100. Presumably all these arrangements would be legitimate under Rawls' scheme. Plattner points out that this indicates how important, after all, economic incentives and the in-

crease of wealth are to Rawls. Plattner also asks why not extend the difference principle to sexual favors and to children. Should the sexually attractive and able be allowed their erotic advantages unless the less desirable and unsuccessful men and women are compensated? And should couples who are fertile give up some of their children to the infertile? See Plattner, "The Welfare State Versus the Redistributive State."

57.   Rawls, A Theory of Justice, pp. 60-108, 511-12.

58.   At least one interpreter claims that there is better grounding for policies that lead to an egalitarian society in Nozick than in Rawls. See Derek Phillips, Equality, Justice and Rectification (New York: Academic Press, 1979), pp. 106-8.

59.   Nozick, Anarchy, State and Utopia, pp. 230-231.

60.   Rawls, A Theory of Justice, p. 277.

61.   Some even more thoroughgoing libertarians would insist that Nozick compromises this position by the admission of the legitimacy of a minimal state, but Nozick attempts to justify this move on libertarian grounds. For evaluations and discussions of Nozick's point of view, see Reading Nozick, ed. Jeffrey Paul (Totowa, N.J.: Rowman & Littlefield, 1981).

62.   For an extensive discussion of Rawls, presenting evaluations from many points of view, see John Rawls' Theory of Justice, H. Gene Blocker and Elizabeth H. Smith, eds. (Athens: Ohio University Press, 1980).

63.   See my Process Ethics, pp. 211-21, for a general discussion and evaluation of Rawls.

64.   Rawls, A Theory of Justice, p. 104.

65.   How would Rawls answer Daniel Bell who wants to know what we are to say if the worst off or the least fortunate are there by their own choice? See The New Egalitarianism, p. 235, note 12.

66.   I have argued for this at length in Process Ethics, pp. 252-63, 278-310.

67.   However, this comes about because of the possibility that those who are making the rules in the OP may end up on the bottom, not because they are motivated by love for the disadvantaged as such. It comes about for practical and self-interested reasons, not as a consequence of ethical principles espoused by the creators of society.

68.   Rawls notes that the rules of society must be such as to evoke the willing cooperation of all. Hence, the rule that all benefits are to be shared equally unless inequalities benefit all would ensure the cooperation of those who are least gifted and least advantaged. However, numerous critics have pointed out that this is a good deal for the disadvantaged, but it is one-sided. What is to ensure the willing cooperation of the better endowed? See Rawls, A Theory of Justice, pp. 100-108; and Nozick, Anarchy, State and Utopia, pp. 189-97.

69.   See Process Ethics, pp. 174-79, 238-52, 260-63, 278-81.

70.   The problem is that many people regard the creation of what I would call produced jointly or in common as produced by the sum total of individual efforts. I see much economic production in systemic or communal terms, i.e., having organic characteristics rather than as the simple total of individual efforts. Individual efforts have little meaning apart from the system of which they are a part. For example, I view the large salaries of sports celebrities as a joint product of many factors and people in a system. Were it not for TV networks broadcasting over public channels and the interest of the people, plus, in many cases, facilities built in part with public funds, etc., not to mention the invention of the games themselves—neither of which is the product of the players—the large salaries would not be possible. Hence, I think it quite just to tax them and redistribute the income produced. It is, of course, possible to view all of this in individualistic or contractual terms, as does Nozick, for example. Given his interpretation of the facts and his view of social reality, I agree with his conclusions. Hence, it

would appear that my disagreement with Nozick arises, at least in part, out of a difference in the interpretation of facts and social reality, not a difference in moral intuitions as such. See Nozick, *Anarchy, State and Utopia*, pp. 160-64, and *Process Ethics*, pp. 295-300.

71.   This approach to social models as ideal types has all the disadvantages of any kind of high abstraction: it loses contact with all the full, rich complexity of the concrete reality from which the abstracting is undertaken. In particular, this approach abstracts from the concrete reality of actual persons in real life circumstances seeking ways to live and developing ideals as paths toward survival and fulfillment. It ignores the fact that ideals reflect particular perspectives of given people in specific historical settings. Ideals may be a defense of vested interests and take the form of defensive ideology. Ideals centering on freedom may be characteristic of the strong, the confident, the gifted, and the oppressor. Ideals centering on equality may be characteristic of the weak, the humble, the poor, and the oppressed. Marxism and the whole enterprise of the psychology and sociology of knowledge have much to teach us here. Conservatives are fond of insisting that the demand for greater equality does not grow out of any passion for justice but out of envy of those who are better off. How does my own socio-economic status, my own life history, my own temperament and psychological development, my own existence as a white, male American, and so on shape if not determine my outlook? Perhaps women see the whole realm of ethics differently from men. (See, for example, Carol Gilligan, *In a Different Voice: Psychological Theory and Women's Development* (Cambridge: Harvard University Press, 1982).) Here I can only acknowledge all these shortcomings and promise to give attention to them elsewhere. Meanwhile, I can only plead that there is some merit and legitimacy in taking the particular approach I have for this occasion. At the very least, I hope that coming at the issue this way might help to clarify underlying philosophical assumptions that give structure and content to moral ideals of justice and the good society.

72.   This paper was read at a Consultation on "Process Philosophy and Forms of Economic Organization" at the annual meeting of the American Academy of Religion in Atlanta, Georgia, on November 22, 1986. I am grateful to members of the Consultation for critical comments that led to important revisions of the present manuscript. I am, of course, fully responsible for the text as it presently stands. It should also be noted that this paper is very similar to Chapter III of my *The Passion for Equality* (Totowa, N.J.: Rowman & Littlefield, 1987).

CHAPTER 6

The Circumstances of Economic Justice: A Response to Kenneth Cauthen

Jon P. Gunnemann

Kenneth Cauthen's paper[1] combines three modes of inquiry: process metaphysics, ethics, and economics. I want to concentrate on his ethical analysis and especially on his analysis of justice and its connection to critical theological questions. I will have some things to say along the way about economics insofar as it bears on the question of justice. My comments on process thought will be more sketchy, taking chiefly the form of some questions and suggestions.

My remarks fall into three general sets: The first has to do with my discomfort at the abstract nature of the argument, the rather arbitrary construction of formal models or types, and my puzzlement at the choice of Nozick and Rawls as contrasting types. I will argue that this approach obscures some of the central issues underlying contemporary theories of economic justice. Second, I turn to "the circumstances of justice," those characterizations of social life which are thought to give rise to problems of justice. Here I will look first at the circumstances of economic justice as understood by Rawls and Nozick,[2] Cauthen's two main dialogue partners, and then offer some critique of those characterizations. These characterizations of the circumstances of justice yield a view of justice as "remedial," a view fundamentally at odds with Cauthen's own in spite of his attempt to combine features of the other two views. Third, and finally, I will suggest a different way of looking at the circumstances of justice, using especially

Michael Walzer's recent work on justice.[3] This view is, I believe, more concrete and historical in its treatment of economic justice, more productive for ethical reflection on our economic institutions, and, I suspect—and this will be more in the form of a question—more consistent with what I understand to be process assumptions. This last point suggests that, in spite of my criticisms of the paper, I am in sympathy with much of what I take to be its aim.

Problems in the Approach

Cauthen's paper sets out to offer a process model of social interdependence, synthesizing features of two opposing models which he calls "individualist-freedom" and "communal-equality" models. He argues that his synthesis of these two models not only offers a more accurate depiction of reality but also is more productive of economic justice.

I am not at all persuaded by the argument and am puzzled by the approach Cauthen takes. Much of the problem lies in the unusually abstract nature of the argument and particularly in the arbitrary and formal construction of his models and types. It is not at all clear what the status of these models or types is: On the one hand, the use of the terms "ideal" and "type" interchangeably with "model" at least hints at Max Weber's "ideal types," heuristic abstractions from social patterns in history. Had Cauthen used "types" in this way, his analysis could have been rooted in concrete historical examples but he makes no attempt at empirical analysis and his types bear litle resemblance to actual societies. On the other hand, Cauthen's suggestion that the types or models represent "social ideals" such as in Plato's *Republic*[4] is not supported by a careful extraction of the models from texts purporting to offer such ideals. Instead, the models are constructed first and then writers found to fit them, and, as his discussion eventually indicates (especially in relation to John Rawls), they do not necessarily reflect in any precise way the positions of actual thinkers. He claims in fact that the models can "be created" by combining different principles in different ways and his procedure does just that: he seems to construct models which he deems useful in providing a contrast permitting him to go in the direction he wants. No compelling social theory and no persuasive theory of justice can be so constructed: the method not only obscures central issues concerning economic life and justice but prevents, I think, a genuinely fruitful dialogue between process thought and current economic thought.

The problem is compounded by the puzzle of making Nozick and Rawls represent the constructed contrasting positions. Quite clearly in some respects they do contrast (Nozick, after all, wrote his book in large part as a critique of Rawls) but in others they do not. The key point is that each represents a different version of classical liberalism in which the individual and individual liberty are given axiomatic priority. Rawls in particular is strained as an example of a "communal-equality" type—certainly Rawls has no notion of persons being "organic parts of a whole," even though Part Three of *A Theory of Justice* makes a strong case for the values of community and for "social union."[5] If one wanted to make "type 2" work, I should think Michael Sandel's communitarianism[6] would have been a better example. Indeed, as Cauthen comes to admit, Rawls in fact spans the two types, beginning on individualist premises not unlike those of Nozick. If so, we do not really have an interesting contrast: there is no genuinely social or relational conception of the self from which to work a synthesis. One must worry in advance that Cauthen will likely stay with a liberal conception of individualism at odds with, if I understand them correctly, process assumptions.

Moreover, this formal account misses the point that neither Nozick nor Rawls is attempting to construct a social ideal but rather is looking at justice in relation to what each perceives to be the actual conditions of human existence, conditions that *require* the priority of right over good, of individual right over social good. This can be seen clearly in the connection between Rawls and Kant, a connection critical to understanding Rawls. Like Kant, Rawls is committed to the position that right precedes good not merely logically but also in actual human societies: it is not good people who make just societies—rather, just social orders make it possible for people to become (relatively) good. Here is Kant's view of the matter:

> "Thus it is only a question of a good organization of the state (which does lie in man's power), whereby the powers of each selfish inclination are so arranged in opposition that one moderates or destroys the ruinous effect of the other. The consequence for reason is the same as if none of them existed, and man is forced to be a good citizen even if not a morally good person.
>
> The problem of organizing a state, however hard it may seem, can be solved even for a race of devils, if only they are intelligent. The problem is, 'Given a multitude of rational beings requiring universal laws for their preservation, but each of whom is secretly inclined to exempt himself from them, to establish a constitution in such a way that, although their private intentions conflict, they check each other, with the result that their public conduct is the same as if they had no such intentions.'
>
> A problem like this must be capable of solution; it does not require that we know how to attain the moral improvement of men but only that we should know the mechanism of nature in order to use it on men, organizing the conflict of the hostile intentions present in a people in such a way that they must compel themselves to submit to coercive law. . . .(A good constitution is not to be expected from morality, but, conversely, a good moral condition of a people is to be expected only under a good constitution.)[7]

This means that the ordering of right and good is not up for grabs for Kant. Neither is it for Rawls. Given that a process position is committed to the proposition that people have goods or a good in common, and that this prevents "right" from having any moral or logical priority, it will not do simply to say, in Whiteheadian fashion, that when confronted with conflicting positions "an effort should be made to transform the opposites into contrasts and to incorporate them into some larger and more harmonious frame of reference." (p. 114) Such an approach ignores the premises on which the contrasting positions are based. In the cases of Kant, Rawls, and Nozick, right is prior to good and to community precisely because there is no common good and no natural community.

This point has at least two versions. In the Kantian version, there is a skepticism about whether people can be sufficiently virtuous, or sufficiently virtuous often enough, to create a just society. Because of this skepticism, Kant's directive is to assume that they "are a race of devils," that is, likely to "exempt themselves" from universal laws, and to construct a society of justice accordingly, that is, in a fashion guaranteeing cooperation in spite of individual intentions. In Rawls, and even more strongly in Nozick, the skepticism is about whether we have morally coherent ends, let alone a common end. In either case, it is critically important to the logic of each position that the establishment of right be possible without resolving the question of ends or of moral intentions.[8]

By contrast, Cauthen simply asserts as a premise of his model that we have a common good which we create. This, I take it, is part of process metaphysics. And, it happens, I am in qualified agreement with this for theological reasons. But the assertion of the point does not itself carry weight against the positions which Cauthen criticizes, nor does it amount either to a synthesis of their positions or to a modification of them. On the contrary, it makes his conception of justice a very different project from theirs, a difference that is demonstrated by his claim that his third model offers "a superior ideal" by comparison to theirs. But an ideal suggests an end which social arrangements can more or less approximate and neither Nozick nor Rawls tries to offer an account of an *ideal* society in this sense. Rather, they attempt to offer conceptions of society adequate to the circumstances of justice, and the circumstances of justice are precisely that we do not have a common end, not necessarily even morally coherent ends. For them the problems of justice arise precisely as a consequence of these circumstances of justice.

In sum, the formal attempt to construct contrasting ideal models of society in which the primary variables are freedom and equality, and individuality and community, obscures the deeper disagreement behind competing theories of justice. This deeper disagreement has to do with the circumstances of justice, that is, the conditions of the world which give rise to questions of justice. The liberal traditions represented by Nozick and Rawls assume that justice is a problem because we lack a common end or *telos*. Cauthen's position is not a melding of these two but depends on the notion that we have a common end. If that claim is going to stick, we have to look more carefully at arguments about the circumstances of justice; and we have to find arguments about the nature of justice different from those offered by either Nozick or Rawls.

The Circumstances of Justice

The chief question is, What problems or circumstances require us to be just, or to be concerned about justice? I will concentrate here on Rawls because he gives a more detailed account of the circumstances of justice, but we may begin with Nozick. For Nozick, justice becomes our concern when persons transgress the bounds of the laws of nature, that is, when they invade others' rights and do harm to one another.[9] The background here is Locke but we do not need either to go through Locke's delineation of the rights dictated by the law of nature or to deal with the puzzle of how, for him, the law of nature is grounded. We need only to understand that, for Nozick, rights are the fundamental unit of morality, and the violation of rights the primary problem of justice. The discussion of good that comes later in the book is a discussion of human *goods*, and these in turn are always understood as goods possessed by individuals—that is, goods are understood as falling under the right of possession or of property.[10] The fact that Nozick never offers an argument for this priority of right over good is perhaps an indication of how critical the assumption is to his project as a whole.[11] In any case, it tells us that we have to look elsewhere for an examination of the premise.

For our purposes, that elsewhere is Rawls. He is explicit on the point, drawing on Hume to distinguish between the objective and subjective circumstances of justice.[12] The *objective* circumstances of justice include the living of many roughly equal individuals within a specific geographical territory, all vulnerable to attack and to having plans blocked by others, and, especially important, all living under conditions of moderate scarcity. These objective circumstances are, I think, not especially controversial, at least for the positions we are discussing here—they are the defining characteristics of economic problems and of economic inquiry.[13] The *subjective* circumstances of economic justice Rawls defines as the absence of a common end: "individuals not only have different plans of life but there exists a diversity of philosophical and religious belief, and of political and social doctrines."[14] As a consequence, individuals act with mutual disinterest, i.e., with no interest in the interests of others.

Now, it is instructive to look at this subjective circumstance of justice in relation to Rawls's "community of saints" passage in his earlier essay,

"Justice as Fairness":

> Amongst an association of saints, if such a community could really exist, the disputes about justice could hardly ever occur; for they would all work selflessly together for one end, the glory of God as defined by their common religion, and reference to this end would settle every question of right. The justice of practices does not come up until there are several different parties (whether we think of these as individuals, associations, or nations and so on, is irrelevant) who do press their claims on one another, and who do regard themselves as representatives of interests which deserve to be considered.[15]

The claim that problems of justice, or at least serious disputes about justice, would never occur among a community of saints, that is, among persons who shared a common end, together with the stipulative denial of a common end as one of the circumstances of justice, suggests, to use Sandel's phrase, that Rawls has a "remedial" view of justice "whose moral advantage consists in the repair it works on fallen conditions."[16] If we did not have fallen conditions, i.e., if we had a common end, we would not need the virtue of justice.

This remedial view of justice accounts, I think, for the relative popularity of Rawls among some recent Christian writers on questions of justice—it has, on the surface, an affinity with the view that after the Fall we must be satisfied in the political and economic realms with justice rather than with love, and with the Pauline and Lutheran view that law and justice are occasioned by sin. Justice is at best a "second-best" morality, but no less important for that. In fact, precisely because we live in post-lapsarian time, we have to focus on justice, not on love and community. Now I want to argue eventually against this theological position, but here I want to point to problems in Rawls and in such theological appropriations of Rawls, even granting for the sake of argument the remedial status of justice.

First of all, there is a profound difference between the claim that human society has a plurality of ends and the claim that it has no common end. The plurality of ends is an empirical matter: we do pursue different ends, the ends often conflict with each others, and our pursuits of ends are often mutually blocked if not incompatible. This observation actually belongs to what Rawls calls the objective circumstances of justice. But it does not follow from this empirical claim that we have no ends in common. It only follows that, even if we had one end or some ends in common, we do not have all ends in common. The empirical point of a plurality of ends is enough to establish the inquiry of economics and to require certain forms of justice without any reference to fallen conditions or to the absence of a common end. The assertion that we have no common end is, by contrast, axiomatic, a virtual article of faith. It abounds in modern economic literature as a stipulation of what economists must assume; and it guarantees a kind of remedial view of economic justice, where the economist occupies a position of the realist who can always say to the latest proposal for economic transformation, "Well, that may be a marvellous ideal but given the realities of economics and of human nature (i.e, that we have no common end), this is what we have to settle for."

But, second, Rawls's apparent remedial view of justice has a surprising outcome: He argues that, if the background institutions are just, a social union will grow in which mutuality and cooperation will become ends in themselves, i.e., in which the mutually disinterested pursuit of private ends in Part One of *A Theory of Justice* is transformed into the mutually interested ends of Part Three. This again is Kant: If you construct a constitution cleverly enough, even a race of devils will find themselves cooperating in spite of their intentions. Moreover, in such a society virtue and a good will are likely to be rewarded, a harmony between noumenal good will and phenomenal consequences is more likely, whereas in an unjust society actions done from a good will surely will not be rewarded and therefore will be rare. Behind this are two inspirations: Rousseau's conviction that social arrangements are responsible for most social discord (the disharmony of ends); and the general Enlightenment confidence that in spite of the apparent discord between individual action and social consequence there is a higher rationality which ultimately unites our actions. Rousseau's dictum that "we must be forced to be free" is picked up in Kant's constitutional engineering and in the artifice of Rawls's "original position": they force a particular outcome.[17]

This aspect of Rawls is ignored in most theological appropriations of his work. Theological pessimists want a remedial view of justice without the remedy—they may find Part Three of *A Theory of Justice* attractive but don't really believe it will come to be since, in spite of Rawls's insistence that his theory is compatible with some forms of either capitalism or socialism, he is essentially describing a more socialist society than we now have in the U.S.

In contrast, theological optimists—and I think Cauthen counts among these—want the remedy without the remedial view of justice: they want more social cooperation and mutuality without viewing justice as remedial and therefore as morally prior to good. In Cauthen's paper the fact of common good is asserted without empirical or theological argument and a basic optimism is displayed in the essentially utilitarian and progressive form of Cauthen's discussion of the priority problem among his three first principles (maximizing good, maximizing freedom and maximizing social equality). (p. 103) To the extent that this characterization is true, we are simply back in the old debate between theological pessimists who argue that some version of free market capitalism is the best we can have and optimists who think we might push for socialism.

I cannot be sure that Cauthen wants to sit simply on one side of this old debate, although his emphasis on individuals and his utilitarian understanding of maximization in the face of priority problems seem less drawn from process assumptions than from an affinity with the optimism of liberal utilitarianism. More importantly, his assertion that we have a common good is not a synthesis of Nozick and Rawls but a fundamentally different kind of position. And his neglect of the central role of the remedial view of justice and of the problems it tries to solve leads him to a position that sounds only optimistic. In my mind, his own position would be stronger if connected to a more nuanced theological delineation of the circumstances of justice.

Theologically, there are two issues here: the first is to clarify the relationship between justice on the one hand and good and love on the other. The second is to relate this to questions of finitude, sin, and discord. Clearly I cannot do this in the context of this response but several clarificatory points may be made.

First of all, it should be evident that the notion that justice is a remedial virtue, a second-best social principle, although enjoying a certain popularity in some forms of Protestantism, is by no means the only theological construal of it—indeed, it is not even the most common construal. Within the Roman Catholic tradition as well as within Calvinism (not to mention much of the Old Testament) there is a strong claim that justice is constitutive of any society independently of notions of sin or the Fall, and that it is indispensible to the workings of love. Cauthen, it seems to me, clearly stands within this tradition: justice is constitutive of any society that is conceivable.

Second, justice may well be complex, having to do not only with the objective circumstances of justice (that is, with any society under conditions of moderate scarcity) but also with the deformations caused by defective human nature, not just in terms of rationality but in terms of will and social deformation, i.e., with the circumstances of human sin. The central problem is learning to talk theologically about a common human end while at the same time recognizing the deformities; and to talk about concrete social possibilities in the light of both. Here again, there are important nuances and differences among theological positions. But given process thought's constitutive understanding of justice, I want to discuss briefly the work of Michael Walzer as a possibly more fruitful conversation partner for it and for theological ethics.

Michael Walzer and the Circumstances of Justice

I must confine myself to a highly schematic presentation of Walzer's position in *Spheres of Justice*. His own understanding of the circumstances of justice, although not explicitly so called, is as follows. As human beings we conceive, create, share, distribute, and exchange a host of goods, and how we do this depends on the meanings we attach to those goods. Justice is the art of differentiation among various kinds of goods (such as power, money, love, security, education), and the determination of principles of distribution appropriate to each kind of sphere. It follows from this that justice is not an independent norm or principle that can be established without reference to shared ends. On the contrary, principles of justice can be articulated only in relation to the shared meanings of a society and these shared meanings are deeply connected to the goods we conceive, create, distribute, and share, the goods which give us our concrete historical identities. In short, to create and to distribute goods is to have a principle of justice; and to have a principle of justice is already to have shared meanings and a theory of goods, that is, to exist in a particular historical community. People who live in historical communities already have

> a history of transactions, not only with one another, but also with the moral and material world in which they live. Without such a history, which begins at birth, they wouldn't be men and women in any recognizable sense, and they wouldn't have the first notion of how to go about the business of giving, allocating, and exchanging goods.[18]

This is a historical notion of goods and of justice—Walzer denies that there are any universal goods (in fact, I think he is ambiguous on this point[19])—with the clear implication that justice is relative to the social meanings of different cultures as well as to different historical periods of the same culture. There can be neither one distributive principle for all social goods, nor the same distributive principle for the same goods for all time. To take just one example: the distribution of the good of education will differ from one culture to another and from one historical period to another because the good of education will mean different things in different cultures and at different times. A good must be distributed for relevant reasons, that is, relevant to its social meaning or meanings.[20] This is a complex, relative notion of justice in which the substantive distributive principles will change as the complexity of a people or culture changes, that is, as the circumstances of justice change.

But there is one principle of justice which does not change: this is the principle that the distributive pattern in one sphere of goods should not interfere with the distributive pattern of another sphere, which is to say that the goods of one sphere may not dominate another. Walzer states it thus: "No social good x should be distributed to men and women who possess some other good y merely because they possess y and without regard to the meaning of x."[21] Political office should not be determined by money, the distribution of education should not be determined by political power or wealth, security should not be based on kinship, and the like. What is especially interesting about this principle is that it is Walzer's remedial principle. It recognizes that the differentiations among goods and the boundaries between their spheres will always be threatened by the tendency toward domination, by the invasion of one sphere by another. Human domination is mediated by social goods, an "elaborate social creation, the work of many hands, mixing reality and symbol." "A dominant good is converted into another good, into many others, in accordance with what often appears to be a natural process but is in fact magical, a kind of social alchemy."[22]

Justice therefore has at least two tasks, corresponding to two different circumstances of justice: it has the constitutive but ongoing task of determining the boundaries between spheres of goods, and the distributive principles relevant to each because of the circumstance that we are historical, social beings who continually create and recreate new goods and social meanings; and it has the remedial task of guarding the boundaries established, of rebuilding the walls broken by invasions of one sphere by another, of correcting the illegitimate social alchemies, that is, the circumstances of social deformities.

This brief account does not begin to do justice to Walzer. I have barely touched, for example, on the notion of complex equality (as opposed to the simple equality of liberalism) which is here presupposed, and I have not been able to say anything of Walzer's intellectual background, the combining of anthropology, Marxist politics, and Judaism, which is a fascinating contrast to Rawls's sources in Kantianism, economics, and psychology. But perhaps this is enough to provide the basis for some concluding remarks about the possible fits between Walzer and process views, and to make some suggestions about the implications of such a direction for economic justice and economic organization.

(1) With respect to the circumstances of justice, Walzer offers an interpretation which is theologically more satisfying than those of either Nozick or Rawls. It permits us to speak of the task of justice as constitutive of any human society, simply because of the circumstances of time and space, the exigencies of concrete historical communities. Moreover, it connects this task both to the differentiation of ends within society *and* to the common meanings a society shares, which is to say that it does not confuse the empirical reality of multiple interests and ends with the question of whether there is a common end. But it also takes seriously the remedial task of

justice, and even though this is not theologically construed, it is open to theological interpretation. Indeed, I am convinced that Walzer's construal of justice and the circumstances of justice hold together best within a theological framework, but that is for another time.

Here I only note that Walzer's complex view of justice is closer to the complexity of theological discussions of justice. It is certainly closer than those remedial views which link the fallen condition of the human race to the necessity of capitalism; and it is closer than optimistic views of human social organization that do not take human deformations seriously. Walzer's view of the task of justice is that we require constant adjustments in our social organization as conditions and social meanings change; and constant vigilance against domination. The idea that justice is constitutive of any conceivable human society without lapsarian assumptions is, I believe, also consistent with process assumptions. It is less clear to me that process thought is as interested in remedial justice, the vigilance against domination and the correction of social deformities. At least in the case of Cauthen's paper I do not see such attention but there should be no principled reason why process thinking could not encompass such attention.[23] But if process thought is to enter into fruitful dialogue with economics, it must attend to this dimension of the circumstances of justice.

(2) The emphasis on social goods and social meanings is not merely a relational understanding of society; it transforms the usual terms of the debate between individual and society, or the relation of individuals to others. The primary focus of analysis is neither the individual nor the social group—it is rather the social meanings and goods which mediate individual and group, which indeed give rise historically to conceptions such as "individual" and "society." This emphasis involves what is now called in several disciplines a "decentering" of the self, where the self is understood to be constituted not so much by others as by language and social goods. This is sharply different from Nozick and Rawls—it cannot be gotten from a synthesis of them. If I understand process thought correctly, the decentering of the self has real affinity with the notion of "the fallacy of misplaced concreteness." Cauthen's thought seems still circumscribed by the assumptions of liberal individualism.

(3) Walzer's construal of distributive justice moves attention away from the question of economic organization to the question of the relationship between economic institutions and other spheres and institutions of society. The fundamental question to be asked of the market, for example, is not whether its distributions are fair but which goods it may appropriately distribute and which not—which exchanges are blocked.[24] We need to know, for example, whether medical care should be distributed by the market or by other means, and in order to do this we have to inquire into

the meaning of medicine and of the good of health. Such inquiry has implications for forms of economic organization, of course, but it does not begin with the question abstractly—rather, it begins with concrete social meanings and concrete institutional arrangements. Such questions in principle must be asked in both capitalist and socialist societies. In any case, the approach does not begin with the capitalism-socialism debate and I consider this an immense plus.

(4) Finally, we need to underline the implications of a point made earlier: that Walzer's conception of distributive and economic justice has no universal substantive principles.[25] This is a marked break with the most commonly articulated views of justice since the Enlightenment in which justice is believed to transcend social systems and local moralities, permitting evaluative comparisons of social systems. Justice in this Enlightenment sense not only permits toleration of wide varieties of beliefs and customs; it in fact requires, as in Rawls, an agnosticism about ends and goods.[26] If we abandon the notion that conceptions of justice can be had independently of the goods we conceive, create, share, and exchange, then we must abandon our agnosticism about the human end—indeed, we will have to plunge directly into discussions of it. We will have to get back into the business of making cognitive claims about the world and about good. This seems to me what process thought wants to do. Theologically, it is what we need to do if we are to have anything to say about justice and economics.

Notes and References

1. This paper was originally given as a response to Kenneth Cauthen's paper, "Process Philosophy and the Social Order: A Freedom-Equality Model," given at the Annual Meeting of the American Academy of Religion, November 22, 1986, Atlanta, Georgia. I have made minor changes in response to Cauthen's revisions.

2. John Rawls, *A Theory of Justice* (Cambridge: Harvard University Press, 1971); and Robert Nozick, *Anarchy, State, and Utopia* (New York: Basic Books, 1974).

3. Michael Walzer, *Spheres of Justice* (New York: Basic Books, 1983).

4. See especially n. 12 of Cauthen's essay.

5. Rawls clearly wants to distinguish his understanding of social union from organic theories of society, rejecting "perfectionist" and "organic" conceptions. His intention is to argue for community from *individualist* assumptions, i.e., from non-organic assumptions. See, e.g., p. 520, and the whole of section 41. Whether this distinction holds is another question.

6. Michael Sandel, *Liberalism and the Limits of Justice* (Cambridge: Cambridge University Press, 1982).

7. Kant, "Perpetual Peace," in *On History*, ed. Lewis White Beck (Indianapolis: Bobs-Merrill, 1957), pp. 112-3. Rawls's "original position" is clearly designed as the functional

equivalent of Kant's cunning use of the laws of nature. On the priority of right over good, and the central role of the "well-ordered society," see Rawls, *A Theory of Justice*, esp. pp. 3ff; 31ff; 395ff; and 446-462.

8. Here is Kant's version: "For it is the pecularity of morals, especially with respect to its principles of public law and hence in relation to a politics known a priori, that the less it makes conduct depend on the proposed end, i.e., the intended material or moral advantage, the more it agrees with it in general." "Perpetual Peace," pp. 125-6. Similar points may be found in his "Idea for a Universal History from a Cosmopolitan Point of View," *On History*, pp. 11-26. The parallel here to Adam Smith's "invisible hand" is extraordinary and perhaps explains why Smith's version of utilitarianism is so easily taken up by Kantian liberals: both wish to make social order independent of human intentions.

9. Nozick, p. 10.

10. See Nozick, Part II, on distributive justice and related problems.

11. The Preface to *Anarchy, State, and Utopia* begins: "Individuals have rights, and there are things no person or group may do to them (without violating their rights)." This premise is never examined or supported in the arguments of the book. When I was an undergraduate at Harvard in the early 1960s, the *Crimson* would run an old piece each examination period on how to get A's on papers and examinations. One of the many devices counselled was "the overwhelming assumption," ranking in its effect alongside "the unsupported generalization." It is good to know that the technique is still alive and well at Harvard.

12. The discussion is in section 22 of *A Theory of Justice*, pp. 126ff. The account follows Hume's in *A Treatise of Human Nature*, bk. III, pt II, sec. ii, and *An Enquiry Concerning the Principles of Morals*, sec. III, pt. I.

13. But they are controversial within some debates about economic justice. In particular, economists and philosophers do not agree on how moderate scarcity is, or how long scarcity will continue to be a problem. The debate about the limits of growth, to name just one, is a debate about the objective circumstances of economic justice.

14. Rawls, p. 127.

15. Rawls, "Justice as Fairness," *Philosophy, Politics and Society*, Second Series, ed. by Peter Laslett and W.G. Runciman (Oxford: Blackwell, 1972), p. 142.

16. Sandel, p. 31.

17. But it is important to note that Rawls has none of the eighteenth century deist assumptions to guarantee a transmutation of individual intention into social harmony. For him, this work is done by economists' game theory.

18. Walzer, p. 8. Pp. 6-10 give an overview of the theory of goods.

19. He is ambiguous because of the special place he accords to recognition and to political goods. He is Hegelian insofar as recognition is a good that we all require and which his theory of justice is designed to protect: see chapter 11. And politics is not merely a sphere of goods but is *the* sphere in which decisions about boundaries among goods are made: see note, bottom of p. 15. The forms of recognition and politics may vary culturally and historically but he has in these conceptions the basis for some kind of theory of universal goods. This may provide a point of contact with process thought. I am grateful to Franklin Gamwell for suggesting a connection.

20. Walzer here follows Bernard Williams, "The Idea of Equality," in *Philosophy, Politics and Society*, Second Series, ed. by Peter Laslett and W.G. Runciman (Oxford, Blackwell, 1962), pp. 110-131. In Williams, however, the relevant reasons seem dependent upon an intrinsic meaning of the goods while in Walzer the meanings are always social.

21. Walzer, p. 20.

22. Walzer, p. 11.

23. I am grateful to Franklin Gamwell for helping me to see this point in response to comments in the draft of this paper.

24. See Walzer, Chapter 4, "Money and Commodities."

25. It does have a formal universal principle: that the distribution of goods from one sphere may not distort or dominate the distribution of goods in another sphere. As Walzer himself notes, this principle is as nonrelative as the classical principle that justice is a matter of giving each person his or her due. But as with the classical principle, there is no universal substantive principle of distribution.

26. Because of various criticisms, including especially that of Michael Sandel, Rawls has more recently moved away from his apparent Kantian universalism, arguing for a far more historical conception of justice in which his own theory is appropriate only in societies already having liberal democratic traditions. See Rawls, "Justice as Fairness: Political not Metaphysical," *Philosophy and Public Affairs* 14, no. 3 (1985), pp. 223-251. In my view, this is a significant modification of the original theory: it implies not merely an agnosticism about ends and goods but leaves only historical foundations for the principles of justice themselves, for "right."

CHAPTER 7

Beyond Production
and Class:
A Process Project in
Economic Theory

Robert Cummings Neville

I.

The invention of mathematical physics during the European Renaissance successfully united the modes of quantitative and qualitative thinking so admired by the Greeks and became the model for theoretical understanding. It had the disastrous effect, however, of excluding valuational thinking from theoretical status. Since then, politics, ethics, aesthetics, and normative aspects of philosophy of education, art, and religion have had an impossible time defending themselves as properly cognitive in light of the Renaissance or "modern" mode.[1]

The social sciences have been in a particularly embarrassing bind, vacillating between a hypocritical positivist claim to value-freedom and a social engineer/religious prophet's claim that all theory should be frankly biased to serve some ideology. New paradigms of thinking that reconstruct a proper relation of valuation to quantitative and qualitative analysis are imperative before the obviously value-laden subjects of the social sciences can be approached with appropriately formed theories.[2] The social sciences cannot be theoretically framed areas of discourse until a new paradigm of theory is adopted. I want here to discuss some of the problems that lie in the way of this task insofar as it is applied to economic theory.

If indeed a valuative paradigm for social science theory is required, then the conceptual apparatus of economic theory should display and explain the values involved in its subject matter. By "values" I don't mean only the values commonly identified as economic, such as use, exchange, or labor value. I mean also the historical and civilizational values of economic arrangements, values vis-a-vis the environment, values in the impact of the economic system on other social systems such as the law, religion, politics, social and class structure, and gender relations; and most particularly the values embodied in the different economic roles of producer, consumer, manager, etc.; the values these roles have in and for the individuals who play them relative to their degree of wealth, power, social standing, ambitions, and inherited cultures.

Except in special circumstances, "value" does not mean the "idea" by which a person or group estimates the actual value of something, as when we speak of the "values" a person or culture stands for. It means the worth achieved in the thing itself. A proper theoretical understanding should indicate how an economic system disposes worths in its diverse values, and explain to whom, in what ways, and by what means it achieves that.

Most approaches to economic theory, such as the Marxist and Liberal capitalist, in part recognize this need to attend to values.[3] But in larger part, the ways by which the major economic theories highlight specific values are implicit and underground. An opposing theoretical perspective is often needed to point out that a given theory's structure highlights some values and obscures others, thus serving some parochial interest. Overall, it is fair to say that our major theoretical approaches to economics obscure rather than display and explain the values in their subject matters. The reason for this is that both Liberal capitalism and Marxism, as well as socialist and mixed economies, share the metaphysical assumptions of modern philosophy that separate facts from values, believing that theories should explain only the facts.

Process philosophy has provided an alternative to these metaphysical assumptions, an alternative that recognizes facts as achievements and embodiments of values, and that can offer new directions to economic theory. My purpose in this paper is to explore what can be called the "axiological requirements" of a proper approach to economic theory, building on a base of process philosophy. The classical philosophy of Whitehead and his students broke the ground; if extensions, modifications, and criticisms of his theory need to be made in the course of planting, cultivating and harvesting the implications of process philosophy for social science, that is only a tribute to Whitehead's revolutionary importance. Indeed, Paul Weiss, one of the most important contributors to a viable contemporary understanding of persons and social structures, was a student of Whitehead's. Of course there are many requirements besides the axiological ones for a viable economic theory, requirements that economists will recognize far more readily than the axiological ones. The axiological argument, however, may be the beginning of a dialogue between economics and metaphysical philosophy.

To argue for an axiological dimension to economic theory is of course to call for a restructuring of the conceptual apparatus of social science. But it is also, and more fundamentally, to make a metaphysical point. The reason that Marxist, capitalist, and other modern Western analyses deal with values in such restrained ways is the limitation of their metaphysics. By metaphysics here I mean the broad range of vague, abstract concepts that are assumed when an economic theory formulates its own assertions, concepts about the nature of being a thing, of relation, causation, space-time, change, and so forth. These metaphysical notions are informally vague in the sense that they can be assumed without examination and without even the consciousness that they are assumed at all. The metaphysical notions are formally vague in the sense that a more specific level of theory must be added to them before they can be applied to concrete phenomena.[4] Causation is such a vague notion, and it needs specification as economic causation (according to one theory or another, e.g. Marxist historical materialism), material mechanics, psychological motivation, or some other, before we can apply it. What really happens, of course, is that we slip in some specifying theory unnoticed. The specifying, relatively concrete theoretical levels are also vague, though less so; they too need to be specified by more particular levels of analysis, perhaps including appeal to paradigm individual cases. Hidden metaphysical assumptions, and hidden ways of parsing these in specific applications, are the original "false consciousness" or ideology, though not necessarily with (hidden) malevolence.

Although I claim that both Liberal capitalism and Marxist theories share that part of the metaphysics of modern philsophy asserting a separation of facts from values, there are important metaphysical differences between them. A brief exploration of those differences is in order, first, to illustrate the level of abstractness at which philosophy can provide a non-modernist alternative in economics and, second, to formulate criticisms justifying the need to move beyond those forms of economic analysis to an axiological one.

Marxist analyses often criticize the capitalist mode of production for dehumanizing people because wage labor—the meaning of labor in a theory emphasizing price, supply, and demand—recognizes nothing more of individuals than their capacity to be place-holders in an impersonal economic system, and steals the due rewards of their labors.[5] Expressed in metaphysical language the personal lives of individuals are externally related to the economic system in capitalism, and irrelevant to it so long as the individuals are capable of playing the system's roles. On the other hand, the economic system has a deep effect on people's lives and thus is internally related to the individuals within it. Capitalism thus presupposes at the metaphysical level an asymmetrical relation between individuals and the economic system: the system is internal to the individuals whereas the individuals are external to the system. This is unjust on the one hand, Marxists say, because individuals are at the mercy of the system and exploited in their labor, and unstable on the other hand because the system is essentially untouchable by human wit and blindly runs according to its own evolving laws, tending (according to classical Marxism) toward overexpansion and crash. With respect to the values of things, the asymmetry in relations determines that the individuals must internalize the abstract values of the economic system but cannot re-embody their own human values in the system: the system is strictly impersonal.

The opposing metaphysical critique capitalism would make is that Marxist theory mistakenly assumes symmetrical relations between individuals and the economic system, internal in both directions. That is, the personal element is now supposed by the Marxists to be incorporated into the system through joint management, etc., and the system, now made personal, is incorporated back into each individual.[6] Symmetrical internal relations constitute both sides as mere analytically distinct elements in a totalitarian whole for Marxism, according to capitalism. Value would belong to the totality, the state or collective, and not to individuals, as capitalism thinks necessary. For individuals to be valuable in themselves, according to capitalism, they must be somewhat external to the economic system. Whether and where they enter the economic system must be external to the system itself, a matter of the individuals' choices.

The metaphysical reason for capitalism's insistence that individuals remain somewhat external to the system is its deep commitment to a particular theory of what it is to be a thing, a theory perhaps naively but influentially articulated by Locke.[7] To be a thing is to be a possessing of properties, not to be some underlying substratum that does the possessing. A person, on this theory, exists in the owning of personal things, primarily one's acquired experiences and body, secondarily one's labor and the fruits of it; a person exists finally in one's powers over one's ownership as exercised in transferring title, buying, and selling. Capitalism's culture can admit that an economic system is internal to a person's nature, but only as the medium through which the person exercises ownership, which is both self-expression and self-control. By the same token, the system itself doesn't include the individuals because it is only the medium of transferring ownership, not ownership itself. Only individuals can own, and the system, not being an individual, is a personally neutral set of relations. Value within the capitalist metaphysics is a function of individual willingness to buy and sell on the one hand and of the system's arranging reciprocal willingness to sell and buy on the other. The system itself has no intrinsic values, only the function of relating individual wills so as to fix value.[8]

The metaphysical reason for Marxism's sharp attention to internal and external relations has to do with its conception of identity and change. In general agreement with Hegel, Marxist analysis interprets the identity of a thing in terms of how it has internalized things so as to overcome oppositions, and in terms of how it alienates things and thus stands in further oppositions. From this perspective an isolated individual could hardly claim to have achieved ownership of anything but his or her own brute nature. Both human socialization and ownership of goods are achieved not by the dialectical activities of isolated individuals but by a complex social process. Values are to be determined not by exchange alone but by the various factors of achievement-overcoming-alienation within the social process. A person's work takes its value less from its contributions to the person's own existential definition than from the roles it plays in the dialectic of the situation. What one notes about the value of something in a Marxist analysis is its factual character as overcoming certain oppositions or alienations and falling into certain others, not the nature and degree of worth.

I believe we need to move beyond a capitalist economics of production limited to the values demanded by a metaphysics of ownership. Without questioning the worth of the individual liberty upon which Liberal capitalism insists, the metaphysics of ownership is simply too partial to give an adequate account of personal life. The Marxist criticism of capitalism's brutality is generally well taken, to judge from experience. The relatively powerless people in a capitalist situation are made to conform to such appalling conditions that their freedom to trade their goods or labor is worth too little. The powerful, on the other hand, become seduced into believing that they are fulfilled by the successful playing of economic roles alone, and all other domains of life get shoved into the private sphere or diminished entirely, resulting in boredom and alienation.[9] An economic theory that improves upon capitalism requires a metaphysical foundation that expresses more generally the nature of individual lives in terms of many connections, systematic or otherwise, people typically have with the world. In particular, an improved metaphysics must be able to represent not only how economic values are responsive to the sense in which people are what they own, but also how economic and other values impact upon all the typical dimensions of human life.

I believe also that we need to move beyond the Marxist economics that relates individuals to the economic system by treating them as members of an economically defined social class. Although Marx and Marxists have never said that individuals are nothing but ciphers in their social class, they have often indicated that the other dimensions of human experience are somewhat blindly run by the dynamics of class roles: hence, the therapeutic emphasis on class solidarity. Yet people take part in many systems, and in unsystematic connections, besides economics. No matter how powerful one's theory of social class, it's unlikely that any one set of variables defining social class would give a complete coordination of all the social systems to which a person belongs. Marxist social analysis and prediction have run afoul of uncoordinated ethnic systems in Russia, vivid religion in Poland, the American assimilation of unionism to the love of lodges rather than to revolutionary politics, and so forth. The concept of social class, then, is inadequate both for a total definition of human life and for a far-reaching determination of how people are related to an economic system, for any such relation can be mediated by religion, ethnicity, or any number of other systems or historically particular conditions with which economic participation must be integrated. What's required of an economic theory improving upon Marxism is a metaphysics showing that individuals can be members of many systems at once, that these memberships bind the people together in some ways but not all ways, and that the values transferred along the varius systems present both necessities and opportunities for the ways in which they can affect the people involved.

A reminder is in order here about the focus of this discussion on the axiological requirements of an economic theory. Other requirements have to do with understanding how not to go broke, how to relate effort to resources, and how to supply basic needs.

II.

Process philosophy, classically developed by Alfred North Whitehead, has provided the most far-reaching rethinking of metaphysical ideas since the Renaissance invention of modernity.[10] I propose to adopt three of those ideas here for purposes of reshaping economic theory, and then to add three points of my own that move to a metaphysics of human life in social systems.

1. Whitehead's most important and noticed contribution was his model of causation and substance. As is well known, he proposed to say that a fundamental actuality, which he called an actual occasion, comes into being by prehending or including as its own material stuff the actual entities of the past.[11] All of the actual occasions in the emerging occasion's past are taken up initially; but the process of coming-to-be, "concrescence," sorts out some to eliminate and some to keep, and among the latter dismembers and recombines them until a singular, definite, individual integration of them is

achieved. The new entity then is the integration that includes the past entities as modified by the integration plus the emerging entity's own contributions involved in the integration. The emerging entity depends upon the previously realized actualities in its past for the conditions to which it must conform and the resources out of which to make itself. Its own unique contribution is the existential power of integration, resulting in what Whitehead called subjective form. Once the entity is fully emerged, its subjective existential power ceases and its achieved actuality is objectified so as to be available to condition future entities.

In complex entities of the sort comprising human experiences, the means of integration include composite rearrangements of conditions so as to constitute consciousness and what Whitehead called presentational immediacy. This allows for the envisionment of a spatio-temporal field with a future and with objects at a distance, both of which can figure in the integration process.

Charles Hartshorne has developed a subtle philosophy from this model emphasizing the asymmetry in the causal process. An earlier actual occasion conditions a later one, but not vice versa except in the exceptional case in which the earlier occasion anticipates the later and chooses to react to it. Hartshorne draws out the proper implications of this doctrine for chance in the universe and for human freedom.[12]

Accepting Hartshorne's view so far, I want to shift the stress and emphasize the continuity of value from one occasion to the next. According to Whitehead, an actual entity is an achievement of value. It includes all the values of the entities that it has integrated (as modified in the integration), plus the values emergent in the integration itself, in the having of those values together in just that way. What Whitehead stressed is that the entire actual entity, value and all, enters into the subsequent entities it conditions. If the subsequent entity dismembers it so as to distort or lose its value, that's the responsibility of the particular subsequent process. On the initial metaphysical level, every entity contributes its achieved intrinsic value to the entities it conditions. The conditioned entities may have some limitations as to what elements of value may be retained and re-objectified in their own nature, and they may have some choice about that. But the massive stability of nature consists in the regularities and continuities of values transmitted through multiple lines of causation. This conception of nature as the structured transmission and revaluing of values is the beginning of a cosmology that surmounts the fact-value distinction in modern metaphysics.[13] A theory of a subject matter that acknowledges and traces out these structured value-transmissions and revaluations would transcend the limited conception of theory characterizing the modern period.

There is a decisive limitation to Whitehead's idea of actual occasions, namely that they are momentary. His view cannot give an account of an individual that is temporally thick, with a past, present, and future dynamically shifting with the date; the closest approximation to such an individual is a particular aggregate or society of occasions with highly personal order. The genius of Whitehead's conception, however, is that he shows how causal efficacy and value enter into any present moment of decisive actualization. His point holds good no matter whether the relevant past is another individual or an individual's own past. Therefore his account of occasions can be treated as abstract relative to an account of individuals that are discursive through time, and it would still hold good at the abstract level. His theory will be supplemented below with a theory of discursive or temporally thick individuals.

2. The second major idea I'll take from process philosophy is an enlargement of an aspect of the first, namely that of the freedom of an actual entity to value its conditions up or down. Within the limits set by the conditions it prehends, an entity might be able to integrate them in more than one way. The ways differ from one another not only structurally but in the values to which they give importance. One option might keep certain of the past values intact, enhancing them even by their surroundings, while paring down other past conditions with their values to subordinate instrumental roles, and eliminating yet other past conditions entirely. An alternate option for integration might have a quite different arrangement of what is valuable. With respect to a given conditioning value, this is what Whitehead called valuing up or valuing down.[14]

Process philosophers have sometimes overestimated the extent of this freedom. So far as natural sciences have determined, a great many actual entities are so rigidly conditioned by past entities that there is only one way in which they can integrate their components and come to actuality. This rigidity is lawfulness in nature. Furthermore, it is the source of an important dimension of freedom for human beings, namely, the freedom to exercise control over the intended but distant future results of actions. We employ natural regularities and use craft to increase them in order to gain control; freedom of alternate integration is the last thing we want in the machines we use, for instance. Where the past conditions are partially indeterminate in how they can be integrated, perhaps not all kinds of indeterminacy are helpful to human freedom. The past conditions have to be indeterminate with respect to the important choices for the emerging individual, and this requires being quite determinate with respect to those processes that set up the important choices. For instance, physiological and social systems, insofar as they enter an occasion of choice as conditions, must be stable and regular if the emerging occasion is to deal effectively with them.

The point I want to stress about choice is that although each conditioning element enters an occasion with its own intrinsic value, that value must be modified in order to be intregated with the values of the others, and the modifications might be diminishments as well as enhancements. Where nature is tightly organized according to rigid law, values tend to be transferred intact because the conditions limiting one entity are pretty much the same as those limiting the other entities. But in human affairs where there seems to be a wide range of free play and non-integration, the values of the past can be transformed radically as they pass through agents and institutions. Questions of justice and morality have to do with the transformation of values in process of transmission. Whitehead's account of transmission of values is the means to surmount the exclusion of values from the scientific theories of modernity.

3. The third idea to be taken from process philosophy is that an entity can play roles in many systems at once, and that it may value up or value down these roles, within the limits set by the collection of past conditions. The heart of this idea is that a large group of things can be organized according to a pattern in which each thing plays a role unique to itself. On this conception, each entity plays its role not blindly but by virtue of prehending the overall patterns organizing all the entities and determining for itself the particular role. Part of the solidity of nature is that whole systematic patterns can be "massively inherited" as Whitehead put it, and thus passed down from one generation to another.[15] Of course there are patterns within patterns, tissues within organs, organs within organisms, organisms within environments, structured environments within ecosystems, and so on. Systematic parts of larger systems may have something of a life of their own, only accidentally locked into the larger system and thus setting the larger system at jeopardy of dissolution. Systems can be described as more or less tight, depending on whether the conditions making their parts possible are more or less identical with the conditions that surround the whole.

Social systems such as the economic, religious, or judiciary are not tight. They encompass subsystems: of material artifacts such as trade goods, church buildings, etc.; of ideas and images; of institutions that divide people into social roles by habits, by exercise of authority, by force, by human necessities such as hunger, safety and the like; of a spread of natural and geographical conditions. Each of these subsystems is affected by conditions other than economics, and thus has a partially independent career. Furthermore, the large social systems sometimes but only partially interface with one another, so that economics is affected by politics and religion, but not wholly determined by them.

An individual can play one or many roles in a social system such as the economic, for instance as producer, consumer, manager, or "necessary victim," and the roles themselves may be complex, producing many things, consuming some things but not others, and so forth. Each of these roles in all its nuances conveys values through the system to the individual who must accept them with the conditions necessary to play the role. Insofar as the role-conditions are accepted, the transmitted values partially define the person. Not only does the individual receive and embody the values in the role, but the very playing of the role is to transmit back to the system the role's own contribution. So the system is affected by the individual. More important, if there is more than one way to play the role, then the system is affected by the individual's choice. And if the choices are affected by values coming from the outside the system in question, the individual might make unique and novel contributions to the system. "Unique and novel" is not to imply better.

An individual can play diverse roles in many social systems at once, and this fact is the source of much human freedom. Individuals value up and value down different systems, while playing more or less acceptable roles in all. One person gives priority to job, another to family, another to creative pursuits. Not all social situations allow much free play here—one of the pains of poverty is that it does not. But in most social situations we can both value the diverse systems up or down and also achieve greater or lesser harmony and resonance among them. Wholeness of life is not only playing all the important roles well but also bringing some mutual reinforcement to the lot of them, as differently played over the years of a changing career.

A theory that both traces the transmission of values through patterns of social organization and understands also how individuals integrate their multiple roles is true social theory. European theories focusing on individuals' intentions may miss the regularity in social patterns, and American theories stressing structure and function may miss the individuals. A properly formulated social theory would focus on the transmissions of values both through systems and within individuals participating in systems. The process model of entities integrating diverse massively inherited systems is a good beginning.

III.

Whitehead's model, and that of most of his followers, deals mainly with individual actual entities prehending and playing roles in patterned societies of actual entities. Yet in my exposition I have slipped over into speaking of individuals as if they were people and of roles as if they were recognizable organized processes that take long periods to play and involve many groups of actual entities and larger individuals. With my own three points supplementing Whitehead's let me now backtrack and make the translation from actual entities to people and affairs of the human scale. These points sustain the positive contributions of process philosophy, but abandon its negative polemic against substance philosophies.[16]

1. According to Whitehead's process philosophy, the sense in which a single actual entity constitutes part of a larger organism with other entities in its past consists in the fact that each of the entities displays a pattern common to the others.[17] The pattern may be relatively simple as when a group of entities exists as a unified and enduring vector of force; or it can be as complex as a system in which different entities play different roles. There is nothing except this reiteration of pattern to discriminate between the continuities with each other of the occasions in an enduring person and the continuities of external occasions with those within the person, according to Whitehead. Yet the distinction between intrapersonal relations and person-environment interrelations is enormously important. For instance, in morals, a person's earlier actions give a moral character to that person's later life, depending on what the individual later does, yet without a coercive reiteration of pattern. Another person cannot so obligate an individual in the same ways, although other people and events provide the content for a person's obligations. Without a device for articulating the continuity or endurance of persons, process philosophy is not in a position to show how persons can make up identity of their own while participating in many social systems.

Therefore, it is necessary to develop new terms to give a categoreal definition of what I called above a "discursive individual." A discursive individual is a concrete, temporally thick being. Such a being exists in three modes of time: past, present, and future. Existence in the present may be modelled on process philosophy's account of the actual occasion, but that existence is only an abstract part of the whole existence of the person. This point assumes that time indeed has three modes, each with an integrity and essential features of its own, and that discursive individuals relate to time by having the three temporal modes. Process philosophy's signal contribution is having explicated the internal nature of the present moment, but to the relative neglect of the past and future, or rather to the reduction of past and future to their contributions to the present.[18] My present purpose is not to explore a non-process theory of time but rather to show how discursive individuals can have a past and future related to an ever-changing present.

For this purpose we need to adopt a supplementary metaphysical distinction between conditional and essential features of a thing. Consider that to be determinate is to be complex, both determinately different from something else and positively something in itself. Let us call the features of a determinate thing by virtue of which it relates to and is determinate with respect to other things, its conditional features. Those features by virtue of which it has a positive integrity of its own are its essential features. The essential and conditional features require each other. Without the essential features the conditional features would reduce to the other things without remainder. Without the conditional features the essential features would have no determinate content by which to distinguish the thing from other things. A thing then is an integration of essential and conditional features, and these must be determinate with respect to each other by virtue of their own component essential and conditional features, all the way down.

Instantiated in the cosmological model of process philosophy, the past actual entities entering the coming-to-be of an emerging entity are the conditional features; these are harmonized with the essential features by virtue of being modified or eliminated in the process of conscrescence. The essential features are those that determine the subjective, existential process of concrescence, those spontaneous acts of valuation that value up or down, that disassemble, pare, combine, and harmonize conditions so as to work them into final integration. The spontaneous essential features may give rise to novel properties, which Whitehead called "subjective form" or "eternal objects of the subjective species," that themselves are objectified and may be prehended as conditions by subsequent entities.[19] But within the emergence of the occasion I want to stress that the essential features are the existential elements in the act of coming-to-be. What I have said so far applies to atomic actual entities as concrescing "present" occasions.

An actual occasion within a discursive individual must have not only spontaneous essential features of the existential sort but also essential features deriving from relatively past and future parts of itself. That is, the connection between actual entities internal to a discursive individual such as a person must be itself essential, not merely conditional, although all connections will be at least conditional. A true enduring organism is essentially integrated, not merely conditionally integrated. From the standpoint of the discursive individual, the component atomic individuals are relatively abstract. The essential features of a discursive individual, like those of an atomic individual, are those determining how the conditional features are to be valued and integrated, moment by moment. Since Whitehead was right to see that the existential activity of determining value takes place always and only in a present moment, the essential features of a discursive individual must always relate to some present. That is, in a given moment there are spontaneous essential features, but also essential features deriving from past and future moments of the discursive individual.

A rough example can make the point. A deed in my past is my deed, essentially mine, if it puts obligations on my present actions so as to make me guilty or morally fulfilled by being false or true to it. Another person's past deeds can affect the content of my present actions so that I fulfill or fail some duty by responding to the other's actions; but they do not bind me as my own deeds. Similarly, part of the moral character of my present actions is essentially determined by the obligations they lay on my future actions. The content of my moral character includes the conditions set by many future consequences on things other than myself. Nevertheless, there is a special way in which my anticipatable future life determines the moral worth of my present actions. Whereas all relevant past and future events contribute to the content of my obligations, only the essential connections between my past, present, and future states determine praise and blameworthiness. Praise and blameworthiness are characteristics of a person with an extended career. They cannot be levied on an entity whose ontological status is only momentary; the moral quality of an atomic response can be good or bad relative to the effects on the environment, but not praiseworthy or blameworthy.

If a social science such as economics is to display and explain the ways social systems transmit values to individuals, and the ways individuals respond to those values and alter them, it must have some way of relating the integrity of persons to the causal structures of the system. If a process model be adopted, then some categoreal supplement such as that of discursive individuals is needed. The point is even more general than I have indicated. Not only are there discursive individuals but also discursive events, as in history, and in diachronic unfoldings of systems; these too are not easily accounted for with the emphasis on the present in process philosophy.

2. The next point is that it is necessary for economic theory (or any social science attentive to the transmission of values) to identify the relevant classes of essential features constituting the human. The example of morals is a fairly obvious one. Its obviousness comes from our Western theme of contractual obligation as defining the human, a theme as old as Sinai if not Noah's Landing. What are the additional structures built up through growth, maturation, and learning that constitute the human? Although embodied at every moment of a person's life, these structures exist only with temporal thickness; they build on one another hierarchically, and they interpenetrate, affecting one another both essentially and conditionally as circumstances dictate.

Let us call these structures "essential epitomes" of the human. The word "epitome" suggests both that they are universal structures essential to humanity, and that the structures are vague, requiring specialization in each person and allowing of many different embodiments and developments. To call them "essential" indicates both that they are essential to human life and also that their own identity requires essential features reaching discursively across a person's temporal spread.

Identifying the essential epitomes is an empirical matter that cannot be attempted here. For illustrative purposes, however, I want to mention the list derived and analyzed by Paul Weiss in his extraordinary book, *Privacy*.[20] Each of the following of Weiss's epitomes makes the point that there are structures or habits, or capacities that are temporally thick and bound together by essential features reaching across time.

Sensitivity, Weiss's most elementary epitome, is the capacity to make imaginative contact with what our bodies make available, and to discriminate qualities. It requires a temporal spread because the body must be mastered and unified in experience to the point that it is revelatory of what is beyond it. The more nuanced and mature one's sensitivity, the more one's physical feel of the world can sense moods, dangers, and other subtle qualities. A mature person embodies a cultivated sensitivity. *Sensibility* is the organization of the person so as to be appreciative of values conveyed experientially. Qualities sensed have affective tones that may be registered in experience, but it requires a somewhat developed sensibility to appreciate those tones, to give them organized weight in experience, to seek out and nurture the good and avoid the bad. Sensibility refined becomes good taste and when fully civilized constitutes the human activity of enjoying and cultivating the good. Sensibility is an obvious prerequisite for the moral life.

Need is the organization of the person to seek out things not yet possessed without which one is incomplete. Some needs are relevant to physical existence but others, no less important, are relevant for the development and exercise of the essential human epitomes. There can be yet other needs that are wholly contingent. A need involves the identification of a lack, and of the activities or structures appropriate for fulfilling that lack. Some social systems, including the economic, are essential to human life because, among other reasons, they serve basic needs. *Desire* differs from need in that its satisfaction is motivated and justified by the perceived merit in the object of desire rather than by the perceived lack or incompleteness in the one who needs. Thus while need is always, if justifiably, selfish, desire can be selfless. Desire is responsive to the attractiveness of the object.

Orientation is an epitome of personal structure by virtue of which one relates to an environment, a milieu in which the other epitomes can be exercised. Constituted by activities that use the other epitomes, orientation is the developed organization of activities taking into account one's body, place, basic relations with others, institutions, extent and terrain of movement, and scale of options. No atomic moment alone has orientation, which comes rather from relating one's enduring organism to an enduring environment, both through changes. *Sociality* is the organization of the person not only to interact with others through niches in a social environment but to be accountable to oneself and others for the playing of social roles. With sociality arises the elementary form of the trait that classically distinguishes human rationality. Rationality is not cleverness at problem solving but rather intelligent behavior that takes itself to be representative of any intelligent behavior in the situation. To play a social role is to act as a representative of the social group in the performance of the role. The meaning of playing a role in a society includes identifying oneself as a representative of the society. Sociality requires responding to oneself as a whole, interpreted as a type, and integrated into systematic connections with other people. The essential features uniting a discursive individual must convey this sense of wholeness and sense of type; in most respects, the sense of wholeness derives from an appreciation of the type made reflexively relevant to oneself.

Mind is the epitome of the person that's explicitly representational because it is action in accordance with abstract or eternal principles such as those of logic or mathematics. For mind, activity is normed by the principles that should norm anyone's activities, rather than being normed by its success at satisfying need or desire, for instance. Although the nature of mind is a vast topic that can't be explored here, my point is to stress the temporal thickness of mind and the fact that it is essential for any mental moment to take up a stance not only on the other moments of that mind but on the relation between mental acts and the logical forms that make the acts mental. Of course mentality does not require an explicit identification of the principles, but rather a built-in criticism of potential mental acts according to their participation in the principles. *Resolution* is that organization of the person capable of transforming the various values sensed, responded to with developed sensibility, needed, desired, oriented to one's life, socially structured, and mentally understood, into goals, objectives, ends, and the good. Weiss points out that goals are the objects of preferences, other things being equal; ends, the objects of will in which complex behavior is organized in a commitment to secure the end; and the good, the object of responsibility that seeks to justify its objects by seeing that they are the best. Resolution is the organization of the multitude of habits and activities required for these "voluntary" dimensions of life. Although some people are extremely irresolute, it is essential to their humanity that they have some resolution and be judged accordingly.

Autonomy is not merely separation of oneself from full definition by others but also the positive identification of oneself as vulnerable to moral judgment. The essential features defining autonomy are at the heart of my earlier example of morality. *Responsibility* couples a sense of autonomy with a sense of obligation to what is objectively right or wrong. Of course the determination of objective right or wrong is very complicated. But without some judgment of one's self-identity as oriented to norms as objectively right or wrong there is no taking of oneself to be responsible. Without being responsible one is not a self. The *I* or ego is an ongoing organized activity coordinating other activities with an intentional representation of the self. It is the expression of the person in a self-reflective mode, contoured by its representation of itself to itself. The representation may include not only the particularized essential epitomes but also the particular situational and historical elements of personal identity. Autonomy, responsibility, and the I are intimately interdefined.

Weiss goes on in his analysis, which I have briefly paraphrased here and developed for my own purpose, to explain higher human structures such as the self related to ultimate things, and he connects his account with natural rights. I will stop the list here, however, because the essential epitomes discussed so far are expressions of our common sense. The point has been to identify basic human structures, with essential features of their own interacting across time, that must be integrated into a process model for social science theorizing.

Another limitation to classical process philosophy is apparent here as its model is enriched. What's important for the present about a person's past is not the past actual occasions but the integrated actual structures those occasions achieved. Similarly, the future does not consist of future occasions but of potentialities for the joint action of many "present" creative occasions arrayed, for the future, across space and time. Therefore, the analysis of things into their component actual occasions applies only to things insofar as they are in the temporal mode of the present. The point is even more general. Not only does a discursive individual have an actualized structured past and possible structured future, the entire environment—past, contemporary, and future—is to be grasped according to its coordinating structures. The reason for this is not only that the grasping present moment organizes them that way: this would be merely the reduction of the past and future to their roles for the present. The reason rather is that they *are* that way.

An economic theory, properly to display and explain the values in its subject matter, must be able to show how a given economic arrangement affects the values in the essential epitomes of human life. Otherwise, it can't show how values are transmuted as they pass through the economic system to the individuals, back into the system, and into other systems. Since the earliest attempts at economic theory, we have known that it closely related to an understanding of human life, to philosophical anthropology. My argument here is that the variables of economic theory itself must register the value-effects of transactions on participants in the system.

3. My final point supplementing process philosophy and strengthening the previous remark is that the collection of social systems exists to develop

and to exercise the essential epitomes of human life. Because there is a reciprocity between what culture has developed as the human and what the human demands of culture, it should be possible to define the social and human sciences in an harmonious way. In this essay I have begun with the personal to make contact with social systems, but it is perfectly conceivable to work the other way.

One should not think that each essential epitome is served by a particular social system, although it is tempting to associate economics with need, aesthetics with desire, etc. The list of essential epitomes I've drawn from Weiss is only tentative. Social systems, moreover, are determined by the natural connections and joints of their own media. If economics, for instance, deals with the system framing the production, distribution, and consumption of goods, the proper regularities and variables might be tightly connected with religion in one culture. Social stratification can be close to economics relations in capitalist culture, more distant in Confucian culture. Just as there is a base only of empirical generalization serving to list essential epitomes of human life, only empirical studies can draw the connections of social systems.

A theory of a social system such as economics, in order to trace out the values in its subject matter, needs to trace both the transmission and creation of values within the system and also the interaction of values between the system and each of the essential epitomizations. An economic system that does very well in increasing the amount and quality of goods satisfying a given society's needs and desires might have disastrous effects on the sensibilities, resolution, and autonomy of its people. This is one way to interpret part of the Marxist critique of capitalism. Capitalists criticize the ideals of Marxism for addressing basic need, sensibilities, and resolution at the cost of the elements of the self. A good economic theory would build into its very structure a methodology for paying explicit attention to all these matters.

The list of essential epitomes is of course hypothetical and provisional. So is the organization of our disciplines of social science. If they are correlated and set in juxtaposition for mutual criticism, however, it is possible to envision the development of a unified social-human science, geared to the display and explanation of the transmission of value. This would involve the quantified articulation of structures, but oriented to show how those structures bear and transmit value. Such a theory would be hypothetical and demand empirical, objective testing. But it would also be framed in such a way that issues of justice and morality would be stated directly. Valuational thinking would thus be reintegrated with the quantitative and qualitative thinking characteristic of modern science.

IV.

This argument about an ideal economic theory can be brought to a close with a summary and some remarks about application. The project initiating this essay was to discern what a proper economic theory might consist in, taking into account the initial demand that a theory display and explain the values in its subject matter. The concern for values reflects a metaphysical position vis-a-vis the conception of theorizing characteristic of modernity. I argued that both Marxism and Liberal capitalism have metaphysical deficiencies that should be addressed as such in order to understand their critiques of one another. I then suggested that process philosophy provides a superior metaphysical beginning, though not development, from which to work for a proper approach to economic theory.

Three points were culled from process philosophy. The first is its general conception of causation and substance, giving accounts: of how the factual character of something is an objective achieved value, of how a thing's being caused is its receiving of value, and of how its causing is the further transmission of value. This process conception of nature is the major initiative in overcoming the modern cosmology separating facts in nature from values in thinking. Our goal is an economic theory that identifies the values in its subject matter and their transmission.

The second contribution of process philosophy is its model of alterations of values affected by present activity. In the right circumstances these alterations are the product of freedom. In other circumstances they are products of inexorable law or blind chance. An economic theory identifying the respective alteration points includes the human factor in the economic system and frames economic understanding in the language ready for discourse concerning morals and justice.

The third process conception is that of an entity that can play roles in a larger system such as the economic and at the same time play roles in many other systems as well. An economic theory articulating this will have in hand the variables for tracing the impact of economic values on individuals, the impact of personal freedom on the economic system, and the ways in which economics might relate to other social systems in the cumulative integration of individuals' lives. Such a theory would surmount the mutual critiques of Marxism and capitalism regarding solidarity versus freedom and the internal and external relations of individual and social structure.

The process model drawn from Whitehead needs to be supplemented in three points in order to provide a metaphysical grounding for economic theory. The first point is that a category of discursive individuals needs to be developed by means of a distinction between essential and conditional features. A person has essential structures with temporal thickness, and Whitehead's account of persons as societies is insufficient to account for the essential character of temporally thick structures. A proper economic theory needs an account of such human dimensions if it is to explain the transmission of values through economic systems to individuals and vice versa. Essential features are those valuings that determine how other values are to be weighted in the manufacture of objective reality.

The second point of supplementation is to provide a provisional list of essential human structures, essential epitomes. I adopted Paul Weiss's list including: sensitivity, sensibility, need, desire, orientation, sociality, mind, resolution, autonomy, responsibility, and the I. Each of these is an essential layer of human reality, without which one is not a fully developed human being.

The final supplementary point is simply that an economic system should be understood in terms of the impact it has on each epitome, for it is in all those ways that it exchanges values with individuals. The ramifications of this are obvious. The economic system can be correlated with other social systems regarding their diverse impacts, and the systems can be understood in their differential but cumulative impacts on all the epitomes. In particular, the social systems can be understood in terms of their impact on the typical styles by which the various epitomes are harmonized in people's lives through social position, generation, and age cohort.

A limitation should be noted on all this discussion. I have been speaking principally of the nature of social systems and the systematic nature of individuals: synchronic topics. Yet I began with the historical point that our conception of theory for analyzing social matters arose at the historical point of European Renaissance. Moreover, I have been calling for an historically new theory to supersede it. As Marx stressed, economic systems themselves are in process of historical evolution, and the development of the essential human epitomes is also historical. A full economic account cannot be only synchronic but requires a genetic dimension as well, dealing with the stages of development of each of the important kinds of individuals and institutions. In addition, an economic theory must build in references to particular historical events determining the shape of economic conditions.

The next step in the argument would be to frame a new theory for economic analysis, one as radical in its novelty as Adam Smith's, or Karl Marx's, or Keynes'. Perhaps the metaphysical considerations offered here can provide some guidance as to what might be captured in an adequate theory. Instead of taking that step, however, I am going to speculate about some implicatons of a proper economic theory for economic policy.

Assuming that it is desirable to retain the quantifiable language of economics, a proper economic theory would have extensive implications for the social organization of economic analysis and assessment. Consider something as apparently straightforward as determining the gross national product of a country. It would not be the mere summing up of the exchange value of the products produced in a certain time (this of couse is an over-simplification of the standard procedure); as the Marxists say, that summing up does not subtract the cost in human suffering to determine the real value produced. To be sure, economic production is not only costly, it sometimes contributes "side benefits" such as pride, skill, friendship, and the culture of the workplace. All these costs and benefits would have to be assessed so as to qualify the GNP.

To translate the assessment of those costs and benefits into dollar terms, an enormously complicated machinery would have to be developed, at least for the short run. First, it would be necessary to elaborate models of the transmission of values from the economic system to individuals and other social systems (and historical realities), and understand how these modify one another. These would be empirical models, and thus constantly in a state of modification themselves. Second, it would be necessary to determine a dollar amount to repay the cost or independently sponsor the benefit of the value change in each transmission of values. In some instances this amount can be determined by an experimental market: how much would those affected be willing to pay to offset or secure the change? But in most instances the value-effects are unnoticed or misunderstood by many of the participants; bad architecture, for example, has disastrous psychological and social effects although the people affected may be unaware of the cause and may not themselves be the appropriate ones to pay for changes. Probably *pro bono publico panels* would be required to assess dollar amounts for the value-change of a given transmission.

Changes affect different people in similar circumstances in different ways. Some rough simplifications into ideal types would have to be made. At the minimum it would be necessary to assess the value of a change for people according to their places in the major social systems we can analyze. How does a change play differential value-roles for individuals according to their religion, for instance, their ethnic background, gender, age, social class, education, job, political affiliations? To understand this again requires models for each of these and other appropriate systems that are sensitive to the transmission of value.

Doubtless it will be argued that this is much too complicated, and that determining the GNP is really a straightforward method of summing the value produced. This may not be satisfactory to moralists, theologians and philosophers, it might be said, but why not leave the value questions to them? The GNP determined the usual way is useful for its limited economic purpose.

On the contrary, the GNP determined the usual way is a lie, an abstraction that covers over and distorts what it alleges to measure. It presents its sum without the qualifications of its costs and benefits. The economic costs of production can be measured in the GNP, but not the social and personal costs that also determine its value. The GNP measured the usual way is just bad metaphysics, hence destructive ideology. It is appropriate then to bear with the overly complicated model of measuring the transmission of values, hoping that some simplifying factors will emerge.

The application of economic theory to economic analysis and assessment is closely tied to policies that control such things as the money supply and foreign trade. How does one determine the ideal money supply in a situation, or the right businesses to affect for better or worse by foreign trade? In one sense, the answer is political—the interests with the greatest power get the benefits. But in another sense the answer is that people can't determine their interests without a knowledge of the value-transmissions in the systems involved. The misfortunes of the American automobile industry in the last thirty years testify to the stupidity of the views that management's interest is greater profit and labor's interest is greater wages and benefits. And what are the religious and community interests? The cultural and artistic interests? Thomas Hobbes hoped that self-interest and security would be a reliable natural force, like inertia, on which to build social theory. We know now that true interest is impossible to determine without a fairly settled and attentive knowledge of what is worth our interest.

We may expect the development of a value-oriented economic theory to suggest radical changes in economic policies once the worth of transactions is better known. The values of production are too abstract, and capitalism is thus a distorting ideology. The values of the interest of social classes are also too abstract, and Marxism thus is another distorting ideology. Both kinds of value, however, those of production and those of social class, are sufficiently important to justify the development of an appropriate economic theory and to put in place the analytical mechanisms to allow it to provide data and guide policy.

Notes and References

1. This historical remark is the thesis of my *Reconstruction of Thinking* (Albany: State University of New York Press, 1981); see Chapter 1. In that book I argue for the project of reconstructing paradigms of thinking so as to include valuational elements, in the spheres of imaginative, interpretive, theoretical, and moral or responsibility-pursuing thinking; the book also presents reconstructed models for imagination in some detail.

2. Even the physical sciences falsely prescind from the values in their subjects; but for them, the urgency of a reconstruction of thinking in an axiological direction seems not so great. Nevertheless, environmental disasters and the threat of nuclear war have forced scientists to ask value questions, even if the terms of their scientific discourse are not framed to ask or

answer them well. Furthermore, the recent work of Patrick A. Heelan has shown that not only scientific theories and the use of instruments are structured by interpretive frameworks but also that our perception is so structured. See Heelan's *Space-Perception and the Philosophy of Science* (Berkeley: University of California Press, 1983). The questions then must be asked of physical sciences: Do hermeneutical suppositions screen out the resident values in natural objects? What modes of theory, practice, and perception would be responsive to the nature, presence, or absence of values in things? What cultural values guide our experience and understanding of scientific objects?

3.   Throughout this paper I discuss ideal types or extremes of Marxist and Liberal theory rather than the more prevalent socialisms and mixed economies. The justification for this is that usually my intent is to discuss the structure of theory as such. Where these ideal types as stated by Marx and Locke, say, have been compromised, one way of understanding the compromise is to say that the form of the theory is at fault. Indeed, I'll argue that each side has been compromised precisely to be able to acknowledge the values that are central to the other but cannot be registered within the ideal type at hand.

4.   The formal logical notion of vagueness was developed by Charles Sanders Pierce. He distinguished vagueness from generality by saying that a sign of the former sort requires a further specifying interpretive sign in order to determine an object, whereas the latter determines an object immediately. I have explored and defended the notion with regard to its use in philosophy in *Reconstruction of Thinking*, Chapter 2.

5.   In addition to the classical works of Marxism, this discussion generalizes from more recent works such as Ralf Dahrendorf's *Class and Class Conflict in Industrial Society* (Stanford: Stanford University Press, 1959) and Robert C. Tucker's *The Marxian Revolutionary Idea* (New York: Norton, 1969). On the present point concerning justice, see Tucker's second and third chapters.

6.   The popular capitalist critique of Marxism as totalitarian and statist is rank among American politicians. It is stated more subtly by Paul Samuelson, an advocate of a mixed economy, in his enormously influential text book, *Economics*, e.g., in the 8th edition (New York: McGraw-Hill, 1970) Chapter 42. Marxism does indeed tend toward totalitarian statism at just this point, as I argue in *The Puritan Smile* (Albany: State University of New York Press, 1987), Chapter 4.

7.   Locke's explicit statement of the economic consequences of his metaphysics of property is in Chapter 5, "Of Property," of the *Second Treatise of Civil Government*. The metaphysical underpinnings of the theory that to be is to be an owning of properties is in his *Essay Concerning Human Understanding*, Book II, in which he criticizes the older theory of substance and develops his own. See also David Hume's *Treatise of Human Nature*, Book III, Part II, Chapters II-VI. Adam Smith's discussion is not metaphysical. But he does suggest that the universal human propensity to "truck, barter, and exchange" is either "an original principle in human nature" or, more likely, "the necessary consequence of the faculties of reason and speech." The latter suggestion says more about reason and speech than about economics. See *The Wealth of Nations*, Book I, Chapter II.

8.   While capitalism assumes that individuals always want to buy or sell something or other, the nature of the commodity is metaphysically less important than the fact that the transaction is an instance of change in ownership. Except for vital necessities in the abstract, systems other than the economic determine the content of what people want insofar as that is not affected by its relevance to the virtues of ownership itself. The language of internal and external relations is somewhat alien to capitalism for which relations are paradigmatically those of possession and transfer of possessions.

9.   For a more systematic discussion of the ways by which variable access to social media affect the boundaries of public and private, see my *Cosmology of Freedom* (New Haven: Yale University Press, 1974), Chapter 9.

10.   Whitehead's major metaphysical work is *Process and Reality* (Corrected Edition edited by David Ray Griffin and Donald W. Sherburne; New York: The Free Press, 1978; original edition New York: Macmillan, 1929). See also his *Adventures of Ideas* (New York: Macmillan, 1933), and *Modes of Thought* (New York: Macmillan, 1938). Excellent commentaries include William Christian's *An Interpretation of Whitehead's Metaphysics* (New Haven: Yale University Press, 1959), Elizabeth Kraus's *The Metaphysics of Experience* (New York: Fordham University Press, 1979), and Ivor Leclerc's *Whitehead's Metaphysics* (London: George Allen & Unwin, 1969). Important collections of discussions include Ivor Leclerc, editor, *The Relevance of Whitehead* (London: George Allen & Unwin, 1969), George L. Kline, editor, *Alfred North Whitehead: Essays on His Philosophy* (Englewood Cliffs, N.J.: Prentice-Hall, 1963), and Lewis S. Ford & George L. Kline, editors, *Explorations in Whitehead's Philosophy* (New York: Fordham University Press, 1983). My own interpretations and emendations of Whitehead are in *Cosmology of Freedom* and *Reconstruction of Thinking*.

11.   The phrase "actual entities of the past" is redundant in most senses. When an entity has fully emerged as actual, it no longer has subjective immediacy and exists as past for any entity that can grasp it.

12.   See, for instance, Hartshorne's *Creative Synthesis and Philosophic Method* (Lasalle, Ill.: Open Court, 1970); see also his *Creativity in American Philosophy* (Albany: State University of New York Press, 1984).

13.   On Whitehead's theory of value see particularly *Process and Reality*, Part II, Chapter 4. See also his *Modes of Thought* (New York: Macmillan, 1938). Whitehead's remarks on value, though insightful and provocative, were not extensive or systematic. My own theory of value, inspired by him, is in *The Cosmology of Freedom*, Chapter 3, and in *Reconstruction of Thinking*, Chapter 3.

14.   See Whitehead's discussion in *Process and Reality*, pp. 240-255.

15.   See Jorge Luis Nobo's *Whitehead's Metaphysics of Extension and Solidarity* (Albany: State University of New York Press, 1986).

16.   These are among the points that lead Charles Hartshorne to call me a "deviationist Whiteheadian." See his *Creativity in American Philosophy*, p. 266.

17.   Whitehead's principal discussion of these points is in Section II of Chapter III, "Some Derivative Notions," of Part I of *Process and Reality*.

18.   See Paul Weiss' criticism of Whitehead on this point and development of an alternate process theory of actualities in his first book, *Reality* (Princeton: Princeton University Press, 1939).

19.   Whitehead's discussion is in *Process and Reality*, pp. 291-293.

20.   *Privacy* (Carbondale: Southern Illinois University Press, 1983). Weiss calls these structures epitomizations, from which I derived my own term. Among Weiss's many other books, the most central for the discussion to follow are *Man's Freedom* (New Haven: Yale University Press, 1950) and *You, I, and the Others* (Carbondale: Southern Illinois University Press, 1980). A student of Whitehead's, Weiss early on saw that his teacher's emphasis on creativity results in too great a preoccupation with the present, to the neglect of the other temporal dimensions of enduring things. It is not a surprise, therefore, that Weiss is the first of Whitehead's students to develop a theory of the structures of an individual that require a spread of time in order to be actualized.

CHAPTER 8

On Robert C. Neville's "Beyond Production and Class: A Process Project in Economic Theory"

Clark A. Kucheman

Like the subject matters of the other social sciences, the subject matter of economics—economic arrangements and policies—is "value laden." Hence it follows, Robert Neville argues, that "the conceptual apparatus of economic theory should display and explain the values in its subject matter" if the science of economics is to enable us not only successfully to describe and explain theoretically how the many possible as well as actual economic arrangements and policies would or in fact do function but also correctly to decide which of them we should institute practically.

The economic theories available to us today do not do so, however. On the contrary, "our major theoretical approaches to economics obscure rather than display and explain the values in their subject matters." Why? Because "both Liberal capitalism and Marxism, as well as socialist and mixed economies, share the metaphysical assumptions of modern philosophy that separate facts from values," he answers, "believing that theories should explain only the facts." Consequently "new paradigms of thinking that reconstruct a proper relation of valuation to quantitative and qualitative analysis are imperative before the obviously value-laden subjects of the social sciences [including economics] can be approached with appropriately formed theories." Specifically, we need a metaphysical understanding that "surmounts the fact-value distinction" before we can construct an economic theory that "identifies the values in its subject matter and their transition" and thereby makes it possible for us "appropriately" both to describe and explain the functioning of economic arrangements and policies theoretically and—since "questions of justice and morality have to do with the transformations of values in process of transmission"—to decide what economic arrangements and policies we should institute practically.

Process philosophy meets this need, according to Neville. For "process philosophy has provided an alternative to [the] metaphysical assumptions [that separate facts from values], an alternative that recognizes facts as achievements and embodiments of values." By "recogniz[ing] facts as achievements and embodiments of values" and thereby "surmount[ing] the fact-value distinction," process philosophy comprises a metaphysical foundation for an economic theory that will enable us successfully both theoretically to identify and explain the values in "value-laden" economic arrangements and policies and—since this theory will in turn enable us to "register the value-effects of transactions on participants in the [economic] system"—practically to affect in desirable ways the transmission of values by means of economic policies. Hence his effort here is "to explore . . . the 'axiological requirements' of a proper approach to economic theory" by "building on a base of process philosophy."

In response, let me refer first to what I think is an important contribution Neville makes both to our understanding of process philosophy's implications for economic theory and practice and to process philosophy itself, namely, his explanation of the "continuity or endurance of persons" over time in terms of "temporally thick" " 'essential epitomes' of the human," including especially "autonomy," "responsibility," and "the I or ego."

If individual persons are not enduring substances but only momentary occasions in series of momentary occasions, as process philosophy appears to contend, or, in other words, as Neville puts it, if "process philosophy's signal contribution is having explicated the internal nature of the present moment, but to the relative neglect of the past and the future, or rather to the reduction of the past and future to their contributions to the present," then—within the conceptual framework of process philosophy, that is— "how [can] persons . . . make up an identity of their own while participating in many social systems"? Moreover, I have often asked process philosophers, as does Neville himself, if persons are momentary occasions who do not endure over time, then how can they be morally responsible for acting in the future to keep promises they make in the momentary present?

The answer to both of these questions can be given in terms of the "essential epitomes," Neville shows. Persons are not momentary occasions only. On the contrary, they are enduring "discursive individuals" as well as momentary occasions. For while the *content* of any actual entity—including a person—is determined by what it prehends in its momentary process of coming-to-be, its "process of concrescence," and so is momentary, there are and must also be "essential features" of all actual entities that determine the prehending activity itself, i.e., "that determine the subjective, existential process of concrescence, those spontaneous acts of valuation that value up or down, that disassemble, pare, combine, and harmonize conditions so as to work them into final integration," and so are not themselves momentary but are instead enduring. That which is prehend*ed*—and thereby determines an actual entity's content—is momentary, to be sure; but that which is prehend*ing*—and thereby gives an actual entity, including a person, a continuing identity of its own—endures over time.

In persons, then, according to Neville, following Paul Weiss, these enduring essential epitomes include sensitivity, sensibility, need, desire, orientation, sociability, mind, and, most especially, autonomy, responsibility, and the I or ego. "Although embodied at every moment of a person's life," as Neville puts it, "these structures exist only with temporal thickness; they build on one another hierarchically, and they interpenetrate, affecting one another both essentially and conditionally as circumstances dictate." Hence they can explain both "how persons can make up an identity of their own" and—since autonomy, responsibility and the I are at the top of the hierarchy of the essential epitomes of human persons—how persons can be morally responsible for actions they obligate themselves in the present to perform in the future.

Neville's understanding of the "I" as "an ongoing organized activity coordinating other activities with an intentional representation of the self" is crucial for constructing a scientific economic theory "on a base of process philosophy," I shall argue momentarily. But I wish first to consider the question, Must "the conceptual apparatus of economic theory . . . display and explain the values in its subject matter" if economic science is to be able successfully to analyze the causal functioning of alternative economic arrangements and policies? And I think the answer to this question is that it need not do so.

I do not dispute here that questions of economic organization and policy are "value-laden." Since economic organization and policy shape persons' lives in immensely significant ways, we need to ask what form of economic organization we *should* institute and what economic policies we *should* adopt. Nor—assuming for the moment that process philosophy succeeds in "surmount[ing] the fact-value distinction"—do I dispute the idea that "values . . . and their transmission" can comprise an interesting and legitimate subject matter for empirical scientific investigation. Nor do I deny that the label "economic science" may be used to designate this kind of scientific inquiry. It remains the case, however, that scientific inquiry into the causal laws that govern the functioning of economic arrangements and policies, i.e., scientific inquiry that "separate[s] facts from values" and endeavors to "explain only the facts," is also necessary. For just as in the physical and biological sciences we must know and express theoretically the causal laws that govern the functioning of physical and biological reality in order to have "freedom to exercise control over the intended but distant future results of actions," so in the science of economics we must know and express theoretically the causal laws that govern the functioning of economic arrangements and policies in order to have freedom, by means of arrangements and policies we can implement now, to control their future functioning.

The idea that a person is an enduring "I," i.e., "an ongoing organized activity coordinating other activities with an intentional representation of the self," who—along with other activities—performs subjective "acts of valuation" is nevertheless highly significant for this latter kind of economic scientific inquiry. Indeed, it provides a metaphysical foundation upon which a theory that does explain successfully the functioning of economic arrangements and policies, namely, marginalist supply-and-demand economic theory, can be constructed. For if, in their subjective valuing, persons set ends and allocate the scarce means they have at their disposal in a rational (in the economists' sense of "rational") way so as to attain their ends in the order of the relative value these ends have for them, as Neville's understanding of the essential epitomes—those of "need," "desire," "mind," and "resolution," for example, as well as of the "I"—indicates that they will, then we can derive the fundamental explanatory principles of marginalist economic theory (which I shall not undertake to do here) by tracing out the implications of this "economizing" activity under various assumed conditions.

Thus process philosophy does not provide a foundation for a new or more adequate theory of how economic arrangements and policies in fact do function, it seems to me. But, as amended by Neville's theory of persons as enduring "discursive individuals," process philosophy does provide at least a possible—although certainly not the *only* possible—metaphysical foundation for the marginalist supply-and-demand theory that is prevalent in the science of economics today.

Granting, then, both that there are economic laws that govern the functioning of economic arrangements and policies (which Neville appears to be doing when he states that "social systems, insofar as they enter an occasion of choice as conditions, must be stable and regular if the emerging occasion is to deal effectively with them"), and that marginalist economic theory—which "separate[s] facts from values" and endeavors to "explain only the facts"—provides an accurate understanding of these causal laws, the practical question still remains as to what economic arrangements and policies we *should* adopt. Ought we to have an arrangement wherein the material means of production are privately owned and controlled? Or should the material means of production be publicly owned and controlled? And whichever form, or combination thereof, of ownership and control we decide to adopt, should production and distribution within this form be determined by market competition, by central planning, or by some combination of each? And—what is of special concern to us here—how does process philosophy assist us in making these practical economic decisions?

Primarily, it is by "surmount[ing] the fact-value distinction" that process philosophy assists us in making these practical decisions, Neville answers. For "questions of justice and morality have to do with the transformations of values in process of transmission," he explains and—by "surmount[ing] the fact-value distinction"—process philosophy makes it possible for us to "identif[y] the values in [economic reality] and their transmission" and so to "frame economic understanding in the language ready for discourse concerning morals and justice." Specifically, since "the collection of social systems [including economic arrangements and policies] exists to develop and to exercise the essential epitomes of human life," and since process philosophy's theory of value enables us, in economic theory of the kind Neville proposes, to "show how a given economic arrangement affects the values in the essential epitomes of human life," it thereby also gives us a morally normative criterion for deciding which of the many possible economic arrangements and policies we ought morally to institute. We ought morally to institute those economic arrangements and policies which function most effectively to promote the achievement of value in the development and exercise of the essential epitomes.

Is it really the case, however, that process philosophy successfully "surmounts the fact-value distinction"? At the very least, I am not clear that it does. And even if it does succeed in this, does it thereby provide an acceptable morally normative criterion for economic organization and policy? I think it does not.

According to Neville, following Whitehead, "an actual entity *is* an achievement of value" (my emphasis). Or again, "the factual character of something *is* an objective achieved value" (my emphasis still). But what precisely do we mean by saying this? Do we mean to say that *whatever* an actual entity achieves is an achievement of value, i.e., that it is an achievement of value simply because an actual entity as a matter of fact does achieve it? Or do we mean to say instead that an achievement of value is what an actual entity *should* achieve, i.e., that it is worthy of achieving whether or not an actual entity in fact does achieve it?

If we mean the former, namely, that an achievement of value is whatever an actual entity in fact happens to achieve, then we of course do "surmount the fact-value distinction." But we do so by reducing "value" to "fact." On this interpretation of "an actual entity is an achievement of value," the term "value" has no normative significance; we cannot say that an achievement of value is *worth* achieving, or that it is what *should* be achieved, nor—if whatever an actual entity achieves is, for that reason alone, an achievement of value—can we say that an entity ever fails to achieve value.

If on the other hand we mean to say the latter, namely, that an achievement of value is what an actual entity *ought* to achieve whether or not it happens in fact to do so, or that it is what is *worth* achieving—or is "worth our interest" and so is a "true interest," as Neville puts it—then "value" and "fact" are distinct. We cannot in this case discover what an actual entity should achieve, or what is normatively worth achieving, as over against what it in fact does achieve, simply by observing what it does in fact achieve; "facts" tell us nothing about "values," and so we do not after all succeed in "surmount[ing] the fact-value distinction." Instead, we need yet to determine what *should* be achieved, or is *worth* achieving, in some way other than by empirically examining "the factual character of something."

What is it, then—assuming here that there is some non-empirical way of knowing values—that we should achieve, or that is normatively worth achieving, according to Neville's adaptation of process philosophy? While he does not say so explicitly, by saying, for example, that "the collection of social systems exists to develop and to exercise the essential epitomes of human life" and that "an economic system that does very well in increasing the amount and quality of goods satisfying a given society's needs and desires might have disastrous effects on the sensibilities, resolution, and autonomy of its people," he implies that what is for us worth achieving, or what is intrinsically valuable, is the fulfillment or actualization of the potentialities inherent in our nature as human beings, specifically, the actualization of the essential epitomes themselves, the characteristics "without which one is not a fully developed human being."

For the reason that their fulfillment comprises an "achieved intrinsic value," then, our fundamental moral duty is to act—and hence also to organize and manage our economy policy-wise—in ways that serve most effectively the development and exercise of the essential epitomes of human life. According to Neville's process philosophical assumption, we ought *morally*—i.e., whether we want to or not, or categorically—always to act in ways that best develop and exercise the essential epitomes of human life *because* the fulfillment of the essential epitomes is intrinsically valuable; since the fulfillment of our essential epitomes is an "achievement of value," in other words, it follows that we ought as a matter of moral duty to act so as to do so.

This moral conclusion does not follow, however. For even if we agree that something is intrinsically valuable—whatever it may be, including the fulfillment of the essential epitomes—it does not follow logically that we ought morally, categorically, to act so as best to promote it. It may well be the case, for example, as I indeed think it is, that the experience of hearing Bach's music is intrinsically good. But it does not follow that listening to the music of Bach is morally imperative, or that we act morally wrongly if we never do so. It is of course a good or valuable—in a nonmoral sense of "good" or "valuable"—action to do; *if* we *want* to have an experience that is intrinsically valuable, *then* we *ought* to listen to Bach's music. But to know what is intrinsically valuable is not by itself yet to know what we ought morally—i.e., whether we want to or not, or categorically—to do or not do.

We can add a premise according to which we ought morally to act so as to promote intrinsic value, to be sure, and so impose upon ourselves a moral duty to act in this way. But the knowledge that something is intrinsically valuable—including the fulfillment of the potentialities in the essential epitomes of human life, as well as the experience of hearing beautiful music—does not by itself imply that we have this moral duty. Just as there is a logical "gap" between judgments of fact and judgments of intrinsic value, so there is a logical "gap" between judgments of intrinsic value and judgments of moral duty, and this "gap" must be bridged by a premise or judgment stating that we ought morally to act to promote the achievement of intrinsic value, by which we impose upon ourselves a moral duty to do so, and, at least so far, I do not see that process philosophy provides such a bridge.

If we were to make such a moral judgment, moreover, namely, a judgment according to which an action ought categorically to be performed if it best promotes the achievement of whatever is intrinsically valuable, would our judgment be true? I don't think so. For this judgment is but a slight variation on the utilitarian moral principle and so is subject to the many decisive objections to which the utilitarian principle is subject. Not only is it *not* categorically imperative always *to* act so as best to promote the achievement of intrinsic value (since heroic or supererogatory actions would by implication then be strictly categorically imperative to do), but it often *is* categorically imperative *not* to act so as best to promote the achievement of intrinsic value (as is often the case, for example, when doing so would require breaking a promise).

Hence even if we grant (which I do not) that "the factual character of something is an objective achieved value," and so make possible "an economic theory that identifies the values in its subject matter and their transmission," we do not thereby also make it possible to "frame economic understanding in the language ready for discourse concerning morals and justice." For even if we know "how a given economic arrangement affects the values in the essential epitomes of human life," by means of an economic theory of the kind Neville has in mind, we need still to determine—in some other, non-empirical way—what we ought as a matter of moral duty to do and, consequently, how we ought also to arrange and manage our economic institutions policy-wise.

We can do so, however, while at the same time remaining within the overall framework of Neville's amended version of process philosophy, I wish now to suggest. For just as his understanding of the "I" as "an ongoing organized activity coordinating other activities with an intentional representation of the self" can serve as a metaphysical foundation for contemporary marginalist economic theory, so, in conjunction especially with the essential epitomes of "mind" ("action in accordance with abstract or eternal principles such as those of logic and mathematics") and "resolution" (the "organization of the person capable of transforming the various values sensed, responded to with developed sensibility, needed, desired, oriented to one's life, socially structured, and mentally understood, into goals, objectives, ends, and the good") it can serve as a metaphysical foundation for a moral principle by means of which we can then determine (at least in part) both what we ought morally as individual persons to do or not do and—since a moral right is the observe side of a moral duty—with help from marginalist economic theory's analysis of their causal functioning, how to organize and manage policy-wise our economic institutions so as to implement persons' moral rights.

Put simply, the moral principle I have in mind here morally requires us to act so as to treat all "I"s, including ourselves qua "I"s, always as "I"s and never as mere "it"s. Or expressed more precisely—albeit in a more complicated and perhaps also obscure way—an action (or course or policy or action) ought morally to be done, according to this principle, if and only if not to do it is to treat an "I" not as a thinking and therefore self-determined "I" who wills ends of his or her own but, instead, as a mere non-thinking and therefore other-determined "it" with no ends of its own; and conversely, an action (or course or policy or action) ought morally not to be done, according to this principle, if and only if to do the action is to treat an "I" as an "it." Or, again, if I may express it in Neville's process philosophical language—which hencmforth for the most part I won't try to do—an action ought morally to be done (or not to be done) if and only if not doing it (or doing it) treats "an ongoing organized activity coordinating other activities with an intentional representation of the self" who actively "transform[s] the various values . . . into goals, objectives, ends, and the good" as if this "ongoing activity" or "I" were instead a merely passive or non-active "it."

How then do we know this principle to be so—other than empirically, that is—and what kinds of actions or courses of action does it require us to do and not to do?

In order to answer these questions, I need first to be precise as to what I mean by the expression "I." For an "I" is not as such an individual human being. We individual human beings are "I"s, but, following Hegel here—and I think in substantial agreement with Neville as well, even though I am not putting it in his process philosophical language—qua "I"s we are not coterminous with ourselves qua individual biological, physiological, and even psychological human beings. Qua "I," "I am alive *in* this bodily organism which is my external existence,"[1] to be sure, as Hegel puts it. But "when I say 'I,' I *eo ipso* abandon all my particular characteristics, my disposition, natural endowment, knowledge, and age,"[2] since all of these—including for example the essential epitomes of human life that Neville refers to as "need" and "desire"—are objects about which I think and from which I therefore distinguish or abstract myself qua "I."

Hence qua "I" I am and can only be that which is not and cannot be an object about which I think and from which I therefore cannot distinguish or abstract myself, namely, the subject whose activity the thinking itself is. " 'I' is thought as a thinker," as Hegel says. Qua "I," I am "the ultimate and unanalyzable point of consciousness"[3] in relation to which everything else is an external object, an other. In Hegel's words still, "The ego is quite empty, a mere point, simple, yet active in this simplicity. The variegated canvas of the world is before me; I stand against it."[4] Or if I may modify Neville's view by interpreting the "I" as what is active rather than as being identical with the activity itself, qua "I" I am the thinking "point" whose "ongoing activity [namely, thinking] coordinat[es] other activities with an intentional representation of the self" and "transform[s] the various values . . . into goals, objectives, ends, and the good."

Qua thinking "I," I am self-determined, moreover, at least negatively. I am "undetermined" in other words, as Hegel would say, or "spontaneous," as Neville and other process philosophers might prefer to say. For by virtue of the power or capacity to think, as Hegel explains, "anyone can discover in himself ability to abstract from everything whatever, and in the same way to determine himself, to posit any content in himself by his own effort."[5] By thinking or deliberating, *I* will or decide—in negative freedom from everything external to me, including even my most strongly-felt desires and needs—both what beliefs to affirm theoretically and what actions to do practically. My theoretical beliefs and my practical actions are not *other*-determined *causally* by my desires and needs, say, or by my heredity, environment, and the like. On the contrary, whether I do so explicitly or implicitly, qua thinking "I" I "posit [this] content in [my]self by [my] own effort" and so am in this negative sense free or self-determined, not unfree or other-determined.

To be negatively self-determined, i.e., *undetermined* or spontaneous, is not yet fully to be self-determined, however. For in my negatively, contra-causally self-determined willing or deciding *activity*, I may will or decide to determine the *content* of my theoretical believing and practical doing by subordinating my will or decision as to what to believe and do content-wise to something or someone other than myself qua "I"—as I do if I decide to believe and do whatever my psychological needs and desires lead me to believe and do, for example, or if even out of a moral motive I decide, say, to obey whatever commands a sovereign will might happen to give me—in which case the beliefs I affirm and the actions I do are after all *other*-determined, not *self*-determined.

I am nevertheless responsible for the content of my beliefs and actions if I do this, of course, since it remains the case that I self-determinedly, contra-causally freely, make the decision to determine the content of my believing and doing by obeying something or someone other than myself qua "I." I am *self*-determinedly *other*-determined; in negative freedom from external causes, I *freely* decide to decide *unfreely*—in obedience to an other of some kind—what it is, content-wise, that I should believe theoretically and do practically, and so I am responsible for this content.

So when am I self-determinedly *self*-determined, freely *free*? In Hegel's concise albeit obscure language once again, the answer is that "the will is free only when it does not will anything alien, extrinsic, foreign to itself (for as long as it does so it is dependent), but wills itself alone—wills the will."[6] I am freely free only when, in my negatively, contra-causally free willing activity, I "will the will." I am both negatively and positively self-determined, or self-determinedly self-determined, in other words, when I will my will's *content*—when I decide what beliefs to hold and what actions to do, that is to say—by willing in obedience not to anything external to me whatever but in obedience only to my own self-determined willing *activity*.

Willing is itself an activity of thinking, we need to note here. It is "a special way of thinking," as Hegel says, namely, "thinking translating itself into existence, thinking as the urge to give itself existence."[7] Freely to will to will freely is thus freely to will to will what content-wise to believe and do by thinking freely.

And to do this, i.e., to think freely or to be self-determined in our thinking activity, is to think in obedience to the laws of deductive and inductive logic. For since "in logic a thought is understood to include nothing else but what depends on thinking and what thinking has brought into existence," it is by thinking logically, as Hegel explains, that "the mind [or thinking "I"] is . . . in its home-element and therefore free."[8] I am *freely free*, then, or *self*-determinedly *self*-determined, when I freely will or decide to will or decide what beliefs to hold and what actions to do content-wise freely by thinking or deliberating in obedience to what Hegel calls "the necessary forms and self-determinations of thought"—"pure reason"[9]—namely, the laws of deductive and inductive logic. Self-determined thinking is rational, logical thinking, and therefore qua thinking "I" I am free in my willing or deciding about what content-wise to believe and do—I "will the will," in other words, and so am both negatively and positively self-determined, freely free—only "when I will what is rational."[10] Or expressed (more or less) in Neville's terminology, I am freely free, self-determinedly self-determined, only when I "transform the various values . . . into goals, objectives, ends, and the good" by "act[ing] in accordance with [the] abstract . . . principles . . . of logic."

It is morally imperative for me freely to will to will freely in this sense, moreover. In my negative, contra-causal freedom, i.e., my "ability to determine [my]self, to posit any content in [my]self by [my] own effort," I ought as a matter of moral duty—whether I want to or not, that is to say, or categorically—freely to decide to decide (positively) *freely* what the contents of my theoretical beliefs and practical actions are to be. I ought morally *not* to will freely to will *unfreely*. That is, I ought as a matter of moral duty, or categorically, *not* to decide what beliefs to hold and what actions to do by deciding in obedience to anything external to myself qua thinking "I" and so *unfreely*. Instead, I ought morally *to* will freely to will *freely*. I ought as a matter of moral duty, or categorically, *to* decide what to believe and what to do content-wise by deliberating in obedience only to the laws internal to myself qua thinking "I"—the laws of deductive and inductive logic—and so *freely*.

Why is this so? Because I presuppose that I ought, whether I want to or not, or categorically, to will or decide to determine my thinking or deliberating by the laws of deductive and inductive logic—and therefore also to will or decide content-wise what beliefs to hold (including of course the one at issue here) and what actions to do—even as I try to deny it. Since I can deny that I ought categorically to "will what is rational" only by presupposing at the same time that I ought categorically to do so, it is a dialectically necessary truth that I ought categorically to "will what is rational" and thereby to be positively as well as negatively *self*-determined, *freely free*.

Now, finally, we can understand both what the moral principle I proposed earlier requires of us and why it is true that we ought morally so to act.

The moral duty to treat all "I"s always as "I"s and never as "it"s is first of all a duty to treat ourselves qua "I"s always as "I"s and never as "it"s, and, as we have just seen, this is fundamentally a duty to will (negatively, contra-causally) freely to will (positively, rationally) freely. Qua thinking

"I"s, we ought morally *not* to treat ourselves as mere "it"s, as we do if we will or decide (negatively, contra-causally) freely to will or decide what to believe and what to do content-wise in subjection to anything or anyone external to ourselves qua "I"s and so *un*freely; and we ought morally *to* treat ourselves as "I"s by willing (negatively, contra-causally) freely to will or decide what beliefs to affirm and what actions to do content-wise by thinking in subjection only to the logical laws internal to us qua thinking "I"s and so (positively, rationally) *freely.*

And if we ought morally to treat ourselves as "I"s and not as mere "it"s by freely willing to will *freely* and not *un*freely, then we ought morally also to cultivate and express our capacities for doing so. We ought morally to act both outwardly and inwardly in ways that serve to cultivate and express our potentialities for positive, rational self-determination. For as individual human beings we are "implicitly rational," as Hegel correctly points out, "but [we] must also become explicitly so by struggling to create [ourselves], not only by going forth from [ourselves] but also by building [ourselves] up within."[11]

Hence our moral duty to ourselves qua "I"s to will freely to will freely—our moral duty to will freely to "will what is rational"—implies a moral duty also to cultivate and express our capacities qua "I"s for doing so. We have a "perfect" or "strict" (in Kant's sense) moral duty to ourselves *not* to treat ourselves qua "I"s as mere "it"s by performing actions that damage or destroy this capacity for positive self-determination, and we have an "imperfect" or "broad" (in Kant's sense still) moral duty to ourselves *to* treat ourselves qua "I"s as "I"s by acting creatively outwardly and inwardly in various ways so as to cultivate and express this capacity.[12] Or stated once again (more or less) in Neville's process philosophical terminology, we ought morally to develop and express ourselves as "ongoing organized activit[ies] coordinating other activities with an intentional representation of the self"—"I"s, in Neville's sense—who actively "transform the various values . . . into goals, objectives, ends, and the good" by "act[ing] in accordance with [the] abstract . . . principles . . . of logic."

Our moral duty to treat ourselves as "I"s by willing freely to "will what is rational" also implies a moral duty to treat other "I"s always as "I"s and never as mere "it"s, we now can see. For just as logically valid thinking requires us, in the manner explained above, to treat ourselves always as thinking and therefore self-determined "I"s and never as mere non-thinking and therefore other-determined "it"s, so it requires us—in ways I need now to specify and explain—to treat other "I"s always as thinking and therefore self-determined "I"s and never as mere non-thinking and therefore other-determined "it"s.

Since otherwise I affirm—in violation of the law of contradiction, and so in violation of my moral duty to myself to decide what beliefs to affirm and hence what actions to perform by deliberating logically validly—that the same action simultaneously both is and is not morally imperative to do (or not to do), I must affirm not only that all other "I"s have the same moral duties to themselves as I do to myself, namely, duties to "will what is rational" and hence also to cultivate and express their capacities for doing so, but also, to borrow one of Kant's formulations of the principle of universalizability, that "I ought never to act except in such a way that I can also will that my maxim should become a universal law."[13] I must agree, in other words, that I ought morally always to act toward all other "I"s only in ways that I can will that they act toward me. If I *cannot* will that other "I"s act toward me in a certain way—i.e., if I necessarily will that, whether they want to or not, others ought not so to act toward me—then, whether I want to or not, i.e., morally, I ought *not* to act toward them in this way; and if I *cannot not* will that others act toward me in a certain way, then I ought morally *to* act toward them in this same way.

Now, by willing any end or purpose whatever, including of course the morally imperative purpose of cultivating and expressing my capacity qua thinking "I" for rational self-determination, I necessarily will at the same time—since otherwise I will the defeat rather than the attainment of my purpose, which I cannot possibly do; it cannot be my will that my will be negated—that other "I"s ought, whether they want to or not, i.e., morally, not to treat me as an "it" which neither thinks nor wills and so has no purpose of its own by coercing or manipulating me to serve their purposes rather than my own, and therefore, whether I want to or not, or morally, I ought not to treat other "I"s as mere non-thinking and therefore non-willing "it"s by coercing or manipulating them to serve my purposes. For the reason that I cannot will that others coerce or manipulate me to serve their private purposes and so treat me as a mere other-determined "it" with no purposes of my own, I ought morally not to coerce or manipulate others to serve my private purposes and so treat them as mere other-determined "it"s who have no purposes of their own.

Not only ought I morally *not* to treat other "I"s as mere "it"s by coercing or manipulating them to serve my purposes rather than their own, moreover, but I ought morally *to* treat others as self-determined "I"s with purposes of their own by acting—at least sometimes, when I am able and in a position to do so—to help them to attain their purposes. "It is a duty of every man to be beneficent, i.e., to be helpful to men in need according to one's means," as Kant explains,

For every man who finds himself in need wishes that he might be helped by other men. But if he should make known his maxim of not wanting to give assistance in turn to others in their need—if he should make such a maxim a universal permissive law—then everyone would likewise refuse him assistance when he was in need, or at least would be entitled to refuse.

Since I *cannot not* will that others, whether they want to or not, treat me as a thinking and therefore willing "I" with purposes of my own by acting, at least sometimes, if they are able and in a position to do so, in positive ways to help me to attain my purposes if I am in need of their help, then, on the principle of universalizability, whether I want to or not, I ought to treat others as thinking "I"s who will purposes of their own by acting, at least sometimes, if I am able and in a position to do so, in positive ways to help them to attain their purposes if they are in need. Or in Kant's words, since "the selfish maxim [of never helping others who are in need] conflicts with itself when it is made a universal law," it follows that "the altruistic maxim of beneficence toward those in need is a universal duty of men."[14]

Now if all of us have moral duties qua "I"s not to treat other self-determined "I"s as if they were mere other-determined "it"s by coercing or manipulating them to serve our purposes, or, expressed in the language of the corresponding moral rights, if all "I"s have moral rights against all other "I"s not to be subordinated in this way to others' purposes, then these moral duties and rights must be implemented in our economic arrangements and policies. And assuming marginalism's supply-and-demand theory of economic value to be correct here, then, as over against Marx's labor theory of value, it is clear that, of the available alternatives, these moral duties and rights require a market economy with, for the most part, private ownership of the material means of production rather than a centrally planned economic arrangement with public ownership of the means of production. For at least in principle—although not necessarily also in fact, as I shall indicate momentarily—this arrangement is one within which interactions among individuals are non-coercive or voluntary, whereas in a centrally planned economy the interactions among individuals are in principle subordinated to purposes decided upon by those who formulate the central economic plan.[15]

A market economy with private ownership of the material means of production will not suffice by itself to implement this negative moral right not to be coerced or manipulated to serve externally imposed purposes, however. Monopoly and monopsony power in the market, what economists refer to as neighborhood effects, and "gross" inequalities in the distribution of wealth and/or income, for example, can and often do lead to violations of this moral right. Consequently we cannot rest content with a laissez faire policy toward the market. Not only must we adopt policies to prevent—or if necessary to regulate or even to take into public ownership and control—concentrations of monopoly and monopsony power in the market, which of course entail that some people have manipulative and perhaps even directly coercive power over others, but, since voluntary exchanges between some individuals may impose neighborhood effects coercively upon others (such as the smog which results from voluntary exchanges between consumers and producers of automobiles, to mention an example of considerable importance especially to those of us who live in Southern California), and since at some point inequality in the distribution of wealth and/or income gives the "haves" dominating power over the "have-nots," we must also intervene into the market's functioning with policies of various kinds to prevent at least the most oppressive neighborhood effects and to prevent "gross" inequalities of wealth and/or income from developing.

This negative moral right not to be subordinated to others' purposes is not the only moral right that must be implemented in our economic arrangements and policies, moreover. All of us have moral duties not only *not* to treat other "I"s as mere "it"s by coercing or manipulating them to serve our purposes rather than their own, but also *to* treat other "I"s as "I"s by acting in positive ways, at least sometimes, if we are able and in a position to do so, to help them if they are in need. And corresponding to this positive moral duty of "beneficence toward those in need," there is a positive moral right—the implementation of which also requires intervention into the market's functioning—to conditions of life on the basis of which it will be possible, at least in a minimal way, for all "I"s, including ourselves, to cultivate and express rational self-determination.

For the most part, this positive moral duty of beneficence does not require us to perform actions or courses of action to which others have corresponding moral rights, to be sure. It requires us, "according to [our] means," to act *sometimes*—i.e., not never—in positive ways to help others who are in need to attain their purposes, but it does not specify how often or in what ways to do so. If for example someone should happen to "need" a dish of ice cream in order to fulfill his or her purpose of satisfying a passion for sweets, I do not thereby have a moral duty—to which he or she has a corresponding moral right—to supply the ice cream. I have an "imperfect" moral duty, in Kant's sense, to promote others' welfare along with my own, but I do not have a "perfect" moral duty to perform this specific moral action. There is a progression from "imperfect" to "perfect" under the duty of beneficence, however, depending on the degree of urgency of the others' needs. I have a "perfect" moral duty to perform a specific action, then, to which someone else therefore has a corresponding "perfect" moral right against me, in the degree to which the action is necessary for meeting a basic need, i.e., a need which must be met if it is to be possible for him or her creatively to cultivate and express his or her capacities as a rationally self-determined "I." If and to the extent that my *not* acting will deprive him or her of conditions vital to the cultivation and expression of his or her potentialities as a self-determined "I," then to this same extent I have a "perfect" moral duty—to which he or she therefore has a corresponding moral right—*to* act in this specific way. I have a "perfect" positive moral duty to rescue someone from a burning building if I am able and in a position to do so, for example, to which he or she therefore has a corresponding "perfect" positive moral right to be rescued by me, since in this case my not acting in this specific way would deny him or her not only the possibility of cultivating and expressing rational self-determination but indeed the possibility of life itself.

Insofar as we are capable of doing so, therefore, this line of reasoning can be extended to show, we have positive moral duties, to which there are corresponding positive moral rights, to arrange and manage our economic (and other) institutions policy-wise in ways that provide social and material conditions of life on the basis of which all "I"s, including ourselves, will have effective power and opportunity to act creatively on purposes of their own so as to cultivate and express their capacities as rationally self-determined "I"s. And again, a policy of laissez faire toward the market will not suffice; at least some of these social and material conditions of life can be provided only by means of economic policies that intervene into the market's functioning.

Human beings have a basic need for at least a minimal level of material well-being, for example—an above-poverty level of income, let us call it—if they are to have effective power and opportunity for acting creatively in significant ways so as to cultivate and express their potentialities qua "I"s for rational self-determination. For the reason that market competition distributes income in accordance with what economists refer to as marginal value productivity, however, i.e., as determined by supply and demand, rather than in accordance with individuals' needs, including of course their needs for incomes adequate for cultivating and expressing their potential rational freedom, the market will not assure an above-poverty level for everyone. If an individual supplies a product or service that is scarce in relation to the demand for it, then to this extent his or her income will be high. But if he or she has little or nothing to sell in the market that is scarce in relation to the demand for it—as is in fact the case for roughly twenty percent of our population—then his or her income, and thus his or her power and opportunity to act creatively on purposes of his or her own, will be little or nothing as well. In order to meet this basic need, therefore, we must supplement the market's functioning with anti-poverty policies of various kinds.

So how does all of this relate to process philosophy? The understanding of moral obligation and its application to economic organization and policy presented in the preceding paragraphs derives largely from Kant and Hegel, not Whitehead, perhaps it is needless to say. But I nevertheless believe it to be one the basic content of which could also be derived from Neville's amended version of process philosophy.

If, as John B. Cobb, Jr. and David Griffin once maintained, process philosophy implies that "to be moral is to actualize oneself in such a way as to maximize the enjoyments of future actualities, insofar as these future enjoyments can be conditioned by one's present decision,"[16] i.e., if process philosophical moral theory requires us always to act—and hence also to organize and manage our social institutions policy-wise—so as to maximize the total quantity of "enjoyment," or indeed of anything whatever that is said to be intrinsically good or valuable, then the understanding I have outlined here is incompatible with it. For to act in this way would entail treating "I"s, including even ourselves, not as thinking and therefore self-determined "I"s who will ends of their own but, instead, as "it"s in the service of another, externally imposed end, namely, that of maximizing the total quantity of "enjoyment."

But if within the conceptual framework of process philosophy we emphasize instead, as Neville does, the essential epitomes and, in particular, "mind" as "action in accordance with abstract or eternal principles, such as those of logic and mathematics," "resolution" as "that organization of the person capable of transforming the various values sensed, responded to with developed sensitivity, needed, desired, oriented to one's life, socially structured, and mentally understood, into goals, objectives, ends, and the good," and especially the "I" as "an ongoing organized activity coordinating other activities [including those of "mind" and "resolution"] with an intentional representation of the self," then I think we imply that our fundamental moral duty is—in the manner described above—to treat all "I"s, including ourselves, always as self-determined "I"s and never as mere other-determined "it"s. Even though the language in which it would be expressed would of course be radically different from the Kantian and Hegelian language I have used, the moral and economic content would nevertheless be similar to what I have proposed.

Notes and References

1. G.W.F. Hegel, *Philosophy of Right*, tr. T.M. Knox (Oxford: Clarendon Press, 1962), Para. 47, p. 43. Hereafter referred to as PR.

2. *Ibid.*, Para. 4, Addition, p. 226.

3. G.W.F. Hegel, *Logic*, tr. William Wallace (Oxford: Clarendon Press, 1975), Para 24, p. 38.

4. PR, Para. 4, Addition, p. 226.

5. *Ibid.*, Para. 4, p. 21.

6. G.W.F. Hegel, *The Philosophy of History*, tr. J. Sibree (New York: Dover Publications, Inc., 1956), p. 442.

7. PR, Para. 4, Addition, p. 226.

8. *Logic*, Para. 24, p. 9.

9. G.W.F. Hegel, *Science of Logic*, tr. A.V. Miller (London: George Allen and Unwin, Inc., 1969), p. 50.

10. PR, Para. 15, Addition, p. 230.

11. *Ibid.*, Para. 10, Addition, p. 229.

12. See Immanuel Kant, *The Metaphysical Principles of Virtue*, tr. James Ellington (Indianapolis: Bobbs-Merrill Co.; The Library of Liberal Arts, 1964), "Introduction," pp. 36-73.

13. Immanuel Kant, *Groundwork of the Metaphysic of Morals*, tr. H.J. Paton (New York: Harper Torchbooks, 1964), p. 70.

14. *The Metaphysical Principles of Virtue*, p. 117.

15. This would not be so, of course, if Marx's labor theory of value were true. If all value is created by labor-power's laboring—including the value of labor-power itself—then capitalist profit derives from surplus value created by labor-power, i.e., by workers, but coercively appropriated by capitalists, in which case workers are treated as "it"s in service to purposes imposed upon them by capitalists.

16. John B. Cobb, Jr. and David Ray Griffin, *Process Philosophy: An Introductory Exposition* (Philadelphia: The Westminster Press, 1976), p. 57.

CHAPTER 9

Political Economy: A Process Interpretation

W. Widick Schroeder

I
Introduction

The normatively desirable forms of economic and political institutions and the proper relations between them are the central topics of this essay. The mode of thought which has come to be called process philosophy is used to address this topic. Rooted in the seminal work of Alfred North Whitehead and Charles Hartshorne and deeply in the debt of the Platonic tradition, process philosophy and its correlate, process theology, have become significant philosophical and theological movements in the six decades since Whitehead initiated this style of thinking in several major volumes in the 1920s and 1930s.[1]

In spite of the common debt to Whitehead and to Hartshorne, religious social ethicists informed by the process perspective have not attained a consensus on appropriate modes of economic and political organization and other topics in social ethics.

In their development of process religious social ethics, ethicists have both used and abused process metaphysics. Insofar as ethicists have appealed to process thought to develop generic notions and to formulate propositions applicable to all actual creatures, they have used process metaphysics. Insofar as ethicists have sought to legitimate more specialized propositions by citing more general ones, they have abused process metaphysics, for one cannot derive more specialized propositions from more general ones. One must base specialized propositions on the defining characteristics of particular concrete actual entities or societies of actual entities. One may legitimately set these more specialized propositions in the context of more general propositions, but one must verify them by observing creatures with particular defining characteristics and by using the analogical method.

At this less inclusive level, religious social ethicists informed by process metaphysics disagree about the nature of the pertinent facts, the sequence of priority of formal, dynamic and unifying factors in the several spheres of the human social order, the constitutive and regulative principles of justice, the best conditions and structures to evoke maximal harmony for human beings under the conditions of existence, the plasticity of human nature, the relative importance of form and context in social ethics, the possibility and extent of human sanctification under the conditions of existence, and the probable consequences of alternative public policy proposals.

This essay characterizes the nature of the human social order using categories of interpretation consonant with process metaphysics, formulates principles of justice which are applicable to human beings in this historical epoch, and addresses the bases for persistent disharmony in human life. In the light of these considerations, the essay proposes the most fitting form of human economic and political organizations. In developing these themes, process metaphysics provides the generic notions in relation to which the more specialized propositions pertaining to the topics addressed here are set.

Democratic capitalism is defended as a fitting form of economic/political organization. Both socialism, involving state ownership of the modes of production, and laissez-faire capitalism, involving private ownership unrestrained by the state, are rejected. (Of course, these bald alternatives are ideal types. Under the conditions of existence neither type exists, and many proponents of these types will qualify them in some ways.)

In arguing democratic capitalism is most consonant with the principles of justice and with the nature of human nature, the author takes issue with many religious social ethicists, including both those informed by process modes of thought and also those informed by alternative philosophical or theological perspectives, who promote democratic socialism as the preferred political economy.[2]

The following section of this essay is devoted to a delineation of the spheres of the human social order. This quasi-descriptive analysis is a precondition for the succeeding constructive formulations.

II
The Spheres of the Human Social Order

Human beings are enmeshed in a network of social relations shaped by their locations in the spheres of the human social order. The sequence of events constituting the organizing center of the human being is more fundamental and elemental than abstractions that are derived from it. Consequently, humans transcend and are not unequivocally bound by their location in the human social order, but their lives are shaped by the pattern of relations in which they are set.

The defining characteristics of human beings and the environment in which they find themselves provide the basis for the delineation of the spheres of the human social order. This delineation is necessary in order to set the economic sphere in the context of the other spheres of the social order. By viewing the characteristics of each sphere and by discerning their relations to each other, one can illumine the limits human life places on economic institutions.

The human organism consists of complex societies and sub-societies which are organized hierarchically. Some of the societies and sub-societies can exist outside the human organism. Others apparently depend upon the sustaining environment within the human organism for their survival. The organizing center of the human organism is a sequence of very high-grade occasions, some of which are conscious. They are unified by memory, by their objectification in the Divine Life, and by a formless form so protean it can contain within it all the occasions it encompasses.

The ultimate percipient occasions constituting the human organizing center are partially dependent on the body, partly independent of the body, and partly determinative of bodily activities. Although all occasions have some capacities for novelty of response to circumstances, human freedom is focused in the organizing center. Human rational shaping capacities are also embodied in the organizing center. The peak of consciousness is the negative judgment. In a negative judgment one imagines the absence of something which is present, thus intensifying experience and permitting the development of theory. Compared to other living creatures of which we have any direct knowledge, humans possess the greatest capacity for novelty of response to circumstances. This capacity enhances the ability of humans to live and to live well.

The aim of existence is the evocation of harmony and intensity of feeling. Human freedom should be evaluated by the extent to which human actions maximize harmony and intensity of feeling of the whole.[3] It is easier to formulate this proposition than it is to actualize it. In seeking to maximize the harmony and intensity of feeling of the whole, one must make complex judgments about the consequences of present actions for future events. Because of finitude, ignorance, and the freedom of other creatures, one is never certain of the future consequences of one's actions. One must exercise prudential judgments and humans do not necessarily agree on these judgments. Therefore, one's decisions about actions designed to maximize harmony and intensity of feeling are ambiguous. The best means to attain the objective are never unequivocally clear.

In the delineation of the spheres of the human social order, one must consider human biological, social, rational, and decision-making factors. In addition one must assess the relative importance of formal, dynamic, and unifying facets of human experience in the several spheres of the human social order. The spheres of the social order include the familial, the social, the ethnic, the economic, the political, the cultural, and the religious.

The Familial Sphere

The family and other small primary groups are rooted in biological necessity and human needs for intimacy and inclusive personal relations. Humans can be accepted more fully in the totality of their being in these small groups than in groups identified with institutions in most of the other spheres of the human social order. The form of the person and the sensitivity and fullness of responses which characterize love can best be manifest in the familial sphere and in the religious sphere. (The possibility does not ensure the reality, as heinous activities among people in both spheres starkly reveal.) Power, both linear and reciprocal, is tertiary in family relations.[4] Because the form of the person may be taken more fully into account in interpersonal relations in small groups, reciprocal power and love may be enhanced in primary groups.

The Social and Ethnic Spheres

The social and ethnic spheres of the human social order are rooted in biological necessity, social destiny, and human rational shaping capacities. Persons affirming comparable life styles share a common social status, and persons with a common historical destiny in a subculture may constitute an ethnic group. People in ethnic groups may share common real or imputed racial characteristics. Except insofar as status and ethnic characteristics may condition the formation of primary groups and economic/political interest groups, status and ethnic groups are not directly pertinent to the central topic of this essay. Formal factors are dominant in these spheres; dynamic and unifying factors are set in relation to formal components.

The Economic Sphere

The economic sphere is grounded in biological necessity and human rational shaping capacities. Human needs for food, fiber, and shelter are the basic and elemental factors evoking an economic sphere. Because humans want not only to live but to live well, they have evolved a plethora of economic activities. Indeed, because no human activity can be carried on without some physical base, economic factors are intimately associated with activity in all human social institutions. Nonetheless, economic activity focuses primarily on the production, exchange, and consumption of goods and services.

In earlier historical epochs and in some relatively undifferentiated social systems in the current historical epoch, the spheres of the social order were not as sharply separated and rationally organized as they are in modern post-traditional societies. People often produced the goods they consumed. In such instances, they had relatively simple exchange relations, and they often bartered with one another.

An economy based on a monetary system and the rationalization of production, consumption and exchange relations requires an extensive rationalization of the spheres of the social order, one of the characteristics of post-traditional societies. Cost/benefit calculations and the promotion of the most efficient means to attain given economic ends become much more important in post-traditional societies. People prize technical rationalism in these societies, and they promote its widespread use.[5] Because economic power is shaped by rules and regulations of justice, the legal order is very important in shaping economic life.

Formal rational values dominate economic considerations in the economic sphere in all societies, but they become more salient in post-traditional societies. Because of the primary importance placed on these factors in the economic sphere, a person must be evaluated primarily on the basis of his/her competence in a particular job, not on the basis of his/her general character.

The primacy of evaluation based on rationally delimited competencies precludes the fulfillment of human life in economic relations, for the whole person in his/her rich particularity cannot be central in the economic sphere. Forms are primary in the economic sphere, power is secondary, and the inclusivity of love is tertiary.

The Political Sphere

Social necessity and human rational shaping capacity produce the political sphere in human life. Humans find themselves in social groups. Because of the number of people in the groups and the legitimate and illegitimate desires of people to pursue their own activities, coordination is necessary to enhance the harmony of group life and to defend the group from others. Humans respond to this social necessity by evolving governments to develop rules and regulations of justice to shape and to coordinate human life.

The power given people in the political sphere to make and to enforce the rules and regulations of justice illustrates the primary position of power and the secondary position of forms in the political sphere. Informed in part by the lure of the harmony of life with life and will with will, people in the political sphere are aware of the love which unifies a community and sustains reciprocal power between its members. Love is tertiary in the political sphere, but it works to enhance the degree of reciprocal power and to evoke fitting rules and regulations of justice.

Reciprocal power is "two-way" or relational power. In reciprocal power, agents mutually influence and are affected by each other. This mode of power is central in process thought. According to the principle of relativity, a primary notion in process thought, every being is a potential for every becoming.

The *degree* of reciprocal influence varies widely from creature to creature and may be more fully manifest in some of the spheres of the human social order than in others. Because political leaders cannot ignore public opinion and the responses of people to their actions, power in the political sphere, as in all the spheres of the social order, is reciprocal. However, reciprocity is *not* equal. Political leaders influence the people to a greater degree than the people influence the political leaders. Representative democracy may enhance the reciprocity between the people and their political leaders, but even representativeness cannot eliminate the inequality of relations.

Politicians live in a house of power. Unfortunately, under the conditions of existence, reciprocal power is frequently diminished and the conflict of will with will and life with life often takes place. An approximation of linear or "one-way" power emerges. However, even in the most blatant physical conflicts, the seeds of redemption are present, for humans have at least some vague intuition of the divine evocation of the harmony of life with life and the enhancement of intensity of feeling within and between human beings.

Relations between economic and political institutions have always been problematic.[6] Social necessity, the "natural" ground for political organization, is grounded in the higher phases of experience. In contrast, biological necessity, the "natural" ground for economic organization, is grounded in the lower phases of experience.[7]

Because social necessity is superior to biological necessity, the state, which is rooted in social necessity, in principle has the right to intervene in the economic sphere, which is rooted in biological necessity. In fact, state intervention varies widely, depending upon the dominant values in a given society, the political conditions in a particular given society, and the status of technology and science in the given society.

The enforcement of the rules and regulations of justice entails the apprehension of those persons who have been alleged to violate the law, to try them, and to punish those who have been found to violate the laws of a given state. Without embodying the form of justice and the lure of love in its life, a state cannot long endure. People will withdraw their loyalty to the political leadership and a pre-revolutionary or revolutionary condition will exist.

The Cultural Sphere

Human rational shaping capacities and the free play of imagination combine to produce a cultural sphere. Art, music, drama, sports, literature, poetry, science, and philosophy are all productions of the free play of imagination with the conditions of existence. Institutions in this sphere include those which evoke, sustain, transmit, and store these human cultural creations, such as schools, research institutes, libraries, and museums.

The most generally held cultural values give shape to the forms of social organizations extant in a given society. These general cultural conditions become embodied in a legal order which both legitimates and sustains various social institutions. The legal order also defines the relations which *ought* to exist between social institutions within and between the various spheres of the human social order.

The free play of imagination evokes various forms of definiteness, some of which participate in the harmonization of life. In this manner, justice, power, and love are embodied in cultural forms.

The Religious Sphere

The religious sphere is the final sphere of the human social order. Human awareness of the divine presence evokes religious institutions. Love, entailing an intuition of an ultimate harmony of harmonies and involving reciprocity and sensitivity of response, is the leading component in God-world relations.

It is beyond the scope of this essay to explore this sphere in detail, but the place of religious institutions in the human social order must be noted. Religious institutions' constitutive acts are worship, and these activities are the hallmarks of religious institutions.

Because power and justice are salient in the social, ethnic, economic, political, and cultural spheres of the human social order, human fulfillment can be most adequately expressed in interpersonal relations in the religious and familial spheres where love is primary or secondary.

Economic and political institutions, in which love is the tertiary component, cannot sustain inclusive human fulfillment, but better forms of economic and political organization may enhance it. The contribution of economic and political institutions to the harmony of life with life will be discussed in the fifth section of this essay. Before this discussion can be developed, it is necessary to address the levels and the principles of justice in relation to the spheres of the human social order and to delineate the bases for disharmony in human life.

III
Justice and the Spheres of the
Human Social Order

Power, Justice and Love in the Spheres
of the Human Social Order

Justice is the great regulator sustaining interpersonal and intergroup relations. Because dynamic, formal, and unifying components are embodied in every instance of becoming, these universal components of experience are three-in-relation.

These components are found in every instance of our self-conscious experience. Using the analogical method, one can posit their presence in the becoming of all creatures. Certainly the components are present in all entities of which we have any direct knowledge.

In human social life, power refers to the dynamic facets of human life, justice refers to the formal facets of human life, and love refers to the empathizing and unifying facets of human life. In order to indicate the limits nature imposes on the possibilities for human fulfillment in the spheres of the human social order, the sequence of priority of power, justice, and love in each of the spheres must be elaborated. These priorities were sketched in the discussion in the preceding section, but they need to be set in the context of the discussion of the principles of justice, the focus of this section.

In interpersonal relations, justice is the leading component, love is the secondary component, and power is the tertiary component. The form of the person may be more fully taken into account in interpersonal relations than in any other relations. Reciprocal power, in which each agent directly effects and is directly affected by the other, is potentially and sometimes actually most fully realized in interpersonal relations. In these instances love, which is the secondary component in interpersonal relations, is saliently manifest. Power is tertiary in interpersonal relations, and linear power relations may be minimized in interpersonal relations.

Because the form of the person may be most fully taken into account in interpersonal relations, reciprocity in power relations may be maximized in interpersonal relations. Primary groups potentially and sometimes actually offer the greatest possibilities for human fulfillment, for the particularity of persons can be most richly taken into account in small groups. Such rich fulfillment is not possible in human relations shaped by economic or political structures. Because of the scale of relations in these spheres, the many frequently have to be counted as one, so the particularity of a person is not fully acknowledged. In addition, human relations shaped by institutions in these spheres tend to be circumscribed and less inclusive than relations in groups in the familial, social, and religious spheres.

In the economic sphere, formal components are primary, dynamic factors are secondary, and unifying factors are tertiary, so justice, power, and love constitute the sequence of the triad in this sphere. In societies prizing technical rationalism, the primacy of the formal facet of experience is manifest in the application of cost/benefit analysis techniques to enhance efficiency and to maximize profits, in bureaucratic organization, and in the use of money to assess the value and to facilitate the exchange of the goods and services produced by people in institutions in this sphere.

Power is the secondary component in the economic sphere. Because of the priority of formal components in the economic sphere, peaceful "persuasion" characterizes economic transactions. A stable social order and general agreement about exchange practices are essential to the efficiency of economic institutions. In economic activity, voluntary actions and reciprocal power predominate. Acquisition by plunder is the way of war through political action, not the way of economic interchange.

Power is the leading component in the political sphere, justice is the secondary component, and love is the tertiary component. Through political action the state determines the rules and regulations of justice which define relations between institutions in all the spheres of the human social order. Informed by the general climate of opinion and the political configurations in a given society, the people in the political sphere promulgate, administer, and enforce the rules and regulations of justice in that society.

Without the form of justice and the lure of love, people in a society will not support their political leadership over an extended period of time. *Realpolitik* may be a short-term expedient, but it cannot serve as a long-term policy. Reciprocal power is incompatible with *realpolitik*.

One of the perennial appeals of a democratic polity is its promotion of persuasive and reciprocal power. In democracies politicians must try to persuade the public, and, in turn, they are persuaded by the public.

Nonetheless, reciprocal power is frequently less salient in this sphere than in the other spheres of the social order. In fact, persons representing institutions in the other spheres of the human social order frequently appeal to persons representing political institutions to enforce the rules and regulations of justice by coercing recalcitrant individuals.

The basic reason for the diminution of reciprocal power in the state is its monopoly on the legitimate exercise of physical force within a given geographical territory. (In revolutionary situations, some groups challenge this right, and civil war erupts.) Agencies of the state must ultimately maintain order, peace and harmony within and between the multiple subcommunities in the state. If political leaders fail to persuade recalcitrant individuals and/or groups to obey the law and they consider changes in the rules and regulations of justice to be impossible and/or undesirable, the state must use its coercive power—ultimately physical force—to sustain domestic tranquility. In addition, it must sometimes utilize force or the threat of force to defend its people from external threats.

In the cultural sphere, novel forms and novel propositions are evoked by the free play of human imagination responding to forms embodied in actual occasions in the world. Persuasive power is dominant, for humans are moved toward propositions that are true, actions that are good, and objects that are beautiful by persuasion and not by coercion.

Informed by the general climate of opinion evoked by values embodied in cultural objects and in the feeling tones and intellects of most people in a given society, politicians shape the rules and regulations of justice in a given society.

The slow drift toward greater freedom for more humans in more societies that has characterized the past three millenia is a function of novel ideas and novel technologies. Freedom and destiny have interplayed in this long process.

In the religious sphere, love is the leading component from both the human and divine perspectives. From the divine point of view the sequence is "love, power, and justice"; from the human point of view the sequence is "love, justice, and power." Because reciprocal power is so closely related to love, the intrinsic interrelatedness of the components is maximized in the religious sphere.

Given this qualification, one may say that God first manifests Its love by responding to the contribution the creatures of the world make to Its life and then by seeking to evoke the becoming of new creatures by supplying them with an initial aim. This initial aim ensures that the forms of definiteness appropriated by a new emerging creature can be unified by that creature. In the process, God seeks to evoke harmony and intensity of feeling. After this creature unifies itself, it is then objectified in the Divine Life, and the process is repeated.

From the human point of view, God's subjective aim evokes the human's initial aim. The human rightly or "justly" appropriates forms of definiteness from creatures in its causal past and from the primordial facet of God's nature.

The creature actualizes itself through a dynamic process of unification of data from its physical and conceptual poles. In this process it is guided by its subjective aim. After it is actualized, the emerging creature in its role as an object is a "power" which affects all subsequent creatures.

Religious institutions ought to be shaped by persuasive love. If this is the case, human associations shaped by religious institutions provide rich opportunities for inclusivity and relationality. Along with the family and small friendship groups, they potentially offer the greatest opportunities for rich and inclusive human relations.[8]

This discussion of the sequence of priority in the various spheres of the human social order sets the stage for the discussion of the levels and the principles of justice. These notions provide guidance for the discussion of the normatively desirable relations between the economic and political spheres.

The Levels of Justice

There are three dimensions or levels of justice, intrinsic, legal, and transformative. Intrinsic justice refers to the defining characteristics of a particular actual entity, subsociety, or society. For example, rocks, trees, animals, and humans possess different defining characteristics and hence differ in claims for intrinsic justice. Human capacities for deliberation, reflection, and sensitivity of response to changing circumstances exceed those of any other creatures of whom we have any direct knowledge. Humans have an intrinsic claim to be treated as centered, deliberating, sensitive creatures. Intrinsic justice acknowledges the legitimacy of this claim.

In the human realm, there are two other dimensions of justice. The first is a formal or legal dimension analogous to the classical idea of distributive justice. The second is a dynamic dimension analogous to the classical notion of unifying, creative or transformative justice. In this dimension formal justice is surpassed for the sake of justice.

Creative or transformative justice is essential to human life, for no formal rule or regulation of justice is fully applicable to a given circumstance. In addition, circumstances change, and laws applicable to one historical epoch may be inappropriate to succeeding ones.

Creative justice is grounded in the primacy of the dynamic side of experience and in the unifying facet of experience. In process thought, this dynamic primacy is reflected in the ultimacy of the category of creativity. Creativity stands beyond the forms and is inexplicable by the forms. It is always manifest through the dynamic realization of actual entities, but it is never exhausted by the realization of actual entities. It is the universal of universals. Because of its ultimacy, it cannot be demonstrated by appeal to a penultimate principle. The sole appeal is to intuitive insight. One may employ linguistic symbols to focus one's attention on creativity, but one cannot demonstrate its ultimacy by appeal to linguistic symbols.

The unification of the dynamic and formal aspects of experience is a result of creative synthesis or creative transformation. By analogy, this elemental unification is seen in the surpassment of particular rules and regulations of justice for the sake of justice. A process social ethic is ultimately a contextual or situational social ethic.

Because of the dynamic bias in emergent evolution, life would be unbearable without creative justice. At the same time, without legal or distributive justice, life would be chaotic and arbitrary. In human life, transformative justice evokes changes in legal justice to help legal justice more closely fit new and novel situations.

The state is necessarily concerned primarily with legal justice. However, the widespread prevalence of the pardon of human actions or commutation of juridical sentences among human communities points to the ubiquity or at least implicit awareness of the ultimacy of creative justice.

Principles of Justice

Every society evolves rules and regulations of justice. These rules and regulations are more formally rationalized in some societies than in others. General cultural conditions determine the extent to which the rules and regulations of justice are elaborated and formalized. In the Occident, the rules and regulations have been richly elaborated, and lawyers and judges have become key agents in this extensive rationalization of the legal order.

Three general principles of justice stand behind and are embodied in the specific rules and regulations of justice shaping social life in a given society in a given historical epoch. The three principles are self-determination informed by excellence, equality appropriate to form, and order/peace/harmony. These principles are rooted in the dynamic, formal, and unifying aspects of our experience.

As noted earlier, creativity is the ultimate category, inexplicable by any other notion. In human life, it is manifest in the dynamic aspects of our experience, including our capacity to deliberate and to make decisions. This capacity for freedom and self-determination is too widespread and too foundational to be put aside as a misconstruction. Purposiveness, valuation, and responsibility inform the entire tone of human life.

Freedom is the constitutive principle of justice. However, freedom understood merely as the ability to do what one wants to do or has the power to do is a sophistic view of freedom. Freedom needs to be informed by excellence. The person who is authentically free seeks to act so as to enhance the harmony and intensity of feeling of the whole.[9] It is much easier to state this maxim than it is to actualize it. Because humans are finite, ignorant of some things, and make excessive claims for themselves, it is impossible to actualize fully the principle. The implications of this observation for political economy will be considered subsequently.

The quest for excellence is rooted in the divine lure for harmony and intensity of feeling. The initial aims of the ultimate percipient occasions constituting the human soul are derived from the divine subjective aim. The internal relatedness of an emerging creature to creatures in its causal past and the immanence of the future in the present underscore the social character of existence and concern of the individual occasion for the many constituting the universe as a whole.

The other two principles of justice, equality appropriate to form and order/peace/harmony, are regulative rather than constitutive. Equality is grounded in human rationality, and order/peace/harmony are grounded in human community. They impose limits on the actions of the individual. People abuse their freedom, freedom and equality are not perfectly compatible, and the community can oppress as well as support human freedom. Consequently, the three principles of justice cannot be perfectly harmonized.

Equality is a mathematical ideal grounded in the notions of oddness, evenness, and congruence. It is never fully manifest under the conditions of existence, for no two creatures are *exactly* equal. In reality, the principle must be applied to creatures who are roughly equal, or who are equal for purposes of specific rules and regulations of justice. At a minimum, the principle requires that laws be applied equally to all the persons in the categories designated in the applicable law. The qualification "appropriate to form" is affixed to the principle of equality to acknowledge the legitimacy of the qualification to the principle of equality.

In spite of this general legitimacy, the precise limits which form imposes on equality in human life are subject to debate and review. No one denies that age legitimately limits equality. Young children are not expected to obey laws applying to adults. At the same time, there is ambiguity about the age at which children should be considered adults.

This biological limitation on equality is even more ambiguous in relation to human sexuality. Some sexual differences must be taken into account in formulating the rules and regulations of justice, but the extent to which they should inform the rules and regulations of justice is ambiguous. The limits which sexuality imposes on equality have undergone substantial change from one epoch to another and vary substantially between societies in the same historical epoch.

Social function also limits the principle of equality. Presidents, prime ministers, and chancellors are afforded some privileges by law which are not available to all people. The legitimacy of wage and salary differences among various types of employees rests in part on the implicit or explicit acknowledgement of the legitimacy of different rewards for various social functions. (The legitimacy also rests on consumer preferences, for the demand for various labor skills varies with the demand for the goods and services those skills can produce.)

Political conflict often emerges between those advocating a narrower and those advocating a broader understanding of human equality. The relative importance of human freedom and the limits the state may legitimately impose on people are other facets of this conflict.

The third principle of justice is order/peace/harmony. Rooted in God's harmonization of the forms of definiteness in Its primordial nature and in the derivative human experience of the lure for harmony and intensity of feeling, this principle recognizes the legitimacy of the quest for order, peace, and harmony in the life of a living community and in the relations between various living communities.

The tension between the rights of the individual and the rights of the community is reflected in the interplay between the three principles of justice. The freedom of individuals is both enhanced and repressed by the claims of equality and of the rights of the community. The proper balance between individual freedom and equality and between individual freedom and the claims of the community is not static. Changes both in the general climate of opinion and in technological developments affect the balance.

In one's constructive work, one is guided by one's assessment of the relative importance of the three principles in a given context, by one's view of the limits imposed on the harmony of life with life under the conditions of existence, and by one's prudential judgments about the likely consequences of particular public policies and particular forms of economic and political organization for human life.

The next section examines the bases for the frequently experienced disharmony of life with life. The concluding section draws on the delineation of the spheres of the human social order, the principles of justice, and the bases for disharmony in human life to develop a normatively desirable form of the arrangements between economic and political institutions.

IV

The Sources of Disharmony in Human Life

One of the persistent issues in religious social ethics is the basis for the disharmony in human life. In process thinking, evil is interpreted in aesthetic categories. Experiences which are evil evoke intense disharmony. Experiences which are good evoke heightened harmony and intensity of feelings. The embodiment of fitting principles of justice enhances harmony; their absence evokes disharmony.

The Bases of Evil in Human Life

The bases of evil in human life in order of the increasing level of intentionality evoking the evil are finitude, sloth and lethargy, ignorance, and inordinate self-interest.

The basic source of evil is finitude. Things perpetually perish. From the human point of view events embodying peak experiences pass away. The present fades into the past; objectification entails loss. Because some of the vivid experiences of the present evoke intense disharmony, some of this loss may be for the better. Unless succeeding creatures can encompass intensely disharmonious events as minor contrasts in a higher synthesis, the way of anesthesia is the way of peace. In spite of this positive evaluation of loss, the fact remains that the highest aspects of human achievement are lost.

Finitude also entails exclusion. If one decides to actualize some potentiality, other potentiality is not actualized. Coupled with the other factors contributing to disharmony in human life, the limits finitude imposes on human life may exacerbate the disharmonious aspects of experience.

The second source of evil is sloth and lethargy. Humans find the drag of the causal past to be greater than the lure for creative innovation in the present. Human acts of omission enhance evil patterns of social organization and creaturely practice. Sometimes humans simply do not have the willful energy to do that which needs to be done to reduce evil and to promote the good.

Ignorance is the third source of evil in human life. At a lower level, ignorance of the probable consequences of certain activities and/or of the understanding of certain laws may evoke substantial disharmony. Ignorance of certain laws, natural or human, is illustrative of this level of ignorance. Inadequate medical knowledge may lead to a prescribed course of treatment which is ineffectual or injurious. Inadequate economic knowledge may lead to public policies which evoke economic depressions and widespread human suffering.

At a higher level, ignorance of decisions contemporaries are making may evoke disharmony. The internal freedom of contemporary occasions prevents any one of them knowing unequivocally what its contemporaries are doing. A shared past and the ordering capacity of the divine subjective aim assure that contemporary occasions will not make utterly incompatible decisions, but these factors do not assure that contemporaries will make maximally compatible decisions.

Because human capacity to respond in a novel manner to the events of the causal past is greater than the capacity of other creatures on this planet to do so, humans are less certain than are members of sub-human species that the consequences of their actions will be the foreseen ones. Consequently, the prudential judgments one makes based on one's assessment of the probable consequences of particular public policy proposals and of particular courses of action are always more or less problematic. If unanticipated responses to one's actions occur, the actions may prove to be harmful.

Inordinate self-interest is the final source of evil in human life. All too frequently, human beings pursue their own self-interest excessively, placing their own interests and the interests of their family above the concerns for the well-being of the whole.

The boundary between legitimate self-interest and excessive self-interest is obscure. Some self-interest is necessary for a creature to actualize itself. Even if one acknowledges that authentic self-interest requires an interest for well-being of the whole, some self-interest is obligatory. Because of the necessity to become *some* thing rather than *no* thing, self-interest is inherent in the nature of things. One has the right to be just towards one's self.

The heightened human capacity to entertain contrasts, and contrasts of contrasts, and to exercise negative judgments—the peak of consciousness—both exacerbates human self-interest and also promotes altruism. Most humans are concerned both with their own being and well-being and also with the being and well-being of the whole. In fact, the two are intrinsically interrelated, for a wholesome sustaining environment is essential for personal well-being.

In advancing public policy proposals and in positing a desirable form of political economy, one must take account of the pervasiveness and the persistence of self-interest and of the intermingling of egoism and altruism in human actions.

Implications of the Bases of Evil
for Economic and Political Life

People differ in their assessments of the degree of harmony of life with life possible under the conditions of existence, the plasticity of human nature, and the effect of the rearrangement of social institutions on the transformation of human nature.[10]

It makes a great deal of difference for social policy and for one's view of desirable forms of social organization whether one locates the sources of disharmony within the human being, in social institutions, or in some combination of the two. If one thinks that the locus of disharmony is essentially within the human being, one will be relatively disinterested in the transformation of social institutions. If one locates the sources of disharmony in factors external to the individual, one will be very interested in social transformation as *the* means to enhance the harmony of life with life possible under the conditions of existence.

If one locates the sources of disharmony as both internal and external, the situation is more complex. Both personal and social transformation may be seen as important ways to enhance the harmony of life with life.

One's views on these matters usually inform one's prudential judgments. If one is persuaded that both inordinate self-interest and also concern for the community as a whole are perenniel aspects of the human condition, one will be concerned with promoting social institutions that enhance the good of the community, protect the individual from the power of the community, promote the good of the individual, and protect the community from the power of individuals.

In the author's view, the loci of disharmony are both internal and external to the organism, and egoism and altruism are intermingled in human conduct. He bases these notions on personal experience and on the widespread experiences of humankind as embodied in the literature produced by the race. The constructive views advanced in the following section of this essay are informed by these notions and by the principles of justice enumerated here.

V

Capitalism and Democratic Polity: A Fitting Mode of Economic and Political Organization

Introduction

In the conclusion of this essay, the issues addressed in the foregoing sections are considered conjointly to develop a normative view of the fitting form of economic and political organization most likely to facilitate the following policy objectives:

1. Promote the embodiment of the principles of justice in the rules and regulations of justice.
2. Blunt and deflect widespread and persistent human propensities to promote their self-interests inordinately in economic and political activities.
3. Encourage and support widespread and persistent human propensities to promote the good of the community.
4. Protect the individual from the inordinate demands of the community.
5. Protect the community from the inordinate demands of the individual.
6. Foster growth and efficiency in the economic sphere.

The combination of a capitalist economic system and a democratic polity is best able to promote the six policy objectives just cited. This combination promotes individual self-initiative and self-determination, reduces gross inequalities, and facilitates the harmony of life with life in a living community. By separating economic and political power, by promoting checks and balances within and between institutions in the political and economic spheres, and by legitimating political intervention in the economic sphere for the sake of social justice, this arrangement blunts human self-interest and directs it into constructive channels. It also facilitates a concern with the whole by promoting democratic decision-making. The diffusion of power and the sustenance of multiple centers of initiative protect individuals and minorities from the powers of the community. At the same time, the community can limit through legal means the activities of individuals and corporations who violate the common good.[11]

The dynamic and emergent character of human life and the persistence of values and behavior patterns developed in other historical epochs underscore the need for flexible and innovative patterns of economic and political life. However, the direction of economic life should not be placed directly in the hands of politicians now or in the foreseeable future. The foreseeable future means at least several generations—beyond our present ability to discern the possibility. If human nature is substantially transformed, such full direction may eventually be warranted; but the author is skeptical about the likelihood of the radical transformation of human nature due to the structure of the human organism, the nature of the socialization process, and the necessity for some creaturely self-interest. At the same time, limited transformation has occurred, as the extension of freedom in some parts of the planet in the past three or four millenia shows. Moral progress is possible, and conditions for fostering moral progress should be encouraged.[12]

Because the well-being of the community is intimately related to its economic productivity, one must consider the impact both of the structural relations between economic and political entities and also of specific public policy proposals upon growth and efficiency in economic enterprises. This area is treated very lightly by most religious social ethicists, who are frequently more concerned with the common good of the community and the promotion of greater equality than with the growth and efficiency of economic enterprises. This omission is most unfortunate, for the unanticipated negative consequences of policies which diminish the growth and efficiency of economic enterprises endanger the quest for community as well as for the reduction of gross inequality.[13]

Democracy: A Fitting Form of Political Organization

The rule of the one, the some, or the many has characterized human political organizations. Monarchy, aristocracy, and democracy, the good forms of the rule of the one, the some, and the many, have been contrasted with despotism, oligarchy, and anarchy, the bad forms of the rule of the one, the some, and the many. It is beyond the scope of this essay to sort out the nuances between these types, but these broad formulations can serve to highlight the options available to humankind.

Democracy is most compatible with the constitutive principle of justice, i.e., freedom informed by excellence, for in a democracy many participate in the governing process. In large scale societies, representative democracy is required, for there are simply too many people for all to participate equally. Finitude is not the only limiting factor, for the necessity of a centered decision-making process demands that selected political leaders act on behalf of the group in any period of crisis.

Human capacity for justice is one of the bases for democracy, for human freedom and human concern for the well-being of the whole make democracy possible. Human capacity for injustice is the other basis for democracy. As noted earlier, humans not infrequently pursue their own self-interest inordinately. Human capacity for injustice makes democracy necessary, for democracy curbs the inordinate self-interest of political leaders by providing for their periodic election. The system of checks and balances within and between the executive, legislative, and judicial branches of government further blunts inordinate self-interest.

Universal suffrage furthers the principle of equality appropriate to form, for it minimizes the likelihood of inordinate inequality of income or political power in a society. The separation of economic and political power further curbs inordinate concentration of power in the hands of people in the political sphere or in the economic sphere and promotes multiple centers of initiative.

Democratic or Social Market Capitalism

Social market capitalism and democratic capitalism are terms used to describe the forms of economic and political organization that have emerged in several western democracies. The formal patterns considered here do not fit the details of any particular society, but they are embodied more or less fully in several countries in western Europe, the United States and Canada, and in some Pacific Basin countries.[14]

In democratic capitalism (the term used here to describe this arrangement of economy and polity), private ownership of the modes of production is combined with a democratic form of political organization. In such societies the government has the right to intervene in the economic sphere to promote the good of the community, to tax and to regulate economic enterprises, to engage in fiscal and monetary practices designed to promote stability and growth in the economic sphere, and to undertake various income redistribution schemes. At the same time, institutions in the economic sphere are not subsumed by the government.

As an economic system, capitalism possesses the following characteristics:

1. Private ownership of the means of production;
2. Free access to the market as a consumer, a producer, an investor, or a worker;
3. Pursuit of profit as a prime mover for economic activity; and
4. The use of a competitive pricing system to shape the allocation of land, capital, and labor, and to inform economic choices.

To function effectively, a capitalist economic system needs the support of a government and a legal order which (a) sustains voluntary and peaceful exchange through the enforcement of contracts and the maintenance of a viable monetary system, and (b) in most instances (some "natural" monopolies being the exception) prevents monopoly practices which disrupt normal supply-demand pricing mechanisms.

The government can intervene directly in the economic sphere in several ways. It counters monopolistic tendencies with appropriate antitrust actions, undertakes some types of research and development in the national interest, sponsors some forms of basic research, provides for some consumer protection, promotes programs to protect the environment from damage from industrial waste and emissions, maintains land use regulations and restrictions, protects humans from physically injurious products (particularly in health care), and requires reasonable safety standards in the work place.

The state has the responsibility for macroeconomic management through appropriate fiscal and monetary policy. These policies should promote the tendencies toward efficiency and growth fostered by a capitalist enterprise system. Finally, the government should engage in some income redistribution schemes to extend greater liberty to some and minimize inequality. All three principles of justice sustain the idea of some income redistribution. Gross inequality limits the freedom of some and threatens domestic tranquility.

The extent of income redistribution and the means that should be employed to undertake it are matters of considerable political debate. Issues centering around economic growth and efficiency and the appropriate level of inequality of income shape these debates. Because government economic policy should work with rather than against market forces, direct grants to persons needing economic assistance are generally preferable to elaborate government sponsored welfare schemes. Unfortunately, the inability or unwillingness of some of these potential grantees to support their children makes this principle moot in many instances.

One must assess the probable impact of proposed income redistribution schemes on growth and efficiency of the economy and on liberty, for proposals designed to attain greater equality may endager the liberty of some and evoke inefficiency and economic stagnation or decline. If such policies were enacted, less liberty and less equality for most people would be the probable long-run consequences.[15]

In formulating economic policy, one must take into account both the reality of finitude, sloth and lethargy, ignorance, and inordinate self-interest and also human concern for the whole. In addition, one must consider the need to reward individuals who work beyond the norm to promote growth and efficiency and/or make excellent decisions in allocating their resources, and to punish those who are indolent and/or make poor decisons in allocating their resources.

A capitalist enterprise economic system encourages risk-taking and the exercise of human freedom. Because capitalism places the risks for economic decisions on entrepreneurs, people with a very substantial interest in the success of an enterprise are responsible for making decisions and formulating policies.

Income redistribution schemes should seek to reduce gross inequality, but an egalitarian society is both impossible and undesirable.[16] At the foundational level, age grading, sexual differences, and the necessity for different social functions preclude a radically egalitarian society. Even if possible, such a society would be undesirable, for egalitarianism surpresses human freedom inordinately for the sake of equality and the community. Novel and innovative notions and actions do not mesh perfectly with equality and community. Public policy should seek to promote a minimal level of income in accord with the economic resources of a given community, but substantial differences in wealth and income do not necessarily denigrate the well-being of the community. In fact, they may enhance its well-being by promoting growth and efficiency in the economic sphere.

The separation of economic and political institutions promotes multiple centers of initiative in a society. This contribution is very important, for politicians all too frequently pursue their own self-interests inordinately. Politicians are deterred from usurping power and privilege by a democratic polity, the separation of economic and political power, the multiplication of factions, and a balance of power between the legislative, judicial, and executive branches of government. This arrangement—encouraged by tax policies designed to promote them—encourages the proliferation of voluntary associations so characteristic of some western societies and so vital to a vigorous public-serving private sector.[17]

In any economic system, production and consumption are two sides of the same coin. Consumer preference is central in a competitive enterprise system, for the pricing mechanisms based on supply and demand shape both consumption and production of goods and services.

Because of its reflection of consumer preferences, resource allocation based on supply-demand pricing mechanisms accentuates human freedom, the constitutive principle of justice. In spite of the merits of rooting consumption patterns on human choices, human freedom frequently is not informed by excellence. Finitude, sloth and lethargy, ignorance, and inordinate self-interest blunt or obscure the pursuit of excellence. The result is widespread market hedonism, in which people pursuing personal instant gratification degrade themselves and induce public vulgarity.[18]

Moralists have had much to say about conspicuous consumption and misallocation of human resources, but the solution to this condition is elusive. Every society must maintain a minimal level of public morality. Because bigots and fanatics are perennially tempted to try to use the state to foist their own views of proper morality upon others, public standards should not be unduly rigorous. Whenever possible, humans should be persuaded rather than coerced into higher levels of morality.

One of the most effective ways a democratic capitalist society can promote higher standards of morality is by its encouragement of voluntary associations through tax incentives and legal support. Associations in the private sector can contribute substantially to the promotion of higher standards of morality than those legally prescribed and to the development of the higher sensibilities of humankind evoked by the lure for the true and the beautiful. Religious institutions are significant participants in the private cultivation of public morality and in the promotion of the quality of life.[19]

Democratic socialists are persuaded that public ownership of the means of production will further the cause of social justice by enhancing equality and community and by promoting authentic instead of inauthentic freedom. These claims should be viewed with the utmost skepticism. Socialist policies would undercut the constitutive principle of freedom and would place far too much power in the hands of politicians and their families. The promoters of socialist schemes often place too much confidence in the perfectability of human nature, mistrust other people's exercise of human freedom, do not pay sufficient attention to economic growth and efficiency, and are too confident about the transformative capacity of socialist practices.

Democratic capitalist societies do sometimes experience too much inequality, fragmentation of community, and market hedonism. These undesirable traits are not unique to societies with capitalist enterprise systems; in fact, most of those societies with alternative forms of economy and polity suffer from the same maladies, frequently to a greater degree than do democratic capitalist countries.[20]

The government does have a role in countervailing these evils through some income redistribution schemes, appropriate consumer protectionism, protection of the environment, and the cultivation of a climate of opinion promoting community and the higher values of a civilized society—truth, science, art, adventure, and peace.

Nonetheless, perfection is not attainable, some inequality is desirable, and the government's role in these matters should be limited. As noted earlier, voluntary associations should play a major role in enhancing the quality of life in societies with a democratic polity and a capitalist enterprise economic system.

VI
Summary and Conclusions

The formulations developed in this essay are consonant with the propositions of process metaphysics, but these propositions are intermingled here with more specialized propositions pertaining to human beings and to human social institutions. The primacy of self-determination informed by excellence, the constitutive principle of justice, and the inevitable intertwining of harmonious and disharmonious components of experience have guided the constructive views developed here. Human capacity to manifest concern for the whole and human capacity to manifest inordinate self-interest suggest that power be diffused through the separation of the spheres of the human social order, the multiplication of factions, and a system of checks and balances in social organizations within and between the spheres of the human social order.

Utopians and idealists with visionary plans for the reconstruction of the social order grossly underestimate the persistence of inordinate human pursuit of self-interest. Cynics promoting *realpolitik* grossly underestimate human pursuit of justice and human concern for the common good. Neither the harmonies nor the furies prevail in human affairs.

The structure of economic and political institutions promoted here will not produce the perfect harmony of life with life, but democratic capitalism does make a more significant contribution to the enhanced harmonization of life with life consonant with the extension of human freedom than do other forms of economic and political organization now extant or likely to emerge in the foreseeable future.

Of course, no society embodies these forms perfectly; and the evolution of human life, coupled with new technological development, precludes idolization of any particular forms. In the economic sphere, more democratic forms of decision-making and work relations may well emerge.[21] It is conceivable that at some future time much less concern will have to be paid to economic growth and efficiency in the formulation of public policy and in the management of economic enterprises than is now the case. It is also conceivable economic abundance may modify human self-interest so markedly that a democratic socialist political economy would be desirable in some distant historical epoch.

In any event, this future is beyond the capacity of us in this generation to foresee. Although growth and efficiency should never unqualifiedly dominate public policy considerations, they will continue to be very important factors in public policy proposals for a long time to come. The quest for the novel and the innovative—so appealing to some followers of process thought—must be balanced by an awareness of the constraints which existing structures and practices impose on human beings. Some of these constraints may be surmounted in the future; others are intractable.

Process religious social ethicists promoting democratic capitalism assess the tractable and intractable facets of human existence differently than those promoting democratic socialism. Those affirming that freedom is the constitutive principle of justice and acknowledging the persistence of inordinate self-interest among humankind will be sympathetic to democratic capitalism. Those accentuating the principles of equality and community and envisaging the transformation of human nature in the direction of widespread and relatively unqualified altruism will be sympathetic to democratic socialism. In the author's judgment, the former assessment is more consonant with the facts embodied in the widespread experience of humankind than is the latter.

Notes and References

1. The major works of Whitehead which are directly pertinent to religious social ethics include the following: *Science and the Modern World* (Macmillan, 1925); *Religion in the Making* (Macmillan, 1926); *Process and Reality* (Macmillan, 1929); *Adventures of Ideas* (Macmillan, 1933); *Modes of Thought* (Macmillan, 1938).

2. Douglas Sturm is illustrative of persons informed by process thought who promote democratic socialism. In addition to his essay in this volume, the following essays illustrate his

use of process thought: "Process Thought and Political Theory: Implications of a Principle of Internal Relations," in John B. Cobb, Jr. and W. Widick Schroeder, editors, *Process Philosophy and Social Thought* (Chicago: Center for the Scientific Study of Religion, 1981), pp. 81-102; and "Toward a New Social Covenant: From Community to Commonwealth," in Bruce Grelle and David A. Krueger, editors, *Christianity and Capitalism: Perspectives on Religion, Liberalism and the Economy* (Chicago: Center for the Scientific Study of Religion, 1986), pp. 91-108.

Although he does not employ process thought, J. Philip Wogaman promotes a view of political economy close to Sturm's in his *Economics and Ethics: A Christian Inquiry* (Philadelphia: Fortress Press, 1986).

A more balanced view placing somewhat more emphasis on the principles of equality and community and relatively less emphasis on the principles of freedom and on growth and efficiency than is done here is advanced in Prentiss L. Pemberton and Daniel Rush Finn, *Toward a Christian Economic Ethic: Stewardship and Social Power* (Minneapolis: Winston Press, 1985).

Franklin I. Gamwell is less extreme than Sturm, but he also advocates substantially enhanced political participation in the economic sphere. In addition to his contribution to this volume, the following illustrate his orientation:"Happiness and the Public World: Beyond Political Liberalism," in Cobb and Schroeder, ibid., pp. 38-54; *Beyond Preference: Liberal Theories of Independent Associations* (Chicago: University of Chicago Press, 1984); and "Freedom and the Economic Order: A Foreward to Religious Evaluation," in Grelle and Krueger, op. cit., pp. 49-65.

Although they are not informed by process modes of thought, Robert Benne and Michael Novak both support democratic capitalism. Benne's views are most fully developed in *The Ethic of Democratic Capitalism: A Moral Reassessment*(Philadelphia: Fortress Press, 1981), and Novak's views are elaborated in *The Spirit of Democratic Capitalism* (New York: Simon and Schuster, 1982).

The author has addressed the problem of political economy in two other essays which draw on categories of analysis similar to those used here. His "American Democratic Capitalism: A Sympathetic Appraisal," in *Liberation and Ethics: Essays in Religious Social Ethics in Honor of Gibson Winter*, edited by Charles Amjad-Ali and W. Alvin Pitcher (Chicago: Center for the Scientific Study of Religion, 1985), pp. 146-158, addresses this topic directly. His "The Socialist/Communitarian Vision: New Dream or Old Nightmare?" in *Christianity and Capitalism: Perspective on Religion, Liberalism and the Economy* is a critical response to Douglas Sturm's essay in that volume cited earlier in this note.

It is beyond the scope of this essay to explore the relation of process thought to Marxism. In the main, Whitehead himself preferred social evolution to social revolution. The dialectic of negation is not a methodological tool for Whitehead, and the dialectic stops after a creature has become and is objectified in the Divine Life. Charles Hartshorne does address Marx in his *Insights and Oversights of the Great Thinkers: An Evaluation of Western Philosophy* (Albany, N.Y.: State University of New York Press, 1983). In that context he affirms the primacy of freedom and is critical of state controlled economies.

For a discussion of these relations, see Howard L. Parsons, "History as Viewed by Marx and Whitehead," *The Christian Scholar* 50 (1967), pp. 273-289. For a critique of process thought, see George V. Pixley, "Justice, and Class Struggle: A Challenge for Process Philosophy," *Process Studies* 413 (Fall, 1974), pp. 159-175.

In more recent times, process theologians have responded to liberation theologians, many of whom use Marxist modes of social analysis, in a variety of ways. Illustratively, see Delwin Brown, *To Set at Liberty: Christian Faith and Human Freedom* (Maryknoll, Orbis Books, 1981); John B. Cobb, Jr., *Process Theology as Political Theology* (Philadelphia: Westminster Press, 1982); and Schubert Ogden, *Faith and Freedom: Toward a Theology of Liberation*

(Nashville: Abingdon, 1979). None of these texts deals directly with detailed issues of political economy, but none of them explicitly affirms democratic capitalism. They stress community and equality more forcefully than this essay does.

Because so much of liberation theology is indebted to Marxist modes of social analysis, this literature is not directly pertinent to the focus of this essay.

3. This understanding of human freedom is the "freedom informed by excellence" developed later in this essay.

4. Bernard M. Loomer highlights the contrasting views of power in his essay, "Two Conceptions of Power," *Process Studies* 6 (1976), pp. 5-32. The distinction between linear and reciprocal power is elaborated in the subsection, "The Political Sphere" later in this section.

5. Max Weber is the classical figure who most saliently described the routinization and bureaucratization of modern society through the use of technical reason. (Technical reason seeks the most efficient means to attain a given end. It is truncated reason, for in itself it knows nothing directly of its grounding in the forms of definiteness. Ontic reason, which is aware of its participation in the forms of definiteness, must supplement technical reason.)

6. The central focus of this essay is the proper relation between economic and political institutions. Following a discussion of the bases for disharmony in human life under the conditions of existence and the development of the principles of justice which ought to guide human moral decisions, this topic will be discussed more fully than the delineation in this section permits.

7. In human life, both biological and social necessity combine with human rational shaping capacities to produce numerous forms of economic and political organization. In addition, relations between economic and political institutions vary substantially from epoch to epoch and between various societes in the same historical epoch. It is beyond the scope of this essay to deal with these historical matters in any detail.

8. The potential for the emergence of small inclusivistic friendship groups exists in institutions in all the spheres of the social order. These groups frequently develop and "humanize" relations in these spheres. However, in most instances the settings limit the extent and shape of these groups. As noted earlier, most of this discussion is focued on post-traditional large heterogeneous societies. Pre-literate and many traditional societies do not differentiate the spheres of the social order as sharply as modern and post-modern societies do.

9. Franklin I. Gamwell makes a similar point in his "Happiness and the Public World: Beyond Political Liberalism," op. cit. Gamwell is more confident about the ability of humans to formulate transcendent principles than is the author. Gamwell's strong confidence in reason relates him to the rational strand of process thought associated particularly with Charles Hartshorne and Schubert Ogden.

The author retains some residual skepticism about the adequacy of Gamwell's formulations for two reasons. The first has to do with the ambiguity of linguistic symbols. Words have to be used to evoke experience. The "maximization of the harmony of the whole" requires the experience of harmony and the experiential correlation between the word "harmony" and the experience of harmony.

The second has to do with the relations of the forms to each other. The forms are a multiplicity, related to each other by their envisagement by God. Unlike Plato's use of the dialectic in *The Republic* to lead one to a vision of the Good, the dynamic power at the apex of the hierarchy of the forms, Whitehead insists that the forms are a multiplicity, not a class. If they be such, one's faith in rationalism is based on a transrational intuition that there is a relational essence in the nature of things which reason can hope to penetrate.

As a consequence, the author uses the term "quasi-transcendental" rather than "transcendental" to underscore both his hope that humans have been able to formulate some authentic transcendental principles and also his residual skepticism about the ability of humans to formulate a priori universal principles.

10.   In classical Christian social ethics, the debates turned on contrasting views of the doctrine of sanctification and on the nature of human nature. Some felt human self-interest could be constrained, but even the saints continued to be sinners. Others held that the redeemed were indeed sanctified and were called to lead good and godly lives, informed by standards of perfection which were difficult but not impossible to attain. Still others took a middle position between these extremes. They urged Christians to strive toward full sanctification in their present lives, but they knew the goal could not be fully attained, at least for most if not all.

11.   No Protestant theologian in the twentieth century has written more perceptively on these matters than Reinhold Niebuhr. See especially *The Nature and Destiny of Man*(New York: Charles Scribner's Sons, 1949), vol. II, chapter 9, passim; and *The Children of Light and the Children of Darkness* (New York: Charles Scribner's Sons, 1944).

Because Niebuhr also notes the ambiguity of human motivation and formulates comparable principles of justice, the views on political economy developed here are similar to Niebuhr's. For the same reason they are similar to those of Robert Benne in his *The Ethic of Democratic Capitalism: A Moral Reassessment*, ibid., who is deeply in Niebuhr's debt for his constructive formulations.

These convergences occur in spite of the differences in the basic presuppositions informing this essay and the two authors just cited.

12.   Because forms are a necessary part of any moral decision, progress is possible in morality. Better rules and regulations of justice and better forms of social organization can enhance moral decisions. For an illustrative contrasting view envisaging moral decisions involving a free transcendental decision beyond forms, see Paul Tillich, *Systematic Theology*, vol. III (Chicago: University of Chicago Press, 1963), pp. 333-339. Tillich entertains a more radical view of human freedom than does the author. In *Love, Power and Justice* (New York: Oxford, 1953) Tillich develops views regarding the relation of love, power, and justice in interpersonal, intergroup, and Divine Relations similar to those developed here. However, he does not distinguish economic and political groups analytically and entertains a linear view of power.

13.   For a perceptive discussion of the tension between efficiency and equality, see Arthur Okin, *Equality and Efficiency: The Big Tradeoff* (Washington: The Brookings Institution, 1975).

For an illumining analysis of Western economic growth, see Nathan Rosenberg and L.E. Birdzell, Jr., *How the West Grew Rich: The Economic Transformation of the Industrial World* (New York: Basic Books, 1986).

14.   Although facets of the text are somewhat dated, *Capitalism Today*, edited by Daniel Bell and Irving Kristol (New York: Basic Books, 1970), addresses the ideological roots and the multi-faceted meaning of the term "capitalism" and explores the problems and promises of contemporary forms of capitalistic enterprise economies. For extended discussions of democratic capitalism, see Robert Benne, *The Ethic of Democratic Capitalism: A Moral Reassessment*, op. cit., and Michael Novak, *The Spirit of Democratic Capitalism*, op. cit.

For a defense of capitalism, see Irving Kristol, *Two Cheers for Capitalism* (New York: Basic Books, 1978).

15.   See Arthur Okun, *Equality and Efficiency: The Big Tradeoff*, ibid. For some broad discussions of capitalism and equality, see *Capitalism and Socialism: A Theological Inquiry*, Michael Novak, editor (Washington, D.C.: American Enterprise Institute for Public Policy Research, 1979). The essays by Irving Kristol and Peter Berger in that volume are especially evocative.

For a suggestive critique of politically defined efforts to limit growth, see Edward Walter, *The Immorality of Limiting Growth* (Albany: The State University of New York Press, 1981).

It should be noted that economic growth includes both goods and services. Conservation of natural resources is not necessarily incompatible with economic growth. Technological innovation, shifting consumer preferences (which ought to be promoted primarily through the pricing mechanisms and not through rationing), and increased production and consumption of services may lead to economic growth and reduced consumption of non-replenishable natural resources at the same time.

16.   Religious social ethicists sometimes appeal to the notion of creaturely equality before God to legitimate egalitarian ideals.

This notion is a curious one and cannot be justified by any appeal to the common experience of humankind. On the contrary, it would seem that God is supremely responsive to the contributions creatures of the world make to the Divine Life. If that is so, creatures could scarcely be equal before God. It would be a travesty for God to treat the contribution of a society of electrons to Its life equally with the contribution of the sequence of high grade occasions constituting the ultimate percipient occasions of the human soul. The contribution of human occasions to the Divine Life is unequal. Some humans experience richer and more complex feelings than others and hence make unequal contributions to the Divine Life. Even in the life of one individual the contributions of some of the occasions constituting the individual are greater than the contributions of others.

The author finds the views of orthodox Judaism on equality and inequality in human life more suggestive than those Christian formulations utilizing the idea of equality before God to inform religious social ethics.

17.   In 1831 Alexis de Tocqueville in his remarkable *Democracy in America* commented astutely on the proliferation of voluntary associations in America. For contemporary reflections on this phenomenon, see James Luther Adams, *Voluntary Associations: Socio-Cultural Analyses and Theological Interpretation*, edited by J. Ronald Engel (Chicago: Exploration Press, 1986).

18.   For a thoughtful analysis of this phenomenon, see Daniel Bell, *The Cultural Contradictions of Capitalism*(New York: Basic Books, 1976). For a perceptive discussion of some of the issues involved in promoting wholesome public life in America, see Richard John Neuhaus, *The Naked Public Square* (Grand Rapids: Eerdmans, 1984). Plato observed long ago that mediocrity and anarchy were twin dangers to which democracy was especially susceptible.

19.   It is beyond the scope of this essay to address directly the nature and character of religious institutions and their role in a democratic capitalist society. The author has addressed this issue at some length in his essay, "Religious Institutions and Human Society: A Normative Inquiry into the Appropriate Contribution of Religious Institutions to Human Life and to the Divine Life," in Philip Hefner and W. Widick Schroeder, editors, *Belonging and Alienation: Religious Foundations for the Human Future*(Chicago: Center for the Scientific Study of Religion, 1976), pp. 181-218. Briefer observations appear in his other two essays dealing with aspects of political economy cited earlier.

20.   Reliable comparative empirical data on the concentration of wealth in various historical epochs and in various societies in the current historical epoch are difficult to find. Marxists and non-Marxists are prone to use different sources of data and to interpret the same data in different ways.

For a reading that suggests increasingly rigid social stratification in the United States, see G. William Domhoff, *The Powers That Be: Processes of Rising Class Domination in America* (New York: Vintage Books, 1978). In a similar vein is the volume by Jonathan H. Turner and

Charles E. Staines, *Inequality: Privilege and Poverty in America* (New York: Goodyear Publishing Co., 1976).

Others view the situation differently. See, for example, Warren G. Nutter and Henry A. Einhorn, *Enterprise Monopoly in the United States*(New York: Columbia University Press, 1969), and George Stigler, *The Economist as Preacher* (Chicago: University of Chicago Press, 1982).

For a critical assessment of third world development, see P.T. Bauer, *Reality and Rhetoric: Studies in the Economics of Development* (Cambridge: Harvard University Press, 1984).

Because of subsidies and privileges of social function, it is very difficult to compare the inequality in the Soviet Union with Western societies. Although the text is old, a major study by Abram Bergson in 1944 found the pattern of inequality between the highest-paid and lowest-paid workers in the Soviet Union were very similar to those in the United States. *The Structure of Soviet Wages* (Cambridge: Harvard University Press, 1944).

Because the "facts" are only one component in the interpretive contrasts between persons supporting democratic capitalism and those supporting democratic socialism, the debates would probably continue even if there were no evidence of gross income and wealth inequality or significant monopolistic practices. (Of course, socialists would normatively place more value on equality than would capitalists.)

For a trenchant critique of socialism, see Frank H. Knight, "Socialism: The Nature of the Problem," in his *Freedom and Reform* (New York: Harper and Bros., 1947).

Because of the primacy afforded the principle of freedom and the ubiquity of inordinate self-interest, the viewpoint developed here has some affinity to modes of thought informed by nineteenth century liberalism. See, for example, Milton Friedman, *Capitalism and Freedom* (Chicago: University of Chicago Press, 1962).

21.   For one suggestive vision, see Louis O. Kelso and Patricia Hetter Kelso, *Democracy and Economic Power: Extending the ESOP Revolution* (Cambridge: Ballainger Publishing Co., 1986).

CHAPTER 10

Taking Internal Relations Seriously in Political Economy

Warren Copeland

A mutual friend once suggested to me that Widick Schroeder should never speak without a chalkboard available upon which he could diagram his thoughts. Certainly there are times when the reader of one of Schroeder's papers must try to figure out the diagram which was in front of him, or in his head, when he wrote. This paper is no exception. It argues in so many directions with such complexity and with the constant implication that all of this is related as to boggle at least my mind. For instance, I did chart the discussion of the proper role of love, power, and justice in the various spheres of the human social order. It is a rich discussion to which I could not do justice in this relatively brief response even if I did understand just what principles of ordering were at work. So, while all of that complexity is no doubt related to the issues which I want to examine, I shall make reference to it only in passing.

Instead, I shall focus my attention on Widick Schroeder's discussion of anthropology in two senses: the interrelation of the individual and the community and the character and extent of sin. These considerations directly influence his discussions of love and justice, which I shall consider as I go along. Finally, I shall take up the implications of this anthropology for political and economic organization.

"Freedom is the constitutive principle of justice." This assertion, especially given the way Schroeder understands freedom, is the thesis which drives his argument. However, this is not the manifesto of individualism which it might seem to be. Neither Schroeder nor Whitehead could tolerate such simplicity. Rather, Schroeder quickly cautions that freedom is not the power to do what one wants but rather that authentic freedom seeks "to enhance the harmony and freedom of the whole." For any Whiteheadian, the human condition must involve relations to the self, others, and the whole and thus be marked by complexity. However, the ordering of that complexity makes all the difference. As Schroeder discusses freedom and justice, the self takes priority. Freedom (the principle rooted in the self) is constitutive of justice; equality (rooted in others) and harmony (rooted in the whole) are regulative principles of justice. Creativity, grounded in the deliberating and choosing individual, stands at the center of the meaning of human life.

I personally find the descriptions of the Whiteheadian understanding of human action present in the works of Douglas Sturm[1] and Lois Gehr Livezey[2] more adequate to both Whitehead and my knowledge of economic realities. Like Schroeder, both recognize an interplay between individual and community in Whitehead. However, they place much more emphasis upon the role of community both as that from which the individual comes and that to which the individual contributes. As Livezey puts it:

> . . . In process thought the essence of power, divine and human, is that it is community creating, sustaining, and transforming—or destroying. Power is grounded in the fact that our actions issue in a network, a web of relationships, and so makes a difference in the world—for better or worse.[3]

Schroeder recognizes this relationship to the community by requiring that freedom enhance the harmony and intensity of feeling in the whole. However, for Livezey this public is integral to the individual; it seems much more of an external reality to Schroeder.

I am not arguing that Whiteheadian metaphysics eliminates individual agency. Rather, I believe it places that agency within the context of what we know about relativity. The agent does not create freedom from nothing; freedom resides in the capacity to choose among what is given and form it into something new which then helps shape the future. As Douglas Sturm puts it:

> The irreducible individuality that characterizes each self is not an isolated or merely private individuality. It is intrinsically public in its dependency and in its implication. On the one hand, the possibilities of the self are heavily dependent on its forms of social inheritance. In turn, the determinations of the self constitute a legacy to the social future. The self's identity cannot be comprehended apart from its past and its future, its given environment or its creative formation.[4]

Again, Schroeder takes account of both of these aspects of community—that from which individuals come and that to which they contribute. Does he see the individual as "intrinsically public"in Sturm's sense? I think not, at least not in his discussion of principles of justice.

Who is most true to Whitehead at this point? That, of course, is debatable and Whiteheadians certainly like to debate such points at length. What we can be sure of is that individual and community are not separable in reality. Certainly the classical liberal notion of the lone agent is inconsistent with process thought:

> The whole concept of absolute individuals with absolute rights and with contractual power of forming fully defined external relations, has broken down. The human being is inseparable from its environment, in each occasion of its existence.[5]

But Schroeder does not advocate classical liberalism. Rather he recognizes "the internal relatedness of an emerging creature to creatures in its causal past and the immanence of the future in the present. . . ." Yet, his ordering of ethical principles suggests that the emerging creature takes moral precedence; freedom is constitutive while equality and community are regulative. Whitehead recognizes an apparent conflict between harmony and the importance of the individual. However, he contends:

> The antithesis is solved by rating types of order in relative importance according to their success in magnifying the individual actualities, that is to say, in promoting strength of experience. Also in rating the individual on the double basis, partly on the intrinsic strength of its own experience, and partly on its influence in the promotion of a high-grade type of order.[6]

In other words both the individual and the community are to be judged both on their own terms and in terms of their contribution to the other. No priority is possible precisely because each is so integral to the other. By expressing a priority in principle which grows in significance as actual economic and political policy comes under study, Schroeder raises questions about just how internally related he believes the individual and community are.

This understanding of this relationship has important implications for our understanding of both the individual and the community. Ruth L. Smith struggles with the nature of the word agent in her excellent article "Feminism and the Moral Subject."[7] She concludes that it is simply not enough to urge the individual to act for the sake of the community. Rather, we must recognize that the community is a part of the individual from the beginning and so moral human nature is inseparable from social relations. One result of this recognition is that it enables us to account for those cases where groups improve the morality of individuals, a reality documented by Whitehead more than once. Individuals are fundamentally and intrinsically social.

Community also takes on a particular shape. Much of the usual antipathy between individual and community assumes a homogenous form of community which stifles individual creativity. Whitehead describes the ideal community quite differently. Far from being dull, it stresses intensity of experience. It is marked not by conformity but rather by diversity and richness; this is a vital, changing, risky, adventuresome community. While such community is our aim, it is not fully actualized, any more than individuals adequately develop all of their social relations. It is not even the form of community many advocates of community have in mind. It is, however, the sort of community which would be internally related to creative agents. Any human community would have to display some elements of pluralism to be human. In sum, individuality and community which are truly internally related must be social individuality and pluralistic community. If they are understood in these ways there is no need or purpose for giving priority to freedom as an ethical principle. Rather, internal and reciprocal relations between individuality and community can be recognized and even advanced.

This has implications for the second aspect of Schroeder's anthropology, the character and extent of sin. We often proceed under the assumption that Whiteheadians have a more positive view of human nature than other theologians, especially Niebuhrians. I am not at all convinced that this is the case. This is of particular relevance to our consideration of Schroeder's analysis because at the crucial turn of the paper from theology to economics, it is Reinhold Niebuhr and Robert Benne[8] whom he quotes rather than Whitehead. Indeed, I would contend that his conclusions about economic and political structure are at least as influenced by Niebuhr as by Whitehead.

Are Niebuhrians more realistic about human nature than Whiteheadians? I find Niebuhr's discussion of sacrificial love about as unrealistic as anything I have ever read in religious ethics.[9] It is echoed here in Schroeder's suggestions that considerations of love and harmony are more appropriate to personal, family and small group life than to broader social structures. As far as I can tell my personal and family life and my interpersonal relationships are in at least as good a shape as the vast majority of my fellow human beings. Yet, disharmony abounds and matters of justice and power, as well as love, are present. Which dominates is quite unclear to me. By all measures, these aspects of our lives appear much less settled and centered than either Schroeder or Niebuhr suggests. On the other hand, social movements and law have been at least as significant forces for justice and love in such areas as racism, sexism, poverty, peace, and the environment as individual action. Moreover, these expressions of community have not only forced people to be just, but also have inspired greater voluntary justice and love on the part of individuals.

What I am suggesting is that Niebuhr and Schroeder place more faith in the possible disinterestedness of individuals than I do. I am more the realist there. On the other hand, they place much less faith in the community as a source of inspiration to shared interest than I do. I would argue that this contrast arises less from how much we emphasize sin than from our differing understandings of how intrinsically and internally related individuals and communities are. Smith concludes: "The consequences of Reinhold Niebuhr's view for moral agency is the bifurcation of individual and collective morality. . . . Individuals may achieve a level of morality higher than that possible for collectives."[10] I believe the same can be said of Schroeder, as can be seen both in the relative ordering of love, power, and justice in various spheres and his judgments about political economy. The issue, then, is not who believes there is how much sin in human beings. All recognize both sin and love as abiding characteristics of the human condition which must shape our thoughts about how to organize a political economy. The question is just how consistently Schroeder applies the principle of internal relationships in locating sin.

Two examples may help. As Schroeder discusses self-interest as a source of evil in the world the entire matter is expressed as a choice between individual self-interest and individual altruism. Yet many of the most abiding issues of our lives—such as racism, sexism, poverty, peace, or the environment—are matters of social structure as much as of individual choice. Indeed, many good people discover the hard way that no choices they can make as individuals will change these social structures to any significant extent. Rather, it is precisely by drawing upon the moral resources of the community, embodied in the law and social movements, that we have gained much of the practical ground and moral insight we have on these issues. Schroeder recognizes the importance of the social context and urges individuals to act for the sake of the community. Yet, the community remains for him a residual moral concern rather than a moral resource.

The primary regulatory principle that Schroeder does turn to in thinking about the community, as does Niebuhr, is balance of power. It is important to recognize the difference between this balance of power and the sort of pluralistic community Whitehead advocates, particularly since they are so often confused. A balance of power assumes relatively autonomous actors who relate to each other externally. Thus, each limits the action of the other, and in this way the misuse of power by any of the actors is limited. The pluralistic community consistent with Whiteheadian thought recognizes that these actors are internally related to each other and the whole from the beginning. Thus, the interests of one actor do not end where the interests of the others and the whole begin. Rather, the various interests interpenetrate in what is a genuine common interest. Certainly, Schroeder recognizes this difference in principle, but the closer he gets to practice the less important it is in his analysis.

To sum up my criticism of Schroeder's anthropology, I believe there is a consistent individualism in his analysis which makes the community morally less significant. A view which sees the social self and pluralistic community as internally related and of equal moral significance is more true to both Whitehead and our experience. In the case of sin, this latter view locates sin and virtue in both the individual and the community. It is not necessarily either more naive or more realistic in the aggregate than those who emphasize the individual, as Schroeder does.

As we move from anthropology to political economy it is useful to ask first what the general purpose of political and economic institutions is. Douglas Sturm contends:

> . . . The constructive political orientation of process philosophy with its principle of internal relations is not individualistic liberalism. It is a form of communitarianism. The central value of its political ethic is not the creative act of the individual soul taken by itself, but how fully the creative act is responsive to the communal ground of its being and how richly it contributes to the communal future. The aim of communitarian politics is not simply the fulfillment of the individual, but the conjunctive participation of each person in a unity of adventure.[11]

It is critical to recognize that what we have here is a family disagreement. Schroeder would surely agree that individualistic liberalism is inconsistent with process philosophy. He specifically discusses the need for the individual to contribute to the community because it provides a social context for individual creativity. For this reason, Schroeder advocates a social market democratic capitalism not free market capitalism. What I have argued is that in principle the individual and community are equal in moral standing in process thought. Schroeder seems to believe that individuality takes priority in principle, and Sturm seems to believe that community does.

In light of what we have said so far it should be no surprize that when Schroeder states the objectives a political economy should facilitate, community comes up short. He wants to protect the individual and community from "inordinate demands" upon each other. On the positive side, he seeks to "encourage and support . . . human propensities to promote the good of the community." However, he proposes no comparable goal for the community. Given what I have argued earlier, I would include a goal of encouraging and supporting the community's contributions to the good of individuals. This is not a small difference when we consider its implications for policy. Rather, it is the central point of conflict in our contemporary political economy debate. Those who advocate more government generally have a more social view of the person; those who advocate more market usually downplay the power of social relations in shaping the self. Indeed, as Schroeder discusses the general strengths of democratic capitalism the only function he assigns to the community is negative, i.e. limiting through law those activities which harm the common good.

Schroeder's discussion of the virtues of democracy also mirrors the basic issues we have been discussing. The reader hears at least as many echoes of Reinhold Niebuhr and Robert Benne as of Whitehead. Democracy's greatest value is that it allows for the creative contribution of people while establishing a balance of power which limits the destructive tendencies of human sin. This democracy is a collection of individuals and groups with primarily external relations to one another. It does not take account of the capacity to develop common purposes in a democracy. For instance, it does not recognize the possibility of a democracy providing an educational system which not only requires equal access but also promotes creative interchange across race, sex, and class lines. Not mentioned is the freedom of social movements and voluntary associations to develop visions of a more just society and proceed to persuade a majority through word or deed of its attractiveness. In short, what is missing is a view of democracy which takes pluralistic community as seriously as creative individuality.

When Schroeder turns to economic organization, his position is quite vague at first. He says that the social market or democratic capitalism he favors is that practiced in the industrialized west and Japan. This covers far too many possibilities for us to be sure just what he has in mind. Yet, when he describes the appropriate functions of government the picture clears up quite a bit and a neo-liberal capitalism appears. In this system ownership is private, markets decide most matters, and government intervenes to facilitate markets and to redistribute income a bit. This is hardly the mixed ownership and developed welfare state of various western European countries or even the cooperative capitalism of Japan. I believe that several questions can be raised about the claims Schroeder makes for his version of democratic capitalism, and that those questions are related to the earlier theoretical discussion.

First, Schroeder notes with great appreciation the argument of Arthur Okun and others that there is a "great tradeoff" between equality and efficiency.[12] Okun may be correct about certain ways of creating equality, such as welfare grants which do not allow recipients to work, but economists such as Lester Thurow and Robert Reich[13] have contended with considerable force that equality and efficiency may go hand in hand. It is interesting to note that our most successful competitors, Japan for example, have more equality than we do. Thurow and Reich suggest three good reasons why inequality may lead to inefficiency. First it may help produce a section of the labor force which is unskilled and, therefore, unproductive especially in today's labor market. Second, inequality may make teamwork between labor and management difficult, an area in which our competitors have done much better than we have. Finally, inequality may undermine the basic sense of fairness which would make it easier for the society to ask its citizens to sacrifice in order to become more efficient, by spending more on education for instance. On these grounds, Thurow, Reich and others conclude that greater equality would make possible greater efficiency. In all three cases, I believe Thurow and Reich are taking much more seriously the social character of individuals and the community's contribution to individuality than does Schroeder.

A second question that can be raised about Schroeder's view of capitalism is whether it does in fact produce all of the individual freedom and creativity which he claims. Schroeder, himself, notes that human freedom is often not informed by excellence resulting in conspicuous consumption and misallocation of resources. Since Schroeder locates the problem in the individual consumer, he sees no solution except consumer education. Again, this assumes an individualistic bias, in relation to sin in this case. Large community structures called corporations go to great efforts to corrupt both consumer choice and democratic decision making for their own profit. The sin is social as well as personal. To propose consumer education as an antidote is an inadequate solution consistent with Schroeder's bias toward individual freedom.

The final question I would raise about Schroeder's discussion of political economy concerns his rejection of democratic socialism. The serious advocates of democratic socialism in the United States, such as Michael Harrington, simply do not propose for any near future what Schroeder rejects. He rejects government ownership of the means of production. Harrington proposes an expansion of the welfare state, government investment to promote full employment, worker ownership where possible, increased public planning, and government ownership where appropriate (e.g., a passenger rail system).[14] Many others who consider themselves democratic socialists would not go that far and many who might be called social democrats would advocate a mixed capitalism which is still much less market oriented than Schroeder seems to be. For Schroeder to dismiss in this way the alternatives which stress community more than he does is equivalent to me rejecting Schroeder for being a free market capitalist, which he is not. Just as he advocates a more social form of individualism, others can propose a pluralistic form of community. It makes the choice more difficult, but much more real. Once again we can see the theoretical discussion of the relation between social individuality and pluralistic community reflected in a more proximate matter of political economy.

I suggested earlier that I thought Douglas Sturm's principled advocacy of a communitarian political economy could be contrasted with Schroeder's principled individualistic one. I would content that in principle both represent essential considerations for a political economy. Creative agency in social context and community inclusive of such creative agency require each other for their fullest expression. Therefore, I would argue in principle for a political economy which seeks to maximize both creative individuality and pluralistic community.[15] Since they are mutually supportive it is both possible and best to do both at the same time. In practice, however, I would stress community at this time in the United States because it is my practical judgment that we have been stressing individualism at the expense of community. The result is not just impoverished community institutions, witness our schools, but as a result also individuals who lack the social context within which to develop as creative agents. At another time in another place I might well argue that the community has lost its pluralism so much that the advocacy of creative agency was in order.

Whether my present support for community would take me as far as full democratic socialism anytime soon, I am not sure. That would depend, in part, upon what we discovered as we moved more in that direction. However, I am convinced that a social democracy to the left of what Schroeder supports is necessary. In the final analysis, I do not believe, consistent with my reading of Whitehead, that we can get much more specific guidance from philosophic principles. Concrete practical judgment not general philosophical principles must fill in the details. Moreover, Schroeder's formulations of a democratic capitalism informed by process thought is a vast improvement upon those based on a supposed rugged individualism precisely because it recognizes the importance of social context. As a result, in the present political climate, I might well even vote for it as a step in the right direction.

Notes and References

1. Douglas Sturm, "Process Thought and Political Theory: Implications of a Principle of Internal Relations," in John B. Cobb, Jr. and W. Widick Schroeder, editors, *Process Philosophy and Social Thought* (Chicago: Center for the Scientific Study of Religion, 1981), pp. 81-102; and "Toward a New Social Covenant: From Community to Commonwealth," in Bruce Grelle and David A. Krueger, editors *Christianity and Capitalism: Perspectives on Religious Liberalism and the Economy* (Chicago: Center for the Scientific Study of Religion, 1986), pp. 91-108.

2. Lois Gehr Livezey, "Goods, Rights, and Virtues: Toward an Interpretation of Justice in Process Thought," *The Annual of the Society of Christian Ethics: 1986* (Knoxville, Tennessee: The Society of Christian Ethics, 1986), pp. 37-64.

3. *Ibid.*, p. 40.

4. Sturm, "Process Thought and Political Theory, *op. cit.*, p. 90.

5. Alfred North Whitehead, *Adventures of Ideas* (New York: The Free Press, 1967), p. 63.

6. *Ibid.*, p. 292.

7. Ruth L. Smith, "Feminism and the Moral Subject," in Barbara Hilkert Andolsen, Christine E. Gudorf, and Mary D. Pellauer, editors, *Women's Consciousness, Women's Conscience: A Reader in Feminist Ethics* (New York: Harper and Row, 1987), pp. 235-250.

8. Robert Benne, *The Ethic of Democratic Capitalism: A Moral Reassessment* (Philadelphia: Fortress Press, 1981) is the best of the ethical defenses of capitalism. Basically it justifies capitalism along the lines of Reinhold Niebuhr's description of democracy as allowing for the best in humans while preventing the worst. I believe Schroeder's analysis here takes the same direction.

9. An excellent discussion of the inadequacy of sacrificial love in practice even in our personal lives is Christine E. Gudorf, "Parenting, Mutual Love, and Sacrifice," in Andolsen, *et al, op. cit.*, pp. 175-191.

10. Smith, "Feminism and the Moral Subject," *op. cit.*, p. 240.

11. Sturm, "Process Thought and Political Theory," *op. cit., p. 99.*

12. Arthur Okun, *Equality and Efficiency: The Big Tradeoff* (Washington: The Brookings Institution, 1975).

13. Lester C. Thurow, *The Zero-Sum Society* (New York: Basic Books, 1980) and *The Zero-Sum Solution* (New York: Simon and Schuster, 1985) and Robert B. Reich, *The Next American Frontier* (New York: Times Books, 1983).

14. Michael Harrington, *The Next Left* (New York: Henry Holt and Company, 1986).

15. Warren Copeland, *Economic Justice: The Social Ethics of U.S. Economic Policy* (Nashville, Abingdon Press, 1988) represents the full development of my own position.

CHAPTER 11

Democracy, Capitalism, and Economic Growth

Franklin I. Gamwell

It is a widely recognized but still remarkable fact that modern political democracy has flourished only within societies which have also displayed capitalist forms of economic organization (see Friedman, 10; Lindblom, 162; Heilbroner, 1985, 126). This is not to say that the converse is also true; on the contrary, capitalism, at least by some meanings of the term, has thrived in politically oppressive or nondemocratic societies, including Italy and Spain under fascist regimes (see Friedman, 10), contemporary South Africa, and, for American blacks, the United States during most of its history (see Heilbroner 1985, 125). But if capitalism is not a sufficient condition for democracy, it remains that all instances of the latter have also been instances of the former, and there has been a considerable debate about the importance of capitalism to democratic politics. Of course, an answer to this question depends upon what one means by "democracy" and what one means by "capitalism." For present purposes, I will simply stipulate definitions of these two terms. The definitions may be controversial, but I believe that they are sufficiently minimal to be of service.

I will understand democracy to be, in the first instance at least, a political principle or political theory, that is, an inclusive ideal for the associational order as such. Of course, the term also refers to a theory or ideal for the specifically political association generally called the state. But the ambiguity which is involved in using democracy in both of these senses becomes a systematic one if the state is defined as a second-order association whose distinguishing purpose is to govern or provide order for the society as a whole and, for this purpose, is granted the legitimate use of coercion. In contrast to other kinds of associations, then, the distinguishing purpose of the state cannot be properly identified without explicit reference to the ideal for the associational order as such. I will further understand democracy to be the specific form of political theory which affirms the right to freedom of all members of the society. It is true that this formulation is vague with respect to the meaning of "freedom;" thus, alternative proposals which seek to give precision to that term constitute the basis for alternative democratic theories.

I will define "capitalism" as an economic order in which decisions are predominantly nongovernmental. In other words, both the means of production and the goods and services produced are, for the most part, nongovernmentally owned, so that economic activities are, for the most part, nongovernmentally coordinated through market exchange. Precisely because it is politics and not economics which orders associational life as a whole, one must identify capitalism in relative terms. As even the most forceful advocates of capitalism have insisted, capitalism could not exist for a day independently of the state's power to constitute the order within which economic decisions are made (see, e.g., Friedman, 15)—including the state's power to define nongovernmental ownership and to specify and enforce the conditions of contract or exchange. Hence, property is not exclusively nongovernmental, at least in the sense that the state has power to tax in order to execute its own proper activities, and exchanges are never completely nongovernmental, at least in the sense that the state defines what a legal exchange is. Accordingly, capitalism must be defined as an economic order in which decisions are *predominantly* nongovernmental.

Given these definitions, to ask about the importance of capitalism to democracy is to ask a political question. Only an understanding of democracy, in other words, can provide the terms within which to assess the proper place of economic activities within the social order and, therefore, the respects in which economic decisions should be nongovernmental. The political arguments for capitalism are generally clear. The democratic right to freedom is threatened especially by the concentration of political power, it is said, because this power is granted the legitimate use of coercion. Hence, when economic life is predominantly independent of governmental decisions, freedom is insofar protected from the tyrannical potentialities of the state. Moreover, a capitalist economy removes from control by the existing political regime the economic means which any effective political dissent requires (see, e.g., Friedman, 7-21). Again, insofar as the democratic affirmation of freedom implies an affirmation of the welfare of citizens, it is important that a competitive capitalist social order more efficiently allocates economic resources. A society which seeks to dispense with reliance upon the market has no alternative except to assume that the detailed coordination of economic activity may be purposefully or deliberately effected. But this alternative founders, especially in massively complex societies, upon the fallible and fragmentary character of human knowledge (see, e.g., Lindblom, 247-52).

In opposition to democratic capitalism, it is argued that the system concentrates economic power and that this concentration is all the more objectionable because it is not democratically accountable. Moreover, the same consequence gives a privileged place to capitalists within the political process. Again, the coordination of economic activity by market prices does not account for the increasingly significant "external costs" of economic activity, and the efficiency which the market is said to serve is always relative to the prevailing distribution of income. I will not pursue these issues in this essay. I will later suggest reason to conclude that a capitalist order might properly be supervised or constituted in substantial measure by the state. But I am persuaded and will here assume that there is sufficient merit in the considerations advanced on behalf of capitalism to give one pause about rejecting a predominant reliance upon nongovernmental economic decisions.

I make this assumption in order to focus attention upon another issue by virtue of which one might question the importance of capitalism to democracy. A growing literature in recent decades has argued that western democracies, perhaps the United States in particular, are being overwhelmed by their economic success. As massive corporations have become the dominant institutions of the economy, we are told, these same institutions have become the dominant forces in the social order. Notwithstanding the material affluence which "advanced" economies have achieved, economic goals continue to identify the telos of the social order, and unending economic expansion or growth persists as the dominant social purpose. John Kenneth Galbraith, to choose one example, has insisted that "the new industrial state," of which he takes American society to be the principal example, assumes more or less without question that the growth of the economy is the principal purpose of the social order. "It is the genius of the industrial system that it makes the goals that reflect its needs—efficient production of goods, a steady expansion of their output, a steady expansion in their consumption, a powerful preference for goods over leisure, an unqualified commitment to technological change, autonomy for the technostructure, an adequate supply of trained and educated manpower—coordinate with social virtue and human enlightenment" (Galbraith, 345).

Among other consequences, we are told, this commitment to growth as an end-in-itself so "commodifies" or "commercializes" life as to impoverish the intellectual, aesthetic, and communitarian pursuits of the human spirit. There is, writes Robert L. Heilbroner, "a hollowness at the centre of business civilization—a hollowness from which the pursuit of material goods diverts our attention for a time, but that in the end insistently asserts itself." This hollowness involves, he continues, "the tendency of business civilization to substitute impersonal pecuniary values for personal nonpecuniary ones" (1976, 113). Qualified only by a few fundamental rules of personal virtue, the good life is equated with the enjoyment of material benefits, so that the pursuit of a better life becomes, more or less by definition, the pursuit of greater economic rewards. It is this same pursuit of "pecuniary values" which, many have argued, leads to a strictly instrumental relation to the natural environment, and, unless the commitment to economic growth is strictly qualified by "in the long run," this relation threatens so to exploit the subhuman world as a means for expansion and repository of wastes as to imperil the human community itself. Insofar as there is validity in this critique of western democracies, one may ask whether or to what extent the fault lies with their reliance upon a capitalist economic order and, in that respect, question the importance of capitalism to democracy.

To be sure, the merit of this critique is itself a subject of controversy. In my judgment, however, that controversy has been significantly compromised by that fact that critics have not developed and defended a political theory in accord with which the issue is to be clarified and resolved. As I have already suggested, the importance of economic activities generally and capitalism in particular to democracy is a political issue. Thus, to criticize the extent to which the social order pursues economic growth is implicitly to assert some political principle in terms of which this evaluation is justified. But the case against western democracies in this regard has been characteristically thin at precisely this point.

No serious participant on either side of the discussion asserts that maximal economic growth, even maximal economic growth in the long run, is the *only* social purpose, such that all other social activities are justified only insofar as they serve it. Even those who applaud maximal economic growth do or would concede that pursuit of this telos should occur within the context of certain political conditions whose claim limits the legitimate means to economic goals. Slavery is immoral, to choose an extreme example, even if it could be shown that in specified circumstances it would serve economic expansion. More generally, it is universally agreed that the protection of certain specifically political rights or liberties, such as those affirmed in the amendments to the United States Constitution, takes precedence over the calculation of economic goals. Further, at least some parties on both sides of the controversy affirm that economic growth should be similarly constrained by attention to the fair distribution of economic rewards. There is, of course, considerable disagreement about the meaning of "fair distribution," and some may be persuaded that only minimal changes should be made in the distribution effected by a capitalist market. But there are very few who dissent from the claim that some minimal economic provision for all must take precedence over the calculation of maximal production.

Of course, a critic of economically "advanced" democracies might contend that distributional constraints upon growth should be far more substantial, presumably far more directed toward equality of distribution, than is presently the case. As I have already suggested, however, the criticism of economic expansion in affluent societies generally intends to be of quite another order. To take issue with the distributional pattern of the contemporary economic order is not to dissent from the place which economic values occupy in the social order. In other words, one might still be committed to the pursuit of maximal economic benefit and differ from others so committed only in one's insistence that this benefit be more equally enjoyed. To the contrary, the indictment of western democracies has generally been a criticism of the extent to which economic goals themselves consume contemporary life and is advanced in the name of noneconomic values. It is for the sake of clarifying these noneconomic values that a political theory is wanted.

For instance, values such as the conservation of the natural environment and the solidarity of local community life have sometimes been advocated. Typically, however, these are not formulated in a principled manner, such that one could decide when they should override economic goals. Somewhat more fully, Galbraith once provocatively suggested that aesthetic values should be "accorded priority" (352) in contemporary industrial societies, and, on this basis, he argued for defense of the natural environment, control of the specific forms of economic development, and promotion by the state of the arts and architecture (348-55). "That one must pause to affirm that beauty is worth the sacrifice of some increase in Gross National Product shows how effectively our beliefs have been accommodated to the needs of the industrial system" (352). But Galbraith, perhaps because his principal purpose was to clarify the character of our "new industrial state," did not tell us why aesthetic goals should be prior or provide a political principle in terms of which this priority might be given comprehensive formulation. Heilbroner has ventured that "a major force for the [long-run] transformation of business civilization will be a new religious orientation, which will include a high degree of political authority" (1976, 119) and "the elevation of the collective and communal destiny of man to the forefront of public consciousness" (1976, 120). Because his discussion of future possibilities is principally predictive rather than prescriptive, however, Heilbroner does not offer a statement about how this communal destiny should be understood, so that one cannot find in his prediction a principle which might inform a political theory.

The intent of this essay is to pursue an understanding of democracy in relation to which the place of economic growth in the social order and, in this regard, the relation between democracy and capitalism may be assessed. In other words, I will seek to advance toward an answer to the complex question: By appeal to what political principle should economic growth be assessed, and in what respects, if any, is capitalism consistent with this assessment? As this formulation implies, I will not attempt to decide the empirical question of whether western democracies are in fact inappropriately committed to economic growth but will focus upon the question of political principle by appeal to which that evaluation might be achieved.

I judge that the criticism of contemporary economic growth has been typically thin with respect to political principle because its understanding of democracy is informed in significant measure by a political theory which in fact cannot adjudicate the issue which this criticism seeks to raise. I will call this the political theory of established liberalism, and I will first attempt to clarify the character of this theory and to display its inadequacy to an evaluation of economic growth. Subsequently, I will seek to formulate the principle for an alternative democratic theory and to assess the place in the social order which it assigns to economic growth. Finally, I will return to the relation of democracy and capitalism and ask whether what has been achieved provides the basis for a critique of a capitalist economic order. In order to limit the discussion, I will abstract from the intersocietal relations of a given social order; it is my opinion that the recommendations which I will make would not be altered by so expanding the scope of attention.

I

Given that democratic theories generally are identified by their common affirmation of the human right to freedom, I suggest that the dominant democratic theory in the modern West has understood freedom in the following, more specific sense: The moral meaning of freedom is independent of the ends or purposes for which individuals exercise their right. In other words, the moral principle by which this political theory is constituted does not imply a criterion or standard by which the purposes of individuals might be evaluated. It is this theory which I will call established liberalism. John Dewey similarly asserted that a form of political liberalism based upon a notion of "separate individuals" has dominated modern democratic thought (Dewey 1963, 54), and we might also say that the meaning of liberty is, in established liberalism, separated from the ends or interests of citizens. With this reading of Western political theory, the intimate relationship between democracy and capitalism in the development of the modern West is readily understood. The affirmation of human freedom in a sense which is independent of the purposes for which it is exercised clearly permits if it does not require an economic order in which decisions are predominantly nongovernmental or beyond the reach of legitimate coercion.

I propose to call freedom so understood "private freedom," for two related reasons. In its most general meaning, "private" usually refers to aspects of human experience which are not shared among human individuals, and the freedom in question is "private" in the sense that its exercise is not bound by any shared or public criterion or norm. It is true that the human right to freedom is itself a public norm, such that the exercise of freedom is always morally bound to respect the freedom of others. But the point is that this moral requirement does not imply a criterion for the interests which humans might pursue; on the contrary, it is a constraint upon the means which are legitimate in that pursuit and, therefore, presupposes the independent or private determination of those ends. It then follows that freedom is also private in the sense that human association, in which human experience is communicated or shared, is not itself an intrinsic moral good for which freedom ought to be exercised. As a matter of political theory, associations themselves must be understood as instrumental to whatever purposes individuals elect.

One apparent consequence of this political theory is that it at least permits what I will call the priority of private-regarding associations in the social order. The implied distinction between private-regarding and public-regarding associations refers to the identifying or distinguishing purposes of the associations in question. When this purpose is nothing other than the creation of human association or communication, the association is public-regarding, and when the distinguishing purpose is something other than human communication, the association is private-regarding. In the nature of the case, of course, all private-regarding associations do create human association, and the individuals within the association may indeed prize the communication which occurs. Moreover, the distinction might be considered analytic, in the sense that some associations have a complex purpose which includes both the creation of human association and something else. In referring to the identifying purpose of the association, however, I have in mind the controlling or overriding purpose, in terms of which conflicts between or among two or more aspects of a complex purpose would be adjudicated, and, in this sense, at least most associations are either public-regarding or private-regarding. Although an automobile manufacturing organization might include within its purpose certain humane relationships among its employees, for instance, it remains that the production and sale of automobiles is the controlling purpose, and, therefore, the association is private-regarding.

It is, then, just because human association is not an intrinsic moral good for established liberalism that this theory of democracy at least permits the priority of private-regarding associations, that is, a social order in which public-regarding associations are instrumental to private-regarding ones. Given that the purposes for which freedom is exercised are private, it might be thought that *all* associations should be private-regarding. But to draw this conclusion is to ignore that the state and its constitutive organizations must be public-regarding in character. The distinguishing purpose of specifically political associations, namely, to govern or to participate in governing the associational order generally, is nothing other than the creation of human association. Hence, it is more appropriate to say that the established liberal state may be subservient to the purposes of private-regarding associations; the activities of the former are then strictly instrumental to the activities of the latter.

We may now take a further step by equating private-regarding with economic associations. "Economics" is one of those terms the meaning of which often seems so apparent that few attempt to give it precise definition. Still, the common understanding that this realm of human activity is concerned with the production and distribution of goods and services is, absent some qualification, too general to be theoretically useful. Since human association or human community may be considered a "good" that is "produced," this understanding threatens to make the term "economic association" coincident with "human association" as such. Some further specification is suggested by the common assumption that economic relationships may be understood as matters of exchange. Since exchange may be identified as an interaction which is instrumental to the diverse purposes of the individuals involved, the goods and services which specifically economic activity is concerned to produce and distribute may be understood as things other than human association itself, so that economic organizations may be equated with private-regarding associations. Given this equation, the priority of private-regarding associations which established liberalism at least permits is also the priority of economic associations. We may now say that this political theory permits economic growth to be the dominating purpose of the social order. For the priority of economic associations implies that the social order should be so designed that other associations are subservient to the distinguishing purpose of economic ones and, in that sense, to maximal economic growth.

It is true that this conclusion leaves unspecified the morally required restraints upon the means by which economic growth may be legitimately pursued, so that established liberal theory might specify its permission of maximal economic growth to a greater or lesser extent depending upon the extent of such requirements. Still, enough has been said to conclude that established liberalism cannot justify any candidates for this status other than those concerned with the distribution of economic advantages or rewards. This is precisely because the moral meaning of freedom is independent of the purposes for which freedom is exercised. Hence, even the abiding commitment of all established liberal theories to specifically political freedom or to civil liberties must be understood as required by the fair or moral distribution of private resources or opportunities. Democratic participation in the activities of the state is, then, a necessary condition for the rightful freedom of each to pursue his or her private purposes.

But if the only moral constraints upon economic growth are distributional in character, it is now apparent that established liberalism cannot provide a foundation for the critique of economic growth which I previously reviewed. Distributional constraints, as I have mentioned, do not take exception to the dominance of the social order by economic goals; indeed, one may remain committed to maximizing economic benefit and differ from others so committed only in the insistence that this benefit be more equally enjoyed. Thus, those who remain under the theoretical influence of the established liberal tradition even while they indict the contemporary pursuit of economic growth in the name of noneconomic values find themselves without the theoretical resources through which to clarify the issue which they seek to raise, and it is often for this reason, in my judgment, that the critique wants for an adequate political theory.

Given this analysis, one might decide that the critique of contemporary economic expansion is simply without merit. In other words, one might continue to affirm the established liberal theory of democracy and, therefore, embrace the implication that maximal economic growth, subject to the constraints of appropriate distribution, is at least morally permissible. But I now wish to argue that this conclusion is untenable, such that established liberalism not only fails to ground the assertion of noneconomic values but also fails to provide an assessment of economic growth. This conclusion is required, as I will now attempt to show, because established liberalism is finally an incoherent political theory and, therefore, not an adequate principle for any evaluation at all. In order to approach this conclusion, I propose briefly to review an abiding dispute within the liberal political tradition between two types of established liberalism. Other students of the tradition, to whom I am indebted, have developed a similar distinction (see, e.g., Wolff, Sandel), and some have further argued that one type, which I will call libertarian liberalism, was more dominant during the nineteenth century, while the second, which I will call welfare liberalism, has become more dominant in the twentieth (see, e.g., Wolff).

Both types agree that the human right to private freedom includes or implies the right to specifically political freedom, which we may summarize, as I did a moment ago, as the right to democratic participation in the activities of the state. Given that private freedom cannot imply any moral constraints upon economic growth other than distributional ones, it is not surprising that the two types are distinguished by their respective understandings regarding the distribution of resources for the pursuit of private purposes. Generally speaking, the libertarian type asserts that private freedom is simply the right to noninterference by others, such that the distribution of resources is not the concern of the state so long as this distribution is effected through free and voluntary exchanges which assume some previous distribution. Subtleties aside, then, the government is properly limited to the protection of such voluntary exchanges. Except in the most extreme formulations of this type, the affirmation of market distribution is qualified by some minimal commitment to the support of the helpless; but, in the present context, the relevant point is that this qualification is indeed minimal.

In contrast, then, the welfare type of established liberalism asserts that the right to private freedom includes the right to a significant measure of resources, such that the state may justly limit the resources available to some in order to ensure that others are not deprived. It is, in my judgment, a confirmation of the extent to which established liberalism has indeed been established that a large measure of political contention in modern democracies, certainly in the United States, may be understood as a debate between these two interpretations of the right to private freedom. To be sure, that contention includes disagreement about the relation between specifically political freedom and the distribution of resources and, in particular, the extent to which unequal distribution compromises for some the right to democratic participation. Nonetheless, the proper activity of the state with respect to the distribution of resources cannot be settled solely on these grounds. For it is also true that the meaning of democratic participation depends in part upon what one takes to be the right to resources.

The philosophical problem within established liberal theory is revealed in the fact that the principle of private freedom cannot adjudicate the controversy between these two types. Precisely because the moral meaning of freedom is independent of the ends or purposes for which it is exercised, this principle offers no grounds upon which to decide what distribution identifies the proper purpose of the state. In other words, a proper distribution would be a purpose for which freedom ought to be exercised, but the moral principle does not include a standard or criterion by which purposes may be evaluated. Accordingly, there can be no moral conclusion about the resources included within the right to freedom.

If this reasoning is sound, some may be led to say that established liberal theory implicitly affirms any distribution of resources at all as morally permissible. No doubt this claim, even if it were implied, would be sufficiently counterintuitive to make this political theory highly problematic. In truth, however, the claim is a non sequitur. To say that diverse alternatives are all morally permissible is to say that they are all morally good—and, moreover, equally good. But if there is no moral criterion by which purposes may be evaluated, then, the principle of freedom is simply silent with respect to the distribution of resources, and one must conclude that the availability of such resources is neither good nor bad. Morality is not concerned with whether there are any resources at all, because the purposes for which freedom is exercised are likewise of no concern to morality.

Surely, this implication reveals that something in established liberal theory is fundamentally amiss. Without any resources at all, there could be no human freedom. As I see it, the fundamental problem is that private freedom is a self-contradictory notion. An exercise of freedom *is* the choice of some purpose. Thus, if no purpose is morally good, freedom itself cannot have moral worth. In short, established liberal theory seeks to separate the inseparable. But if this theory of democracy is based upon an incoherent political principle, then it is clear that the entire controversy about economic growth in contemporary western democracies will remain confused as long as this understanding of democracy implicity or explicitly informs the debate. The place of economic growth in the social order cannot be assessed by this appeal, and resolution of the issue waits upon a more adequate political principle.

Although I cannot document the judgment in the present context, I am persuaded that the tradition of established political liberalism is profoundly indebted to the moral theory of Immanuel Kant—or, at least, to the most influential reading of Kant's moral thought. On this reading, Kant's justly famous claim that "nothing can possibly be conceived in the world, or even out of it, which can be called good without qualification, except a *good will*" (1949, 11) asserts, in its most profound meaning, that the moral law must be identified independently of any end or telos which human action might pursue and is, therefore, radically nonteleological. Kant's reasons for this conclusion are the following: Given that moral imperatives are categorical in the sense that they legislate obligations which one cannot reasonably choose not to have, the moral law must be *a priori*, that is, must be implied by the exercise of human freedom or practical reason as such. Were this not the case, one could choose to deny the moral law without self-contradiction, and the obligations which it prescribes would be hypothetical, that is, they would bind one's choice only *if* one simultaneously chose to affirm the law in question. But if the moral law is *a priori*, Kant continued, it cannot be identified by an end or telos which human action might pursue, because no telos or possible state of affairs is implied by the exercise of human freedom as such.

Of course, this argument depends upon the claim that no telos is *a priori*, but showing the truth of precisely that claim is one of the principal burdens of Kant's magisterial *Critique of Pure Reason*. Summarily stated, that first critique argues that a transcendental inquiry into human knowing may establish the *a priori* conditions of human experience but not the nature of the things experienced. We have knowledge of things-as-they-appear, that is, as they are constituted by understanding, but never of things-in-themselves. Accordingly, the Western metaphysical tradition, which has at least included an attempt to understand the transcendental conditions of reality as such or being qua being, has been an exercise in "transcendental illusion" (1965, 300). It also follows that all claims about what does or might exist are empirical or *a posteriori* in character and, therefore, can be denied without self-contradiction, and it is this conclusion which reappears in the radically nonteleological character of Kant's moral law. Thus, the moral law can only be: So act as to respect the freedom of all rational beings, where freedom is understood independently of the purposes for which it is exercised. Nothing is good without qualification except a good will.

It is, then, this reading of Kant's moral law which informs the established liberal affirmation of private freedom. But if this latter affirmation is self-contradictory, then the same must be the case with Kant's radically nonteleological ethic. Just because the exercise of practical reason *is* the affirmation of some purpose, the notion of a good will has no meaning if there is no criterion or standard in accord with which purposes may be called good. Kant's ethic, on the reading which I have briefly reviewed, also seeks to separate the inseparable, and, if this reading is correct, there is merit in the claim of many subsequent philosophical ethicists that Kant's categorical imperative is empty. Still, that conclusion does not invalidate Kant's insistence that the moral law must be *a priori* or implied by practical reason as such. On the contrary, I am inclined to believe that this insistence represents the enduring legacy of Kant's ethics to contemporary moral theory. If that is so, then the Kantian claim which must be rejected is his denial of an *a priori* or transcendental telos, and this conclusion argues for a reconsideration of the Western metaphysical enterprise as the basis for moral and political theory. It is that implication which I will now pursue by seeking to articulate a moral and political principle informed especially by the achievement of Charles Hartshorne (see especially Hartshorne 1948; 1970). Given the scope of this paper, I will not so much argue for Hartshorne's proposal as I will seek to explicate the evaluative principle which it includes. Still, I will attempt to provide enough argument to recommend that his metaphysical project merits careful attention within the discussion of moral and political theory. Following this attempt to introduce a more adequate understanding of democracy, the final section will return to the relation between democracy and capitalism.

II

In response to the assertion that political theory is properly informed by a metaphysical principle, some may object that this supposed alternative only condemns us to the established form of political liberalism. To be sure, a metaphysical principle of the good may allow one to escape the contradiction which is involved in a radically nonteleological ethic, because it provides a criterion by which purposes may be morally evaluated. But just because a metaphysical telos is transcendental or implied by the exercise of freedom as such, does it not follow that all possible purposes are good, such that there is no moral distinction among them? As a consequence, this objection concludes, morality cannot be concerned with which among possible purposes a given agent chooses, since all are equally good, and political theory is left with an affirmation of the right to private freedom. As a further consequence, any distribution of resources is as good as any other, and one is still faced with the futile contention between advocates of the libertarian and welfare types of established liberalism.

But this line of reasoning also involves a non sequitur. It is indeed correct to say that a metaphysical telos means that all purposes are good, but it does not follow from this that all purposes are *equally* good, such that there is no moral distinction among them by which an agent's choice ought to be informed. On the contrary, purposes all of which are good in some measure may differ in the extent to which they realize the good—or would realize the good were they fulfilled. In other words, a metaphysical telos or principle of the good may be a variable in accord with which alternative possible purposes may be compared, so that some are evaluated as better than others, and one is morally obliged to choose that purpose which maximizes the good.

The conviction that metaphysical principles are variables is constitutive of Hartshorne's proposal, at least in the following sense: The character of reality as such may be expressed as a cosmic or comprehensive variable of which all conceivable concrete things are exemplifications. Concrete things or actualities are the "final real things," in the sense that anything else of which it might be said that it is real or that it exists must be either an aspect of one or more actualities or a composite of two or more actualities. It is true that Hartshorne typically speaks of "cosmic variables" rather than a single variable and thereby implies a plurality of characteristics which are exemplified in actualities as such (see Hartshorne 1937, 111-25). But his point is that a plurality of concepts is required fully to explicate the character of final real things, and it is clear that for him each of this plurality implies all of the others. Given that they identify all *conceivable* reality, in other words, all metaphysical characteristics are logically necessary, and the relations among logically necessary characteristics can only themselves be logically necessary. It is for this reason that there must be one kind of "final real" or concrete thing, and, for the same reason, one may speak of the many cosmic variables as aspects of one comprehensive variable.

Although all conceivable actualities share the same metaphysical identity, it is apparent that they also differ. This latter follows from the fact that there simply are different things in the world. Indeed, absent these differences, there could not be a plurality of things at all; were everything identical, there would simply be cosmic identity. Further, it is clear that actualities could not be different if their characteristics were all metaphysical, because metaphysical "differences" would all imply each other so that the things could not be genuinely different. Hartshorne expresses this by saying that actualities exemplify not only the comprehensive variable but also diverse local variables, that is, characteristics in accord with which two or more but not all concrete things may be compared. Of course, local variables are also specifications of the comprehensive variable, since the latter identifies all conceivable things. But the point is that the specific characteristics cannot be logically derived from the most general characteristics of concrete things, so that there are logically contingent differences among actualities.

In seeking to understand the comprehensive variable, metaphysics also seeks to understand the character of the good. A metaphysical principle of moral evaluation, in other words, can only oblige human freedom so to choose as to pursue actualities and composite states of affairs which maximally exemplify the comprehensive variable; the metaphysical telos can only be the greatest possible realization of whatever it is that identifies reality as such. Thus, the fundamental question of moral theory might be formulated in the following manner: What is the comprehensive variable or measure in accord with which all conceivable actualities may be compared and thereby evaluated as better and worse?

The conviction that practical reason implies an answer to this question is one reason why Hartshorne is a theist. Human freedom becomes, in other words, the premise of a moral argument for the existence of God, and the argument might be summarily stated as follows: A comprehensive comparison of all things requires a comprehensive actuality in which all actual and possible things are together. Because the comprehensive variable provides the terms with which all things may be compared, it might be objected that a comprehensive actuality is unnecessary. But the point is that the concrete differences among actualities can only be compared or evaluated concretely. The comprehensive variable identifies any given actuality as *some* greater or lesser exemplification of itself. In what measure differing things exemplify this variable can only be determined if those things are compared concretely. Accordingly, there must be a supreme or all-inclusive exemplification of the variable in which all actual and possible things are together, and this supreme exemplification may be called the divine actuality precisely because it is inclusive of all other good and, therefore, must be supremely good. Hartshorne also calls it "the divine relativity," by which he means that this exemplification is constituted by its complete or fully adequate internal relations to all actuality and possibility.

Precisely because a concrete comparison or evaluation of all conceivable things is completely relative to all actuality *and possibility*, the divine actuality occurs with respect to a particular temporal reference. As the future becomes past, possibilities are actualized and the all-inclusive reality is different. In other words, Hartshorne distinguishes between past and future in terms of the distinction between actuality and possibility. The past is identified by reality that has been actualized or made fully determinate, while the future is identified by reality which remains indeterminate or merely possible. The present, then, is the referent of determination, the becoming determinate of what was heretofore indeterminate, and, for this reason, actualities may also be called "activities." Accordingly, one must distinguish between the divine as an activity and the divine as an individual. An individual may be understood as a series of activities or actualities which is sequentially ordered and has genetic identity; no two of the activities in question are coterminous, and the characteristic which distinguishes the individual in question from all others is exemplified in any later activity by virtue of its relativity to earlier ones. Thus, the necessary existence of the divine should be understood to mean a sequentially ordered series of actualities whose distinguishing characteristic is "complete relativity to all actuality and possibility." The divine is an everlasting individual whose present determination always includes all things. Because there must always be a divine actuality, we may say that the divine is the metaphysical individual, that is, the one individual which is distinguished from all others metaphysically.

All other individuals, then, must be distinguished or identified by characteristics which are nonmetaphysical and, therefore, local variables. In speaking of a human individual, for instance, Hartshorne means a sequentially ordered series of experiences which is at least sometimes self-conscious or self-reflective and, so far as we know, is only possible because those experiences are intimately relative to a human body. Because there can be only one metaphysical individual, the identity which distinguishes any given human individual from all others must be logically contingent. This follows also because human activities, as all other nondivine exemplifications of the comprehensive variable, must be relativities which differ from the divine and, therefore, are fragmentary or partial rather than all-inclusive. Nondivine actualities are relative to some but not all actuality and possibility, and an individual whose experiences or activities are partially relative cannot be specified or distinguished from all others except by some logically contingent characteristic.

Thus, the comprehensive variable of which all actualities are exemplifications may be formulated, "relative to all or some actuality and possibility," where "relative to all" refers to the activities of God, and "relative to some" refers to all of the actualities of the world. Given that the variable may also be formulated "relative to some but not all of the determinate past and the indeterminate future," we can understand why Hartshorne speaks of the metaphysical character of reality as "creative synthesis" and thereby appropriates Alfred North Whitehead's category of "creativity": "the many become one and are increased by one" (Whitehead, 21). In any actuality, relativity to past actualities is synthesized in a present which is also constituted by the necessity that this synthesis become one of the past many to which future actualities will be relative. Alternatively, the variable of creativity may be understood as unity-in-diversity. Creative synthesis is a unification of diverse relations to the past and to the future as such.

It now follows that the metaphysical measure in accord with which actualities are greater or less and, therefore, better or worse is the measure of creativity or unity-in-diversity. Since greater and lesser good can only be determined in the comparison of the divine relativity, it also follows that greater creativity is better precisely because it increases the divine unity-in-diversity. To be more creative is, in other words, to be more distinct and thereby to increase the diversity to which the all-inclusive actuality is relative. But now one may say that the possibilities for creativity in any actuality depend upon the diversity to which it is relative. Greater possibilities are a gift to the present from the diversity of the past. Unlike the all-inclusive character of the divine, however, all nondivine actualities are partial or fragmentary, so that greater possibilities for good require a past with *relevant* diversity, that is, diversity which is so ordered that fragmentary actuality can indeed be relative to it, rather than so extreme that it is chaotic and thereby compromises subsequent creativity.

We are now in a position to return to the moral law and, through it, to political theory. Having said that the variable of creativity is the metaphysical measure in accord with which actualities are better or worse, it follows that the possible purposes among which human action must choose are morally evaluated in accord with the following principle: So act as to maximize creativity in the future as such. In other words, maximal creativity in the future as such is the metaphysical telos of human action. Of course, we must also say that the moral law obliges human choice to maximize the actuality of God. But these two formulations of the law are identical in meaning, because the future as such is nothing other than the future of the individual whose actualities are all-inclusive.

We may return closer to the discussion of liberal political theory if we recognize that the pursuit of maximal creativity may also be formulated as the pursuit of maximal freedom in the future as such. If the comprehensive variable is creativity, in other words, it is also freedom. Hartshorne insists that the unification of diversity (and, therefore, each of the final real things) is in some measure a free choice among alternatives. His point is that determination of what is indeterminate can never be completely a product of what is already determinate. Were it so, the present would not be different from the past. But if this means that no actuality can be completely other-determined, it does not mean that any actuality is completely self-determined, for complete self-determination would mean that there is no past at all. Unity-in-diversity is, then, partially self-determined, namely, in its unification of that diversity. Hence, the metaphysical claim that every actuality is free does not identify in what measure this is so for any given one; conceivable freedom varies from the unimaginably trivial to the unimaginably profound.

Within the world that we know, freedom is apparently greatest within the activities of human individuals. Indeed, it is because the capacity for self-conscious or rational freedom is apparently so much greater than the freedom of subhuman existence that we may speak for many purposes as if humans were the only self-determined individuals in the world. Since creativity is greater insofar as relativity is greater, the conditions of greater freedom are always more diverse other-determination, and the reasons why humans characteristically enjoy greater self-determination include the fact that human activity is always intimately relative to the immense diversity ordered within the human body, especially the human brain.

But if the moral law requires the pursuit of maximal freedom in the future as such, then we may also say that all humans have the right to optimal freedom, that is, each has the right to receive the measure of ordered diversity in its world which optimizes its own creative possibilities. In other words, Hartshorne's metaphysics provides the foundation for a liberal political theory. The term "optimal" rather than "maximal" is appropriate in defining this fundamental human right precisely because all humans have the right; the rightful claims of each are constrained by the rightful claims of others, and the general principle of this constraint can only be the telos of maximal creativity in the future as such. But the fact that one individual's claim is limited by the rights of others does not mean that rights are necessarily competitive. On the contrary, one's freedom is enhanced by greater ordered diversity in one's world, so that, ideally, the greater freedom of each is a condition for the greater freedom of all.

Strictly speaking, it is not simply human individuals which have the right to freedom but rather all individuals, for the metaphysical telos is the maximal creativity of the future as such. Assuming that human freedom is not only the greatest in the world but also dramatically greater than that of subhuman existence, however, the human future occupies a preeminent place in the moral enterprise. Indeed, we may say that the creativity of the subhuman world is greatest insofar as that world is ordered so as to maximize the freedom in the human future, and, for purposes of deliberation, the moral law may be reformulated: So act as to maximize the creativity of freedom of human existence as such. But if human freedom is the greatest in the world, it follows that human creativity will, if properly ordered, contribute the greatest diversity to subsequent human existence, that is, the greater freedom of each is, ideally, the condition for the greater freedom of all. For purposes of deliberation, then, the moral law may also be reformulated: So act as to maximize the creativity communicated among humans.

I will call the creativity which is communicated among humans "the public world," so that human action is morally bound to pursue the maximal public world—and, by implication, in the long run. If Hartshorne's metaphysical proposal affirms the fundamental human right to freedom and, therefore, provides the backing for a liberal political theory, it is now clear that this theory departs from the tradition of established political liberalism. In contrast to the notion of private freedom by which that tradition is constituted, the telos informs a principle of public freedom, and this in two related senses: Freedom is now public in the sense that its exercise is subject to an objective or public norm. It is also public in the sense that that norm is identified by the maximal public world. So far from providing a solely instrumental setting for private purposes, human association is intrinsically good, because it creates the public world. I will call the political theory constituted by this notion of public freedom the theory of reformed liberalism.

I suggested earlier that established liberal theory at least permits the priority of private-regarding associations. In contrast, reformed liberal theory prescribes the priority of public-regarding associations. Properly speaking, in other words, economic associations are teleologically subservient to associations whose identifying purpose is nothing other than to create human communication and, thereby, the public world. This is not to say that economic associations are teleologically subservient to specifically political associations. It is true that the latter are public-regarding, because their identifying purpose is nothing other than to govern or to create the order of associations as such. But public-regarding associations also include those whose identifying purpose is not participation in the process of governing but is rather to create human communication about matters of common interest—and I have in mind the order of educational, cultural, civic, and religious associations which, as I use the term, properly constitute the class of "independent associations" (see Gamwell).

It is also important to stress that the subservence of the economic order is teleological in character and, therefore, does not minimize the importance of economic preconditions for human creativity. In the absence of some significant measure of biological health and material security, human freedom is, as a general rule, profoundly impoverished. Moreover, the artificial world which humans build, including the products of major technological advances which some societies have in the last century come to enjoy, provides in many respects an essential context for an enhanced public world. Indeed, one may say that the possibilities for substantial participation in public-regarding associations occur in a widespread manner only within societies which have become so economically productive that large numbers of individuals are released from persistent demands of survival and minimal security and are provided with resources for the creation of the public world. In principle, then, a reformed liberal theory prescribes the pursuit of economic productivity in such manner as to establish the preconditions for the higher possibilities of human creativity—and, in situations of massive economic want, this means that the economic problem properly commands an overwhelming measure of attention. Finally, the economic order, precisely as it becomes technologically advanced, also increasingly becomes an occasion for human communication and, therefore, the creation of the public world, and this has been especially true in the more specialized aspects of complex private-regarding institutions.

But it remains that reformed liberalism relativizes economic institutions to noneconomic values, that is, evaluates the economic order by virtue of its relations to an inclusive telos that is not economic. Thus, the subservence of private-regarding associations to the maximal public world informs a political theory in accord with which one might criticize a given society for the extent to which the social order is consumed by economic goals or by the pursuit of economic growth. If this does not settle the empirical question which is raised by the recent indictment on just this charge of American society or Western societies generally, reformed liberalism does offer a political principle in relation to which that question may be clarified and debated. It is worth noting, moreover, that a development of this theory might appropriate the noneconomic values that have been suggested by Galbraith and Heilbroner and which were mentioned earlier. Galbraith's proposal that the aesthetic values of the natural and artificial environment be "accorded priority" may be appropriated on the grounds that beauty in the nonhuman world is a condition and a consequence of the higher forms of human creativity. Indeed, unity-in-diversity is, for Hartshorne, an aesthetic variable, so that pursuit of the maximal public world may also be expressed as pursuit of maximal beauty communicated among humans. Heilbroner's prediction that business civilization will in the long run be so transformed as to elevate "the collective and communal destiny of man" may itself be transformed into the prescription that the maximal public world ought to be taken as the long-run telos of the social order.

I know of no modern thinker who has more clearly developed a reformed liberal theory of the kind which I have only suggested than has John Dewey. To be sure, Dewey did not pursue metaphysics in the sense which I judge necessary if one is to provide an adequate foundation for the moral enterprise. That difference aside, however, one may find in his political writings a clear appreciation both of the massive contribution which modern economic success has made to the human adventure and of what I have called the priority of public-regarding associations. We require, he once wrote, "a form of social organization that should include economic activities but yet should convert them into servants of the development of the higher human capacities" (1963, 31-32). It is, then, significant that Dewey's "guiding intention may be summarized as the attempt to further the realization of democracy in every sphere of life" (Horowitz, 746). A liberal theory constituted by the right to public freedom is a reformed theory of democracy. "Democracy has many meanings," Dewey also wrote, "but if it has a moral meaning, it is found in resolving that the supreme test of all human actions . . . shall be the contribution which they make to the all-around growth of every member of society" (1957, 196). If one substitutes for "growth" the term "creativity," a synonym of which I believe Dewey would approve, one may say that the moral meaning of democracy is the telos of the maximal public world.

III

Given this theory of democracy, I now return to the relation between democracy and capitalism. At the outset of this essay, I assumed sufficient merit in certain considerations advanced on behalf of capitalism, especially those concerned with the distribution of power and the coordination of economic activities by market prices, to give one pause about rejecting a predominant reliance upon nongovernmental economic decisions. I also noted my judgment that a capitalist economic order might properly be supervised or constituted in substantial measure by the state. The intervening outline of a reformed liberal theory provides the context in which to offer some reasons for that latter judgment. The overriding reason is, of course, that the economy is properly subservient to the maximal public world. Prima facie, then, it is appropriate for the state to prevent the system of nongovernmental economic decisions from so invading the integrity and beauty of the natural environment, the conditions of communal diversity and solidarity, the flourishing of cultural activities, or the democratic process of the state itself as to compromise the maximal public world.

Moreover, this reformed liberal theory also provides a principle in accord with which the political process might seek to adjudicate the distributional questions which, I have argued, established liberalism can only beg. The claim that economic associations serve a noneconomic telos is also the claim that economic distribution should serve that same telos. Given that the public world is the greater insofar as a greater diversity of human creativity is more fully shared or communicated, there is a prima facie imperative to provide for each individual the resources required to optimize his or her creativity. There is, in other words, a prima facie loss to the public world insofar as the potential creativity of any individual is compromised by ill health, poverty, the want of education, and, in general, the absence of those economic conditions required for the higher human achievements. To say this is simply to repeat that the constitutive principle of reformed liberalism is the right to optimal public freedom, where the latter is understood as the opportunity to be creative.

But if these considerations at least leave open an affirmation of capitalism within a reformed liberal theory of democracy, that affirmation cannot be sustained without attention to the claim that capitalism is in fact inconsistent with the priority of public-regarding associations. Critics of capitalism have repeatedly argued that this form of economic order is identified by the unending drive to accumulate capital. It is fundamentally for this reason, the argument continues, that the economic institutions of "advanced" industrial democracies dominate the social order and that such societies are committed to the unending pursuit of economic growth. So far as I can see, the supposed relation between capitalism and unending accumulation is finally an empirical claim. Nonetheless, this characteristic is taken to be so fundamental to capitalism that the claim, if true, would provide prima facie reason profoundly to doubt that a capitalist economic order can be contained within an economically "advanced" democratic polity whose inclusive or overriding commitment is to noneconomic goals. One recent and lucid statement of the claim is found in Heilbroner's *The Nature and Logic of Capitalism*, and some brief attention to this work will help to clarify the issue.

The distinction between capitalist and precapitalist societies, Heilbroner argues, does not consist in the extraction of "surplus" from the "broad working body of society" (33) for the use of a restricted group or class. On the contrary, such extraction of wealth has been characteristic of "all

societies that have made the leap from primitive communities into civilizations" (34). In contrast to capitalist societies, however, others have typically
channelled this surplus into "desired objects"—those of luxury consumption, public monuments, military power, or religious edifices. Wealth, in
other words, has taken the form of "use values" (34). What is peculiar to
capitalism, then, is that wealth is used "not as an end in itself, but as a
means for gathering more wealth" (35). In other words, "wealth inhabits
material things only transiently" (35). Capital is invested in resources and in
"labor power" and through them in a product only for the purpose of turn-
ing the product back into wealth, and, moreover, wealth that is greater in
measure than that with which one began. Capitalism is a "continuous
transformation of capital-as-money into capital-as-commodities into
capital-as-more-money," and this is, Heilbroner summarizes, "the famous
M-C-M' formula by which Marx schematized the repetitive, expansive
metamorphosis through which 'capital' manifests itself" (36). Hence,
"without *the organizing purpose of expansion*, capital dissolves into
material building blocks that are necessary but not sufficient to define its life
purpose" (37, emphasis added).

It is essential to Heilbroner's understanding of capital as a process rather
than a material thing that capital is also "a relationship of domination" (40),
in which those who do not own capital are dependent upon those who do.
As a matter of historical fact, Heilbroner argues, the emergence of
capitalism involved "a protracted revolution" in which both peasants and
urban workers were separated from their ownership of productive means;
"established rights of direct access to one's own product were replaced by
new rights by which peasants and workers were legally excluded from access to their means of livelihood" (42). The peculiar power of capitalism,
Heilbroner continues, is not that of direct coercion but the power to
withhold capital from productive use. To be sure, the "proletarianized"
workers may also withhold their "labor power." But in fact the concentration of wealth means that the worker's need for employment is far more
immediate than the capitalist's need to place capital in use, and, accordingly, the inequality of power is constituted. "'In the long run '" Heilbroner
quotes from Adam Smith, "'the workman may be as necessary to his master
as his master is to him, but the necessity is not so immediate'" (41).
Heilbroner's point, then, is that this inequality is required if capital is to expand. For the increase from M to M' depends upon an extraction of surplus—or, in more common terminology, the realization of a profit. The
legal provision by which capitalism is constituted stipulates that "the product itself belongs to the owner of the capital resources that are used in production, not to the owners of the labor resources" (67), and it is the
dominating position of capitalists which allows them to hire labor for a

wage that is less than the value of labor's contribution to the product—and thereby to realize a profit.

But if domination is required in order that capital might be a process of expansion, we have not yet clarified why this process is fundamental to capitalism. Heilbroner locates "the rationale of this endless process" (42) in the drives for prestige and power which he takes to be constitutive of human nature. "It is uncertain whether all societies possess prestige goods, but there is no question that all humankind possess the capacity, rooted in infantile narcissism, to project psychic energies and fantasies into objects that then become extensions or embellishments of the person"(44). But "the drive for prestige . . . ," is only a necessary, not a sufficient condition of the drive for wealth (44), for wealth is "a social category inseparable from power" (45, emphasis deleted), because it "confers on its owners the ability to direct and mobilize the activities of society" (45). Heilbroner finds the "roots of the power relationship" in the "prolonged infantile dependency, the uniquely and universally human experience out of which social behavior is formed" (48). That experience, he continues, leads to both "unappeased and unappeasable needs for affect" and "a submissiveness acquired in coping with adult wills" (48), so that it prepares individuals for both the positions of dominator and dominated into which the social order casts differing people.

Capitalism, Heilbroner insists, adds a certain instability to the drive for power. This is in part because all forms of wealth are reduced to "money terms" (55). By the very abstract nature of this measure, "there are no bounds imposed on the size of the wealth by which power and prestige are symbolized, in contrast to the limitations often imposed by the sheer physical bulk of material riches"(55). Equally important is the "constant state of vulnerability" (56) into which capital is placed in the M-C-M' circuit or by "the process of competition" (57, emphasis deleted) and without which there could not be an economic system in which decisions are predominantly nongovernmental. In part, then, continual expansion is a continual quest for self-protection. If I understand Heilbroner rightly, the abstract nature of capital permits and the vulnerability of capital requires that the capitalist expression of the drive for prestige and power be unbounded, so that continual expansion is fundamental to capitalism.

It is clear that Heilbroner's own appeal to human nature in order to explain endless accumulation is dependent upon his appropriation of theories in empirical psychology. But his case need not rest upon that appeal. His discussion of the drives for prestige and power and the insatiability promoted in part by the insecurity of power reminds one of nothing so much as Reinhold Niebuhr's classic analysis of the inauthentic mode of human existence. Consistent with the theistic foundation of moral life which I described above, Niebuhr holds that self-conscious freedom finds its meaning only in relation to the totality of all things in the kingdom of God. But if the greatness of the human spirit consists in its capacity "to survey the whole" (1949, I, 17), it remains that "man is a finite spirit," and "he easily commits the error of imagining himself the whole which he envisages" (1949, I, 181). The "will-to-power" is, then, an attempt to find within one's own achievements and, therefore, within oneself the source of meaning which in truth cannot be found anywhere in the world, and the fact that the very worth of life itself consists in one's power means that the inescapable insecurity of power makes the "lust for power" insatiable.

If this "sin of pride," as Niebuhr characteristically called it, is "the primal sin of self-love" (1949, I, 233), he also argues that the inauthentic mode of human existence may be expressed in the attempt to abdicate the demands of freedom in "the sin of sensuality." Having denied the transcendent or divine source of meaning, a human is also unable "to maintain his own will as the centre of himself" and, therefore, seeks "to escape from the self" (1949, I, 233). This expression of inauthenticity, then, may easily be appropriated to explain the submissive aspect of human character which Heilbroner takes to be the inescapable alter ego of the drive to power.

The insistence that a will-to-power or "sin of pride" occupies a central place in human affairs is one reason why some ethicists have affirmed a democratic capitalist economy. In other words, this consideration underscores for many thinkers the importance of preventing the concentration of political power which they take socialism to entail. But the point here is that Niebuhr's analysis might also be called upon to underscore the unending accumulation which, Heilbroner argues, is fundamental to capitalism. Whether the drive to power is indeed as pervasive as Heilbroner and Niebuhr believe is, as I have mentioned, finally an empirical question. In principle, however, the reading seems plausible, and, therefore, one may conclude that there are or could be circumstances in which the forms of prestige and power which capitalism creates are inconsistent with reformed liberal democracy. Moreover, just insofar as one finds persuasive the charge that "advanced" industrial democracies have been overwhelmed by their own economic success and are now irrationally committed to ever increasing economic growth, one may be inclined to think that Heilbroner's analysis has contemporary relevance, so that the relation between democracy and capitalism is a pressing contemporary problem.

The question, then, is whether an economic system which relies in predominant measure upon nongovernmental decisions and, therefore, upon market exchange may be so designed as to be independent of or at least to control a fundamental drive to expansion or accumulation. My own inclination is to think that this is so and that an approach to the problem must begin where Heilbroner's discussion of capitalism begins—namely, with the distinction between capitalists and workers. According to his analysis, it is the legal stipulation that product belongs to the owners of capital which sets up the possibility of extracting surplus and the implied relation of domination. But there is, so far as I can see, no essential connection between this stipulation and predominant reliance upon nongovernmental economic decisions. It would be equally consistent with capitalism as I have defined it were product owned not by the owners of capital but by those who work in an economic association. Capital, then, would be "hired" or borrowed, so that the surplus or profit would belong to the workers, and the direction of the institution would finally be accountable to them. Prima facie, at least, this reconstitution of economic production would remove the possibility that economic surplus is the instrument of excessive power for the relatively few and, therefore, remove the drive to economic expansion which expresses the fundamental human will-to-power.

I do not mean to suggest, in opposition to Niebuhr, that the will-to-power is the creation of a particular institutional order rather than a mode of inauthentic human existence as such, so that it could be overcome by an institutional rearrangement. On the contrary, the reconstitution of economic associations which I have suggested intends to address the problem of economic power in the same way in which Niebuhr sought to address the threat of excessive power generally, namely, by producing insofar as institutional arrangements allow a "balance of power" (see 1949, II, 256-69). Insisting as he did upon the pervasive influence of the sin of pride in human affairs, Niebuhr argued that social and political injustice cannot be achieved by relying solely upon the capacity of individuals to attend to the interests of others. On the contrary, he held, power will always be corrupted by unjust purposes unless it is met with more or less equal power which resists those purposes. Meaning by "democracy" a social process in which the interests of all are represented by such a balance of power, Niebuhr held that "our capacity for justice makes democracy possible"; but he also insisted that "our inclination to injustice makes democracy necessary" (1960, xiii).

The proposal to reconstitute the ownership of economic resources is, in this sense, a proposal for economic democracy. It is important to say, perhaps, that this need not be "direct democracy." The point is not that management of economic institutions would be directly effected in "town meetings" within which all workers in the firm have a vote. On the contrary, it seems clear that large economic organizations could only be governed by a system of "representative democracy." But the officials of the firm would be representatives of the workers rather than the owners of capital and, therefore, the general policies of the institution as well as the distribution of the profit would be accountable to principles established by the "citizens." Of course, none of this changes the fact that all firms would operate within conditions established by the state, nor does it alter the reliance upon the market with respect to interaction among economic institutions and between such institutions and their consumers.

There are, to be sure, a number of questions which have been raised about a system of economic democracy, including whether it would be as efficient as capitalism in its present form and whether it would provide sufficient incentives for entrepreneurial and technological creativity. At least upon first appearances, I do not see why democratic economic institutions would not prize efficiency and provide requisite incentives as much as capitalist-owned institutions do. But a comprehensive defense of this proposal would require an extended discussion of such questions as these. Because I am not competent to engage that discussion, I can do no more at this point than to express my appreciation of Robert Dahl's recent volume, *A Preface to Economic Democracy*, which I take to be a persuasive argument for the kind of economic organization which I intend to recommend.

Granting the merit of Dahl's case, it remains an open question whether all economic organizations should be owned by the workers. It may well be, for instance, that exceptions should be made for very small enterprises and very large economic institutions. Perhaps the former are so extensively the creations of given entrepreneurs that ownership should remain with these individuals. Perhaps very large institutions, especially those for whom the state is a principal customer, threaten so to dominate the government insofar as it relates directly to their interests that they should be governmentally owned. The present argument does not seek to dismiss such differentiations. It is enough that economic democracy might be appropriate for most other economic organizations, and my argument is that this institutional form will allow reliance upon predominantly nongovernmental decisions without introducing a system that threatens to make economic goals the dominant purposes of the social order.

But if this is so, then it is also important to say that economic democracy would also enhance the respects in which economic associations create the public world. There is little serious question that the internal life of economic associations in the American social order, especially large economic institutions, is autocratic (see, e.g. Dahl, 55), such that most of the participants have little opportunity to develop creative capacities and with the consequence that most look upon their work as an activity which is more or less entirely instrumental to other purposes. Established liberal theories have often been unconcerned with this fact, in part because the private purposes for which they seek to protect the worker's freedom have been understood as those of the worker qua customer rather than the worker qua producer. Reformed liberal theory is required, however, to consider the respects in which participation in productive communities is consistent with the right to optimal creativity and the telos of the maximal public world. Economic democracy would not change the fact that economic associations are private-regarding rather than public-regarding in character, since this is true by definition. But participation in the ownership of the product would at least provide the occasion for enhanced creativity and an enhanced public world in pursuit of the institution's purposes. In that respect, economic democracy would not only preserve the contributions of capitalism to reformed liberal democracy but also maximize them.

Works Cited

Dahl, Robert A.
   1985   *A Preface to Economic Democracy*. Berkeley and Los Angeles, California: University of California Press.

Dewey, John
   1957   *Reconstruction in Philosophy*. Boston: Beacon Press.
   1963   *Liberalism and Social Action*. New York: Capricorn Books.

Friedman, Milton
   1962   *Capitalism and Freedom*. Chicago: The University of Chicago Press.

Galbraith, John Kenneth
   1971   *The New Industrial State*, 2nd ed. Boston: Houghton Mifflin Company.

Gamwell, Franklin I.
   1984   *Beyond Preference: Liberal Theories of Independent Associations*. Chicago: University of Chicago Press.

Hartshorne, Charles
   1937   *Beyond Humanism*. Lincoln: University of Nebraska Press.
   1948   *The Divine Relativity*. New Haven: Yale University Press.
   1970   *Creative Synthesis and Philosophic Method*. Lasalle, Illinois: Open Court.

Heilbroner. Robert L.
   1976   *Business Civilization in Decline*. New York: W.W. Norton and Company.
   1985   *The Nature and Logic of Capitalism*. New York: W.W. Norton and Company.

Horowitz, Robert
   1963   "John Dewey." *History of Political Philosophy*. Ed. by Leo Strauss and Joseph Cropsey. Chicago: Rand McNally, 746-62.

Kant, Immanuel
   1949   *Fundamental Principles of the Metaphysics of Morals*. Indianapolis: Bobbs-Merrill.
   1965   *Critique of Pure Reason*. New York: St. Martin's Press.

Lindblom, Charles E.
   1977   *Politics and Markets: The World's Political-Economic Systems*. New York: Basic Books.

Niebuhr, Reinhold
    1949   *The Nature and Destiny of Man.* 2 vols. New York: Charles Scribner's
            Sons.
    1960   *The Children of Light and the Children of Darkness.* New York: Charles
            Scribner's Sons.
Sandel, Michael J.
    1982   *Liberalism and the Limits of Justice.* New York: Cambridge University
            Press.
Whitehead, Alfred North
    1978   *Process and Reality,* corrected edition. Ed. by David Ray Griffin and
            Donald Sherburne. New York: The Free Press.
Wolff, Robert Paul
    1968   *The Poverty of Liberalism.* Boston: Beacon Press.

CHAPTER 12

Reformed Capitalism or Aristocratic Socialism? A Response to Franklin I. Gamwell

Robert Benne

Franklin Gamwell, while graciously bowing to some of the strengths of what he calls "established liberalism," nevertheless has a serious bone to pick with it, in either its libertarian or welfare forms. In the following I intend to sketch the outlines of his critique and alternative project. Then I will reflect critically on his proposal and end with some constructive thoughts of my own.

I

Gamwell's central criticism of establishment liberal practice in our western societies concerns the dominance of economic associations with their private-regarding activities. Private-regarding activities, unlike public-regarding, do not aim at human association and communication as ends in themselves. Rather, they aim at producing and consuming goods and services that can be bought and sold in the market place. Further, according to the critics that Gamwell relies upon, especially Robert Heilbroner, established liberal practice leads inexorably to the blind drive toward growth. This ensures that the dominance of economic goals will go unchallenged and that public-regarding activities will be pushed to the periphery of our social existence. Not only does this lead to the exploitation of workers inherent in privately owned systems of production, it also puts undue demands on the natural world. But, above all, the dominance of economic goals diminishes what is most uniquely and valuably human.

On the theoretical level, the problem is that we have no political theory that can challenge the dominance of economic goals with their private-regarding thurst. (Gamwell, p. 228) Both libertarian and welfare varieties of liberal theory separate the moral meaning of freedom from "the ends or purposes for which individuals exercise their right." (Gamwell, p. 228) Those ends remain "private" in liberal theory because they are held only by individual persons and are not assessed by appeal to common public norms. Therefore, liberalism has no way to prevent the dominance of the economic. This is the well-known "poverty of liberal theory."

The problem of liberal theory has even deeper roots in a fateful philosophical, even metaphysical, mistake. As is often the case with those influenced by process thought, Gamwell traces the mistake to Kant's formalism. That formalism may in turn find its deepest roots in Platonic dualism, but for the Western philosophical tradition the chief sinner is Kant.

Kant locates the morality of action in its formal characteristics and, so the argument goes, gives little attention to its ends or purposes. Liberal political theory based on Kantian ethics—as well as on the philosophical heritage of Locke and Smith—therefore exhibits this empty formalism. It simply does not deal with the question of what freedom is for in a substantive sense. It thereby leaves the field open to the heavy influence of the economic.

II

After this critique Gamwell proposes another alternative. Drawing upon Hartshorne and Whitehead, he argues that their metaphysical perspectives draw both freedom and the purposes of freedom together into "creativity." Since this creativity cannot be achieved except in dynamic human interaction, it is in principle public-regarding.

Gamwell contends that this metaphysical grounding leads to a political theory and practice that, while it prizes freedom, also binds freedom to public-regarding creativity as the supreme end of human life in society. (Gamwell, pp. 240-41) Negatively speaking, it can resist the tendency of economic goals to dominate that life. Positively, it puts to the fore what is essentially human.

Moving from a fundamental metaphysical commitment through a political theory reformed by that prior commitment, Gamwell then sketches a picture of what practice might look like in a society so constituted. His vision certainly does not negate the importance of economic efficiency; it rather makes economic efficiency the means to the end of public activity. It "evaluates the economic order by virtue of its relations to an inclusive telos that is not economic." (Gamwell, p. 241) Generally speaking, this means that:

> It is appropriate for the state to prevent the system of nongovernmental economic decisions from so invading the integrity and beauty of the natural environment, the conditions of communal diversity and solidarity, the flourishing of cultural activities, or the democratic process of the state itself as to compromise the maximal public world. (Gamwell, pp. 242-43)

Though it is difficult to envisage what such a stance means practically (though I have serious reservations about what it *might* mean, about which I shall write later), Gamwell presses on. His view that the freedom of all should be enabled to move toward creativity by all, leads to further governmental intervention in order "to provide for each individual the resources required to optimize his or her creativity." (Gamwell, p. 243) Thus, there is a strong redistributive thrust to his argument.

Further, since human associational activity would be increased and exploitation decreased under a scheme of economic democracy, Gamwell ends his proposal with a resounding affirmation of worker-owned and -managed enterprises. These middle-sized enterprises—the very large ones would be nationalized—would be governed by representative democratic processes and would operate within the dynamics of a competitive market. In other words, we would have a version of the market socialism long hoped for by socialist economists like Oskar Lange.

As Gamwell moves through his argument, he relies on increasingly strident criticisms of liberal capitalism (Heilbroner and Dahl) and proposes alternative ways of relating political and economic power that are positively revolutionary with regard to the present system. Further, all economic activity becomes instrumental to the ends of creativity. Production and consumption would be guided toward support for public-regarding associational activity.

I submit that by this time Gamwell is no longer in the camp of reformed liberalism but rather in what I would call "aristocratic market socialism." Gamwell's vision is aristocratic because it supports governmental stipulation of goals generally associated with high culture. Besides Hartshorne and Dewey, Gamwell seems to be indebted to Hannah Arendt's political thought with its sharp distinction between private and public activities. For Arendt, as for Gamwell, private activities are, among other things, laboring activities devoted to production and consumption. Such activities are cyclical and biological; we share them with the animal world. On the other hand, public activities are actions in the public sphere which have no product; they are ends in themselves. The speech and action of those who are truly excellent are most fit for such public action (Arendt, 23-65).

Besides being aristocratic with regard to ends, it is clear that Gamwell proposes something far different than free enterprise capitalism as a mode of economic decision-making. First, *what* would be produced would be shaped by governmental preference for the goals of creativity. The mode of production would be guided by worker councils. In fact, competitive markets would be one of the few remaining characteristics of the old order. However, it would be difficult to describe those competitive markets as free.

Certainly it is clear in all this that Gamwell remains committed to democratic political processes, though it is difficult to see how citizens within the present order would be persuaded to vote for candidates devoted to such dramatic changes.

III

If this be "aristocratic market socialism" rather than reformed liberal capitalism, what's wrong with that, especially since it is geared to many of the values that many educated and thoughtful people hold dear?

First, there are some internal tensions within Gamwell's argument itself. I do not see how the proposed shift to worker-owned and -managed enterprises will significantly address the question of ends or the issue of incessant growth. The present tendency of workers to get caught up in the round of production and consumption would not necessarily abate under a new system of ownership and management. In fact, the desire for more consumption might be heightened by the increased income workers would theoretically accrue to themselves in such a scheme. Further, since competitive pressures would still operate, wouldn't there be the same tendency to amass capital that Heilbroner thinks is an intrinsic characteristic of capitalism? Firms, even worker-owned and -managed ones, would still have to grow to survive. Indeed, if workers would share heavily in the profits gained from it, growth would likely become a prized goal for the persons involved.

However, Gamwell might respond to this objection by asserting that the ends toward which their increased income could be used would be encouraged toward creativity because the state itself would stipulate what would be produced. Perhaps the plethora of consumer goods and services we have easily available today would simply not be so available in Gamwellia.

This leads to the major problem with Gamwell's project. It simply cannot avoid a heavy-handed, comprehensive role for the state if that state would take seriously the political theory he proposes. The state would radically diminish economic freedom. There would be no free entry into the market for either producers or consumers. Above all, the free movement of capital would be sharply curtailed. These are direct implications of the state stipulating the substantive ends toward which societal life should move.

I am sure that Gamwell means for all of this to be instituted democratically. However, even if it were likely to prevail through democratic process— which it is not, given the current outlook of citizens—it would result in a powerfully interventionist state. The state would have to make a large number of economic decisions and would have to have the knowledge to make them efficiently and the power to make its decisions stick. Those requirements would lead to a far heavier and intrusive state than Americans have ever known or consented to. Gamwellia would not be a reformed liberal state.

Before I move on to a few reflections on what I would consider to be an authentically "reformed liberalism," let me raise a number of smaller criticisms. First, I find it somewhat unfair to the liberal tradition to charge that it has been unconcerned about the purposes or the use of freedom. Smith, Bentham, Mill, Kant and even Friedman *do* have elements in their moral philosophy concerned with ends. *The Theory of Moral Sentiments* accompanies *The Wealth of Nations* in Smith's case. Kant's *Lectures on Ethics* goes beyond mere formalism. Friedman believes there are noble and ignoble uses of freedom. Even libertarians share in that belief. But the liberal tradition insists that those ends be voluntarily claimed. Freedom is not sufficient for a moral life devoted to worthy ends, but it is necessary.

Second, the definitions of private-regarding and public-regarding activities seem too blunt and imprecise to describe the manifold character of human action. Moreover, there is a tendency to apply them too sharply to activities that are highly mixed. For instance, what is a college or university—private-regarding or public? It seems to me it clearly has both elements. On the other hand, is politics itself as public-regarding as Gamwell seems to suggest?

Thirdly, the author seems to rely unduly on the sharpest critics of liberal capitalism. Heilbroner, for example, makes a profession out of pronouncing doom on every facet of liberal capitalism. Perhaps Gamwell should pay a bit more attention to works like Julian Simon's *The Ultimate Resource* or Michael Novak's *The Spirit of Democratic Capitalism*, especially the latter since it too lifts up the notion of "creativity" so strongly.

IV

I must initiate my concluding remarks by confessing that I share many of the misgivings Gamwell has about liberal theory and practice as well as most of the substantive purposes he prizes. I do believe that the crux of our civilizational challenge is the right use of the freedom we cherish. Right now the uses of freedom are pulled downward by the forces of contemporary mass culture. However, I would argue that this downward pull is the result of broad forces of modernization rather than of capitalism *per se*. Be that as it may, a more persuasive approach than Gamwell's would move along more reformist lines than his rather drastic ones.

First, a reformist approach would emphasize the resources we currently have in our voluntary sector for forming persons toward a proper use of freedom. Let's not give up too soon on the voluntary appropriation of a "public-regarding" orientation and leap to political solutions. There will have to be political interventions to protect the natural world, to redistribute resources and to shape public education toward humane ends. But it is premature to legislate purposes so directly. Instead, the indirect route of strengthening our private, value-transmitting associations is crucial. Families, churches, schools, colleges, ethnic associations and cause-oriented associations all have the opportunity to shape the moral character of persons so that they can act with responsibility in all sectors of our common life. A renewed faith in and commitment to the voluntary provide a more fruitful and less dangerous approach to change than the directly political.

Second, our free political, economic and cultural institutions have capacities for self-correction—given a modicum of health in the citizenry—that will respond to the sorts of challenge Gamwell is concerned about. While there is no automatic "fix" in those processes of adjustment, there is also no fated downward trajectory either, witness the current efforts to improve American education at all levels.

Finally, the *sources* for the re-linking of freedom with purpose reside more in the common, ordinary religious heritage of Americans than in the metaphysical schemes of Hartshorne or Whitehead, though those may be useful among the highly educated. Traditions of biblical virtue, or of covenantal models of human existence, resonate quickly and clearly for those brought up in religious communities. Those traditions are inclusive of all sorts of persons, of both private and public activities and of much larger numbers than a philosophically grounded perspective can possibly gather.

Works Cited

Arendt, Hannah. *The Human Condition*, Garden City, N.J.: Doubleday Anchor, 1958.

Gamwell, Franklin. "Democracy, Capitalism and Economic Growth," in this volume.

Kant, Immanuel. *Lectures on Ethics*, New York: Harper, 1963.

Lange, Oskar. *Problems of the Political Economy of Socialism*, New Delhi: Peoples Publishing House, 1965.

Novak, Michael. *The Spirit of Democratic Capitalism*, New York: Simon and Schuster, 1982.

Simon, Julian. *The Ultimate Resource*, Princeton, N.J.: Princeton University Press, 1981.

Smith, Adam. *The Theory of Moral Sentiments*, Indianapolis: Liberty Classics, 1969.
    The Wealth of Nations, Chicago: University of Chicago Press, 1976.

Notes about the Contributors

Robert Benne is Jordan-Trexler Professor of Religion and Director of the Center for Church and Society at Roanoke College. He is the author of *Ordinary Saints: An Introduction to the Christian Life* (1988), *The Ethic of Democratic Capitalism: A Moral Reassessment* (1981), and *Defining America: A Christian Critique of the American Dream* (1974), and many articles on ethics and economics.

Kenneth Cauthen is John Price Crozer Griffith Professor of Theology at Colgate-Rochester/Bexley Hall/Crozer Theological Seminary. He is the author of *The Passion for Equality* (1987), *Systematic Theology: A Modern Protestant Approach* (1986), *Process Ethics: A Constructive System* (1984), *The Ethics of Enjoyment* (1975), *Christian Biopolitics* (1971), *Science, Secularization and God* (1969), *The Triumph of Suffering Love* (1966), and *The Impact of American Religious Liberalism* (1962).

Warren Copeland is Associate Professor of Religion at Wittenburg University. He is the author of *Economic Justice: The Social Ethics of U.S. Economic Policy* (1988), and the co-editor of *Issues of Justice: Social Sources and Religious Meanings* (1988).

Daniel Rush Finn is Associate Professor of Economics and Dean of the School of Theology at St. John's University (Minnesota). He is the co-author of *Toward a Christian Economic Ethic: Stewardship and Social Power* (1985) and several articles on ethics and economics.

Franklin I. Gamwell is Dean and Professor of Ethics and Society, the Divinity School of the University of Chicago. He is the author of *Beyond Preference: Liberal Theories of Independent Associations* (1984) and the co-editor of *Existence and Actuality: Conversations with Charles Hartshorne* (1984). He has also authored numerous articles in religious social ethics.

Jon P. Gunnemann is Associate Professor of Social Ethics in the Candler School of Theology and the Graduate Division of Religion, Emory University. He is the author of *The Moral Meaning of Revelation* (1978), the co-author of *The Ethical Investor* (1972), and the editor of *The Nation-State and Transnational Corporations in Conflict* (1975). He has also written many articles on ethics and economics.

Clark A. Kucheman is Stoughton Professor of Christian Ethics, Claremont McKenna College, and Professor of Religion, Claremont Graduate School. He is the editor of *The Life of Choice: Some Liberal Religious Perspectives on Morality* (1978) and the author of numerous essays, including "Abstract and Concrete Freedom: Hegelian Perspectives on Economic Justice" (1983).

Robert Cummings Neville is Professor of Religion, Philosophy, and Theology, Boston University. He is the author of *The Puritan Smile* (1987), *The Tao and the Daimon* (1982), *Reconstruction of Thinking* (1981), *Creativity and God* (1980), *Soldier, Sage, Saint* (1978), *The Cosmology of Freedom* (1974), and *God the Creator* (1968). He is the editor of *New Essays in Metaphysics* (1987) and *Operating on the Mind* (1975).

George W. Pickering is Professor of Religious Studies at the University of Detroit. He is the co-author of *Confronting the Color Line: The Broken Promise of the Civil Rights Movement in Chicago* (1986).

W. Widick Schroeder is Professor of Religion and Society at the Chicago Theological Seminary. He is the author of *Cognitive Structures and Religious Research* (1970), the co-author of *Suburban Religion* (1974), *Where Do I Stand?* (1973), and *Religion in American Culture* (1964), and the co-editor of *Pastoral Care and Liberation Praxis* (1986), *Spiritual Nurture and Congregational Development* (1984), *Process Philosophy and Social Thought* (1981), *Belief and Ethics* (1978), and *Belonging and Alienation* (1976).

Douglas Sturm is Professor of Religion and Political Science, Bucknell University. He is the author of *Community and Alienation: Essays on Process Thought and Public Life* (1988) and has contributed papers to many books and journals, including "Winstanley, Seventeenth Century Radical: From the Mystery of God to the Law of Freedom" (1988) and "Democratic Theory and Corporate Governance" (1988).

William M. Sullivan is Professor of Philosophy, La Salle University. He is the author of *Reconstructing Public Philosophy* (1982) and the co-author of *Interpreting Social Science: A Second Look* (1988), *Individualism and Commitment: Readings on the Themes of Habits of the Heart* (1987), and *Habits of the Heart: Individualism and Commitment in American Life* (1985).

Subject Index

Author Index

CSSR Publications

edited by

Don S. Browning, Franklin I. Gamwell, Robert L. Moore, and W. Widick Schroeder

STUDIES IN RELIGION AND SOCIETY

Other CSSR Publications in this Series:

Charles Amjad-Ali and W. Alvin Pitcher, eds.,
Liberation and Ethics: Essays in Religious Social Ethics in Honor of Gibson Winter (1985)

John B. Cobb, Jr. and W. Widick Schroeder, eds.,
Process Philosophy and Social Thought (1981)

Bruce Grelle and David A. Krueger, eds., *Christianity and Capitalism:
Perspectives on Religion, Liberalism and the Economy* (1986)

Philip Hefner and W. Widick Schroeder, eds., *Belonging and Alienation:
Religious Foundations for the Human Future* (1976)

Paul E. Kraemer, *Awakening from the American Dream: The Human Rights
Movement in the United States Assessed During a Crucial Decade, 1960-1970* (1973)

William C. Martin, *Christians in Conflict* (1972)

Robert L. Moore and Frank E. Reynolds, eds.,
Anthropology and the Study of Religion (1984)

Victor Obenhaus, *And See the People* (1968)

W. Widick Schroeder, Victor Obenhaus, Larry A. Jones, and Thomas P. Sweetser, SJ,
Suburban Religion: Churches and Synagogues in the American Experience (1974)

W. Widick Schroeder and Gibson Winter, eds., *Belief and Ethics:
Essays in Ethics, the Human Sciences and Ministry in Honor of W. Alvin Pitcher* (1978)

Walter M. Stuhr, Jr., *The Public Style: A Study
of the Community Participation of Protestant Ministers* (1972)

Thomas P. Sweetser, SJ, *The Catholic Parish: Shifting
Membership in a Changing Church* (1974)

Lawrence Witmer, ed., *Issues in Community Organization* (1972)

George D. Younger, *From New Creation to Urban Crisis:
A History of Action Training Ministries, 1962-1975* (1987)

Other Books in the Series:

Thomas C. Campbell and Yoshio Fukuyama, *The Fragmented Layman* (1970)

John Fish, *Black Power/White Control: The Struggle of the
Woodlawn Organization in Chicago* (1973)

John Fish, Gordon Nelson, Walter M. Stuhr, Jr., and Lawrence Witmer,
The Edge of the Ghetto (1968)

W. Widick Schroeder and Victor Obenhaus,
Religion in American Culture (1964)

Gibson Winter, *Religious Identity* (1968)

CRLX